The Electoral College Primer

Lawrence D. Longley and Neal R. Peirce

D1206706

Yale University Press   New Haven and London

The Yale Fastback series is designed to provide timely reports on critical issues of the day. Produced on an expedited schedule, Yale Fastbacks are issued simultaneously in cloth and paper in order to reach the broadest possible audience.

Designed by Sonia L. Scanlon.
Set in Minion type by à la page, New Haven, Connecticut.
Printed in the United States of America by Capital City Press.

ISBN 0-300-07009-8 (cloth)
0-300-07010-1 (paper)

A catalogue record for this book is available from the British Library.

The paper in this book meets the guidelines for permanence and durability of the Committee on Production Guidelines for Book Longevity of the Council on Library Resources.

1   2   3   4   5   6   7   8   9   10

contents

Acknowledgments   vii

chapter one   **The 1996 Election Is Not Quite Decided: A Fantasy**   1

chapter two   **Why Was the Electoral College Created
and How Well Has It Worked?**   16

chapter three   **Recent Crisis Elections**   37

chapter four   **How Today's Electoral College Works**   89

chapter five   **Popular Votes Do Not Equal Electoral Votes**   127

chapter six   **The Electoral College in the 1996 Election—and Beyond**   154

Appendixes   167

Notes   199

Select Bibliography   218

Index   233

acknowledgments

We understand that not everyone is as interested in the mysteries of the electoral college as a means of determining the American president as we have come to be over a period of close to thirty years. Yet, as we argue in this book, the inadequacies of this means of electing the people's president may well, at some point, require an understanding of its strange quirks and important consequences.

We came to our mutual interest in the electoral college by different routes. Neal Peirce, first as political editor of *Congressional Quarterly* and then as a founding editor of the *National Journal,* found himself describing in numerous columns and articles how the electoral college works, and finally resolved to alert the general public to its potentially disastrous possibilities in a book published in 1968.

Lawrence Longley, a presidential scholar and political scientist, found Peirce's book so stimulating that he wrote his own study of the electoral college, *The Politics of Electoral College Reform,* published by Yale University Press in 1972 and revised in 1975. Subsequently, the two of us joined forces in 1981 on *The People's President,* also fittingly published by Yale University Press. This book traced the operations of the electoral college throughout American history and examined the intense efforts of the preceding fifteen years to abolish the beast.

Many people have assisted and stimulated our efforts over the years to clarify this almost inscrutable topic. Neal Peirce notes especially, once again, the advice and counsel of collaborator-advisers James C. Kirby, Jr., John D. Feerick, Robert G. Dixon, Jr., Charles W. Bischoff, and Roan Conrad.

Lawrence Longley continues to be grateful for the challenging stimulation of his fine students at Lawrence University and, most recently, at the Budapest University of Economics and ELTE University in Hungary. Two Lawrence University undergraduates stand out not only as outstanding students but as collaborators in research and books. Alan G. Braun was coauthor of *The Politics of Electoral College Reform,* and John H. Yunker, while still an undergraduate, cowrote several important research monographs and articles. Another then-undergraduate student also deserves special recognition: James D. Dana, now of Northwestern University. Dana and Longley collaborated on several studies measuring the changing biases of the electoral college in the 1980s and 1990s which have received congressional note. One of the special pleasures of teaching at a fine undergraduate school like Lawrence University is having the opportunity of working with bright, young, emergent scholars such as Braun, Yunker, and Dana.

The preparation of this book was invaluably assisted by Vicki Koessl of Lawrence University, who skillfully produced the final manuscript and tables from materials prepared with care by Susan Peter. Their professionalism and unfailing good spirits are gratefully acknowledged. John Covell, senior editor at Yale University Press, provided important encouragement for the book, Harry Haskell was a skillful manuscript editor, and the book's index was well prepared by Cynthia Bertelsen.

In closing, both authors wish to make special note of the support and kindnesses of their wives, Judith Longley and Barbara Peirce. Behind every successful writer there often is a spouse encouraging one to "hit those keys," asking, "Want some more coffee?" or gently suggesting that the author might want to get some sleep. We thank them.

chapter one

The 1996 Election Is Not Quite Decided:
A Fantasy

Peter Jennings of ABC Television sat back in his chair during a station break and surveyed the final results of the 1996 United States presidential election.[1] He had looked forward to broadcasting the conclusion of the contest after months of recounting the twists and turns of this remarkable political year, but he was stunned as the realization sank in that the election was by no means over. No candidate had received a majority of votes in the electoral college; the election had *not* been decided by the popular vote. Instead the result would depend on the future actions of candidates, electors, and members of the House of Representatives. It would be, Jennings saw, a long and continuing story.

How had this uncertainty come about? A major factor was the personal unpopularity of the two major-party nominees. Sen. Bob Dole had finally succeeded in defeating Sen. Phil Gramm, Pat Buchanan, and others to win the Republican presidential nomination, but only at the cost of making broad concessions to the Republican right, positions that had made it difficult for him to appeal to moderates and independents—and had generated a general impression of inconsistency. The result was a candidate who was viewed by many as standing for little except expediency: the nominee of a party dispirited over the commitment (and even vigor) of its own standard bearer.

President Bill Clinton, on the other hand, had presided over a relative love-in at the Democratic Convention in August in Chicago. As the candidate of a unified party—unusual by any measure for

Democrats—he would have done better in November had it not been for deep concerns over the economy and his decision to commit American ground troops to Bosnia. In addition, the personal character issue, which had nearly lost him the presidency in 1992, continued to fester, aggravated by continuing investigations into the Whitewater land deal and by his incessant willingness to compromise and waffle on important issues. As election day approached, many people still saw Clinton, after nearly four years in office, as a questionable choice for the presidency, a candidate "more slick than steady." These doubts were especially strong among political independents and Republican-leaning professionals seeking an attractive alternative to Dole's newfound staunch conservatism and the economic and governing ineptitude that they associated with the Clinton administration.

The chief beneficiary of the general lack of enthusiasm for Dole and Clinton was third-party candidate Ross Perot of Texas. In 1992, Perot had launched a curious on-again, off-again independent campaign, which nevertheless generated more than nineteen million votes—almost one-fifth of the electorate. This was far in excess of the support won by any previous independent or third-party candidate in the history of the Republic. Emboldened by his initial success, and encouraged by evidence of the disenchantment of most Americans with the two major parties and their prospective presidential nominees, Perot announced, in an interview on CNN's *Larry King Live* on September 25, 1995, that he would sponsor a new political party, the Reform party (for legal reasons called the Independence party in some states). One of the party's goals, Perot indicated, was to attract a world-class leader as its candidate. He did not rule out the possibility that he might, in fact, be that person.

The Reform party got off to a promising start by overcoming daunting obstacles to win official ballot designation in the megastate of California on October 23, 1995. It quickly went on to obtain ballot listings in Ohio and Maine, thus establishing that it would be able to get on enough state ballots for respectable popular and electoral vote showings. Assisted by high-powered legal counsel and supported by a network of enthusiastic volunteers (as well as many "paid volunteers"), Perot eventually was able to gain ballot listing for the Reform party in each of the fifty states and the District of Columbia. Some of these successes came easily: in the state of Washington he needed to obtain the signatures of fewer than 200 registered voters. Other states presented more substantial challenges: in North Carolina he needed 51,904 signatures, and in Florida, 65,596. Very specific state requirements concerning the geographical distribution of signatures, short petition circulation periods, and even, in South Carolina, the requirement that petition signers record not only their precinct numbers but also list their personal voter registration numbers, bedeviled his efforts. Many observers had doubted that his party could get on more than forty state ballots; its success in getting listed in all the states (as Perot's independent candidacy had in 1992) provided a major boost to the new party's credibility.

Financing was one problem the Reform party did not face. Despite intense legal disputes over the means used, Perot in effect simply paid most of the party's expenses out of his very deep pockets, personally contributing between $70 and $80 million to its efforts. Direct-mail and other citizen appeals raised an additional $10.8 million during the campaign—an important psychological and political boost for the party's activities.

It came as little surprise to observers when Perot announced, in mid-1996, that he had reluctantly acceded to the request of the leaders of the Reform party that he be its candidate for president in 1996. "They decided that I was the person who could best present the ideals of this citizens' movement. It would be presumptuous of me to stand in the way of the people's will, so I have agreed to run once again. It is no more than my duty as a citizen."

Initially, some had viewed Perot as essentially a "spoiler candidate" who had no realistic prospects of winning a significant number of electoral votes. (Such, in fact, had been the result of his 1992 campaign: despite receiving nearly 19 percent of the popular vote, Perot did not win a single electoral vote.) This perception, however, faded quickly as polls, by the late summer of 1996, reported Perot's support increasing from the low 20 percent range to the mid-30s, and—in a few national polls—even exceeding support for Clinton and Dole. By the close of the summer Perot appeared to have converted the 1996 election into that rarity—a true three-way choice.

September, however, was not a good month for Ross Perot. He found himself hounded and derided by the press as lacking substantive solutions to the nation's problems. In numerous interviews, his tendency to respond with generalities to detailed questions concerning his issue positions began to foster an image of a candidate who lacked real understanding of the problems of the day. His personal traits of both defensiveness and aggressiveness (sometimes exhibited almost simultaneously) were unfortunately well evidenced during these encounters as well. The growing perception of shallowness and personal prickliness became a major setback to Perot's efforts to have his candidacy taken seriously.

Further hurting Perot was the increasing tendency of the national media in the late stages of the campaign to focus on likely state-by-state results. Under the electoral college system, each state's electoral votes are determined as a bloc on a winner-take-all basis. Running second (or third) in a state has no rewards. In the closing weeks of the campaign, voter attention began to shift from the Perot phenomenon to the question of which candidate—Clinton, Dole, or sometimes Perot—was likely to carry a particular state. Many states—especially some of the largest ones—appeared very closely balanced between Clinton and Dole. People began to see a vote for Perot in those instances as "wasted" in terms of the real choice in their state. Perot's national poll figures slowly declined as many Republicans and Democrats returned to their traditional partisan moorings, and as independents shifted and divided between Perot

Table 1 Hypothetical Results of the 1996 Election

Candidate	Popular Votes		Electoral Votes	
	Total	Percentage	Total	Percentage
Bob Dole (R)[a]	41,771,000	39.9	232	43.1
Bill Clinton (D)	39,921,000	38.2	244	45.4
Ross Perot (Reform)	22,271,470	21.3	62	11.6
Others	637,190	0.6	0	0

Dole popular vote margin of 1,850,000. Needed to win: 270 electoral votes.

[a]See Appendix A for a list of abbreviations of political parties.

and the two major-party candidates. By election night, Perot's campaign had lost almost one-third of its strength from its high point in mid-August. Nevertheless, it had succeeded—unintentionally, in the view of most observers—in creating an outcome of consequence: an undecided election.

The final vote was as shown in table 1. Several stunning results were evident. Bob Dole had "won" the election in popular votes, receiving 1,850,000 more votes than Bill Clinton. Dole's popular votes, however, had not been distributed among the states to maximum advantage. A number of his popular votes had been "wasted" in unnecessarily large margins beyond what was needed to carry a state. Clinton's votes had been more economically distributed among the states. He had carried his states by generally thin margins—and he had carried enough such states to lead Dole in electoral votes 244 to 232.

The popular vote and electoral vote results of the 1996 election had provided a divided verdict as to the "winner" of the election. Dole could claim a popular vote win, while Clinton could cite his lead in electoral votes. But neither candidate could claim the victory that counts: a majority of 270 votes in the electoral college. Ross

Perot won his 62 electoral votes from narrow plurality wins in eight states: Texas (32 electoral votes), Oklahoma (8 electoral votes), Utah (5 electoral votes), Idaho (4 electoral votes), Montana (3 electoral votes), and Wyoming (3 electoral votes), together with more geographically diverse Alaska (3 electoral votes) and Maine (where Perot had made his strongest showing in 1992, winning 4 electoral votes). With his 62 electoral votes—the most won by a third-party candidate in American history—Perot had deadlocked the electoral college. No one knew in early November who would be the next president. The decision would depend on actions to be taken forty-one days later, at the meetings of the electoral college on December 16, or possibly on the voting of the House of Representatives starting on January 6, 1997.

Many observers initially assumed that the deadlocked election would simply go to the House in January. Soon, however, it became evident that the next step in the troubled election of 1996 would be neither simple nor certain. Federal statutes call for meetings of each state's slate of electors in the respective state capitals on the first Monday after the second Wednesday in December, which in 1996 would be December 16. Electors are usually assumed to be rubber stamps, automatically confirming the popular verdict of election day. In this case, however, enormous pressures were exerted on Perot electors to defect either to Clinton or to Dole in order to resolve the constitutional crisis.

Clinton needed only 26 more votes to win the election and assiduously appealed—publicly and privately—to each individual Perot elector, most of whom were newcomers to electoral politics and lacked extensive political background. The Clinton appeal rested on a simple argument: the election is now effectively over as far as Perot and his campaign are concerned, and therefore the Perot elector should vote for Clinton, the leader in electoral votes, in order to resolve the crisis. Further, if the election were not decided now, subsequent proceedings in the House would give little recognition to the Perot campaign or its concerns. Perot electors were told that they could perform a public service by voting for the electoral vote winner now instead of delaying the decision for weeks by forcing the election into the House in January. Clinton's appeal to the Perot electors was particularly fervent because his strategists knew well that unless he could win in the electoral college on December 16, his prospects in the Republican-controlled House would be uncertain at best.

Bob Dole, of course, was not inactive during this period. In his press conference on November 7, two days after the election, he cited his lead of nearly two million popular votes over Clinton and stressed "the legitimacy of the popular vote choice." He added pointedly, "I am sure the American people expect the candidate who has run first in popular votes to become president—either by actions of the electors on December 16, or by the constitutionally prescribed procedures beginning on January 6. Any other outcome would be an affront to the Constitution and to the democratic processes of free and fair popular elections."

Quiet and determined contact was also under way between the Dole campaign and individual Perot electors. The Dole appeal to these electors was that the popular will must be respected by the election as president of the candidate who had been preferred by the American people—Bob Dole. A concern of Dole strategists was that unless he could win in the electoral college on December 16, his claim of the legitimacy of the popular vote would be of less importance in the party-dominated House—although continuing Republican majority control of that body offered Dole some solace.

Perot was under perhaps the strongest pressure of any of the candidates. He had run hoping that he could carve out a key position between Clinton and Dole while offering himself as an outspoken fresh face capable of forceful presidential leadership. Instead of winning a majority of the electoral votes—or even a figure comparable to his popular vote of more than 21 percent—he had received less than 12 percent of the electoral votes. Now his contribution to the presidential campaign was seen as that of a spoiler, a creator of crisis in the electoral college. In light of these bitter developments, what should he do?

Although Perot retained many sympathies with Republican issue concerns, he could not contemplate doing anything to enhance the likelihood of Dole's becoming president. The disdain and even contempt he felt toward Dole (more than toward Clinton) as a result of many months of bitter and intensive feuding ruled out offering any help now to the Republican candidate.

Helping Clinton, on the other hand, was a possibility. Only 26 votes separated him from an electoral college majority, and Perot had 62. He could be a king maker by giving Clinton the necessary electoral votes, respect the "electoral vote verdict," and resolve the national uncertainty all at once. Perot, however, could not bear to do it. Clinton, he felt, had been a disaster as a president. If he were reelected, his second administration would be dominated by doctrinaire liberals and congressional insiders. Perot had fought too hard against both to be willing to strengthen their hold upon the presidency.

Accordingly, on November 29, Ross Perot issued a public appeal to his electors to hold fast and "vote according to the expectations of those who had voted for them" by voting for him on December 16. "The electoral college vote must reflect the popular vote results in each state," he said. "The House of Representatives is the constitutionally mandated contingent electoral mechanism for resolving any electoral college deadlock." Off the record, he was said to be hopeful that the House, an institution currently in disdain and comprised of members particularly attuned to constituency sentiment, might be receptive to a candidate who could bring fresh perspective and action to national leadership, and who also had run well in, and even carried, many congressional districts.

On December 16, starting at noon local time, the national television networks reported in continuous coverage the fifty-one meetings of the electors in each of the states and the District of Columbia.

By mid-afternoon, the nation knew the results: Dole had gained 8 Perot electors for a final electoral total of 240 votes, 30 short of a majority, and Clinton had won the support of 7 Perot electors for 251 electoral votes, 19 short of the necessary number. Forty-seven electors had remained with Perot. There could be no second vote of the electoral college; it had completed its work, as inconclusive as it might be. The election now certainly would go to the newly elected House of Representatives, which was to meet on Monday, January 6, 1997, only fourteen days before the constitutionally scheduled inauguration day for the new president.

The House of Representatives contingent procedure is a most curious mechanism for electing the president. Under the Twelfth Amendment to the Constitution, the House choice is limited to the top three candidates for president in electoral votes, and voting in the House is by one vote per state delegation. An absolute majority of state delegations—today, 26—is needed for House election of the president. Delegations that are evenly split cast no vote, but the necessary majority of 26 states still holds. Meanwhile, the Senate meets to elect the vice president from among only the top *two* contenders, with one vote per senator.

Serious problems of fairness certainly exist: in the total exclusion of any representation in these proceedings for the 600,000 residents of the District of Columbia, the inhabitants of which had voted for president in November, and in the absolute equality between huge states such as California and New York and tiny states such as Rhode Island and Delaware. Beyond these problems of equity lurks a more serious problem: What if the House itself should deadlock and be unable to agree upon a president?

At precisely 1 P.M. on Monday, January 6, the Senate and House met in joint session to count the electoral votes as certified by each state. By 2 P.M. it was official: no candidate for president or vice president had the necessary majority, and each chamber would have to act. In light of what was seen as its particular difficulties in choosing among three candidates, the House commenced its proceedings first, at 3:30 P.M. the same day. (The Senate, accustomed to a more deliberate pace, did not begin its efforts to elect the vice president until January 8.)

The House of Representatives found the election of president to be an exceedingly difficult task, in large part because no one party controlled the majority of state delegations. Prior to the 1996 congressional elections, 26 state delegations had been controlled by Republicans, 17 had been controlled by Democrats, 6 had been split and would cast no vote should party lines hold, and one state (Vermont) had been represented by a single congressman, Bernard Sanders, a political independent and self-described Socialist. This apparent Republican domination of the House voting was, however, illusory, even early in 1996. Of the 26 Republican state delegations (the absolute minimum of states needed for presidential election), six were Republican by only one vote—a loss of but one Republican seat in these states in November 1996 would remove it from the Republican column.

As expected, the 1996 congressional elections slightly eroded the Republican strength in the House (a net loss of 11 seats) and, more significant, the number of Republican-controlled state delegations also declined. Three of the previously Republican states (Delaware, New Mexico, and Tennessee) became Democratic and one partisan-tied state (Connecticut) also became a Democratic-majority state delegation. Five states were left with divided partisan control. The apparent state vote then, as of January 1997, was Republican 23, Democrat 21, divided 5, and Vermont represented by Congressman Sanders.

Further complicating matters was the continued candidacy of Ross Perot. Although he had carried only seven relatively small states, along with the megastate of Texas, he had run first in 72 individual congressional districts across the country. Representatives from those districts felt under severe compulsion to respect the preferences of their constituencies. In fact, 24 Republican and 13 Democratic representatives decided to buck party discipline "in order to represent the constituency" and voted for Perot on January 6 and on most of the subsequent votes. This Perot support was enough to make the initial vote for president in the House on January 6 not 23–21–5–1 but rather 21 states for Dole, 19 states for Clinton, 5 states divided and not voting, and 5 states for Perot (including Vermont). A majority of 26 states would prove to be a long time coming.

Over the next days, while the House continued to ballot, tensions built. The stock market, which had been declining sharply ever since the November nonelection, broke into a wild selling decline. Gold prices in London and Zurich, reflecting uncertainty about the status of the U.S. presidency, rose between twenty and forty dollars a day. Renewed fighting in Bosnia threatened U.S. peacekeeping forces there. Foreign nations nervously awaited the determination of American leadership. In the House, ballot after ballot failed to produce a majority.

By January 12, Dole's vote had risen to 23 states—a few Perot-voting Republican representatives finally had been beaten into submission by threats of losing key committee assignments and chairmanships. On January 13, one of the divided states—Maryland—switched to Dole amid rumors of a promised massive Army Corps of Engineers project to rebuild the Baltimore harbor, thus making the Republican total 24 states. Clinton gained one state when Representative Sanders of Vermont announced that he was swinging his vote, and thus his state, to the Democratic candidate. This was quickly followed by a surprise announcement by a DuPage County Republican House member from the partisan-tied state of Illinois that he was becoming a Democrat and would vote for Clinton. Outraged Republicans quickly noted that a large number of Cook County government contracts had been awarded to the representative's family-owned construction firm in the preceding days. With Vermont and Illinois, Clinton now had 21 states to Dole's 24, but there the tally would remain. Despite tremendous pressure on swing representatives—especially in the three still evenly divided states—neither Dole nor Clinton was able to increase his state total above 24 or 21 in the remaining seven days of the most intense two weeks in contemporary American politics.

Events in the Senate were less convoluted but no less indecisive. The Republican control of that chamber had been weakened by the 1996 elections; when the results were in, the chamber was precisely balanced in membership—50 Republicans and 50 Democrats. In the course of normal business in the Senate, ties are broken by a vote by the vice president, but not in the case of an election *of* the vice president. The language of the Twelfth Amendment of the Constitution is quite clear: should the Senate need to elect a vice president, "then from the two highest numbers on the list [the two vice presidential candidates with the greatest number of electoral votes], the Senate shall choose the Vice-President; a quorum for the purpose shall consist of two-thirds of the whole number of senators, and a majority of the whole number shall be necessary to a choice." Senators only would vote; their choice would be limited to incumbent vice president Al Gore or Dole's running mate, Lamar Alexander, former governor of Tennessee; and an absolute majority of senators—51—must favor one of the two if a vice president were to be elected.

The Senate, however, was not to elect a vice president; instead it polarized along partisan lines on this, the most starkly political vote the senators had ever faced. Senate Republican leader Trent Lott insisted on absolute partisan loyalty in his party's ranks, and Democratic Senate leader Tom Daschle of South Dakota fought equally tenaciously to suppress any wavering on the part of his forces. Both party leaders stressed to fellow partisans that this was the absolutely defining issue of party identification. Any deviation would constitute an abandonment of party and principle—as well as personal political future.

Although there were many rumors of possible defections, ultimately party lines held in the Senate, and inconclusive votes of 50 to

50 were held one after another. The Senate proved no more success-ful in electing a vice president than the House was in electing a president.

On inauguration day, January 20, 1997, there was no president or vice president to be inaugurated. The 1996 election was not quite decided. Americans—commentators and average citizens alike—found themselves reaching for the nearest copy of the Constitution for guidance in this extraordinary situation. To the surprise of many, they found that there is reasonably precise language in the Twenti-eth Amendment and in federal law covering the eventuality. The Constitution states: "If a President shall not have been chosen before the time fixed for the beginning of his term, or if the President elect shall have failed to qualify, then the Vice President elect shall act as President until a President shall have qualified; and the Congress may by law provide for the case wherein neither a President elect nor a Vice President elect shall have qualified, declaring who shall then act as President, or the manner in which one who is to act shall be selected, and such person shall act accordingly until a President or Vice President shall have qualified."

Almost fifty years ago, in the Automatic Succession Act of 1947, Congress acted under this constitutional power to provide for the eventuality of a president or a vice president not qualifying on inau-guration day. Under the act, the line of presidential succession goes first to the vice president-elect (if she or he has "qualified"—has been elected by the electoral college or by the Senate). If this is not the case, then the office goes to the Speaker of the House, then to the president pro tempore of the Senate, and finally to various cabinet officials.

Despite furious efforts in the fourteen days between January 6 and 20, 1997, neither a president nor a vice president had been elected by the appropriate congressional chamber. As a consequence, the acting president would be—an astonished nation now discov-ered—the extraordinarily controversial Speaker of the House of Representatives, Newt Gingrich.

It took Gingrich little time to decide to accept this opportunity. Early on the morning of January 20, only hours prior to the inaugural ceremony, Gingrich announced that, as Speaker, he was ordering the suspension of the fruitless House efforts to elect a president, and that as of noon he would resign as Speaker and representative to assume the constitutional responsibilities of acting president. He couldn't help adding, "The difficulties that the nation has endured these past weeks are now over, and as acting president I shall be happy to lead the American people in the advancement of the new conservative revolution and our Contract with America."

Virtually all Americans were amazed (and most also appalled) that the 1996 presidential election had resulted in the presidency being won not by one of the three candidates who had offered himself for the people's choice but by an individual who had not run for president and for whom many voters had considerable disdain and even hostility.

Under constitutional and statutory provisions, at noon on January 20, 1997, the Honorable Newt Gingrich of Georgia became acting president of the United States. The 1996 election was, more or less, finally over, but it had not produced a president—only an acting president. President Gingrich would serve forcefully and controversially "as president," but always subject to the possibility that renewed House balloting, especially following the 1998 congressional elections, might replace him with still-presidential candidate Bob Dole—or even recall former President Bill Clinton from retirement. The presidency and the nation were transformed by these events—the former fatally weakened and made subservient to Congress for its determination and maintenance, and the latter traumatized and divided by months of political and constitutional crisis.

This fictionalized account of what could happen in the 1996 election under the present electoral college system raises some key questions about our system of electing (or not electing) our presidents: How was the electoral college created? How well has it worked in history? What has happened—and what has nearly happened—in recent crisis elections? How does today's electoral college work? What are the differences between popular votes and electoral votes? What is the overall significance of the electoral college to the 1996 election—and beyond? The following chapters will provide answers to these questions. The election of the American president is not a simple matter of votes being tallied by some arcane mechanism. Rather, the electoral college contains the potential—perhaps to be vividly shown in 1996 or in subsequent presidential elections—for profound constitutional and political crisis.

chapter two

Why Was The Electoral College Created and How Well Has It Worked?

A recurring theme in discussions about the electoral college is the "intentions of the founding fathers" concerning the manner of the election of the president. It is entirely possible, of course, to deny the relevance of these considerations to an assessment of the adequacy, in terms of today's needs, of the electoral college. The problem with this position, however, is that much of the debate over the electoral college and its place in the constitutional framework of the American political system utilizes references to, and draws support from, concepts of how the electoral college evolved out of the Constitutional Convention of 1787. Whether the intentions of these radical reformers of nearly two hundred years ago are really relevant today is less important than the fact that in political debate over the electoral college these intentions are given weight and significance. It should also be kept in mind that these same men devised many arrangements that have withstood the tests of close to two centuries. It is not at all inappropriate—and rather illuminating—to consider how this group of intelligent and well-meaning men sought to create a mechanism for selecting their nation's leader that would similarly stand the test of time.

The Birth of the Electoral College System

The Constitutional Convention, which met in Philadelphia from May 25 to September 17, 1787, was beset by massive tensions and rivalries as it sought to draft a new constitution. With profound differences of opinion existing on such questions as the degree of centralized power for the new federal government, the type of special recognition small states would be given, the division of powers among the different branches of government, and the extent to which sectional interests would be protected, the delegates to the convention found themselves engaged in the most difficult of political negotiations in their attempts to achieve consensus—a task so demanding of their political astuteness as to cause John Dickinson of Delaware to cry out, "Experience must be our guide. Reason may mislead us."[1]

During the summer of 1787 successive crises threatened to destroy the work of the convention as delegates fell to bitter quarreling over regional and big-state/small-state differences. The most profound and dangerous of these conflicts was between large-state and small-state plans for representation in the new congress, with proponents of the Virginia Plan, which provided for congressional representation to be based on population, locked in battle with supporters of the New Jersey Plan, which established equal congressional representation for each state. This deadlock was finally broken on July 16 through acceptance of the Connecticut Plan—the "Great Compromise"—which provided for one house of Congress to be based on population and the other on equality of states. As the Constitutional Convention moved, in late August, to determine the means by which the president would be elected, there was little wish to see the conflicts and tensions that had plagued the preceding months of the convention renewed.

On August 31 a Committee of Eleven was commissioned to study various possible methods for the election of the president and to work out a plan on which the delegates could agree. The task of the committee was a formidable one. In the preceding months several different schemes had been advanced, including presidential election by Congress and direct election by the people. Although congressional election of the president was tentatively approved by the Constitutional Convention on four occasions during the summer, there existed strong opposition on the grounds that it would make the chief executive subservient to Congress and unable to develop an independent leadership capacity.[2] The other proposal, that of direct election by the people, had strong support from some of the leaders at the convention, including James Madison of Virginia, Gouverneur Morris of Pennsylvania, and James Wilson, also of Pennsylvania—all three of whom, not very surprisingly, were from large, populous states. Strong objections to direct vote were raised on various grounds, among them being: (1) the lack of awareness and knowledge of candidates by the people, with unforeseen consequences resulting from the scattering of votes by the electorates in the various states among favorite sons they knew best;[3] (2) the loss in relative influence of the South because of its large nonvoting slave population; (3) the dislike, on the part of small, less populous states, of too open an admission of an inferior role in the choice of the president; and (4) the fear of many that direct election of the president would consolidate too much power and influence in one person.[4] With the convention striving for consensus on its proposed constitution, these strenuous objections to both the congressional-election and direct-vote plans meant that some alternate plan would have to be found.

‌   As early as June 2 James Wilson had suggested, as a possible compromise, an *intermediate election* plan involving an electoral college, and during the summer this alternative developed as "the second choice of many delegates though it was the first choice of few."[5] When the Committee of Eleven met in the first few days of September, it turned to this compromise in order to avoid further deadlock and conflict.

On September 4 the committee reported its recommendations for presidential election by a college of electors based on congressional apportionment[6] (thus indirectly reflecting the Connecticut compromise of the preceding month), with the provision that if no candidate received a majority of the votes of the electors, the final selection would be by the United States Senate, choosing from among the top five contenders. With a subsequent change to contingent election by the House rather than the Senate[7]—but with the equality of states maintained through one vote per state—this was the plan adopted by the Constitutional Convention on September 7, 1787, after only brief debate. The electoral college method of selecting the president was the subject of little attention and discussion during the ratification debates following the convention, leading Alexander Hamilton to observe in *The Federalist Papers*, no. 68: "The mode of appointment of the chief magistrate of the United States is almost the only part of the system, of any consequence, which has escaped without severe censure. . . . I . . . hesitate not to affirm that if the manner of it be not perfect, it is at least excellent."[8]

The Constitutional Convention of 1787 thus created out of disagreement a system with broad, if somewhat artificial, support. "What really moved the delegates to accept the electoral system, with little enthusiasm and no unanimity of conviction, were certain practical considerations, dictated not by political ideals but by the social realities of the time-realities that no longer exist."[9]

Among these realities were: (1) the pressure on the delegates at the Constitutional Convention to reach agreement, (2) the lack of immediate concern about the operation of the electoral college, and (3) a major—and soon to be disproved—assumption about the likely dispersion of support for various presidential candidates.

The first of these realities has previously been discussed in terms of the overriding desire on the part of the delegates not to reopen the deep wounds of the first three months of the Constitutional Convention—divisions that had been papered over by the Great Compromise on congressional representation. When plans were advanced concerning the selection of the president that seemed likely to renew conflict, the delegates sought alternatives. In short, the most basic reason that the electoral college was invented was that the convention was deadlocked on simpler schemes like direct election and choice by Congress, and thus invented a system that could be "sold" in the immediate context of 1787. One commentator on this period, John Roche, puts it pointedly: "The vital aspect of the electoral college was that it got the Convention over the hurdle and protected everybody's interests. The future was left to cope with the problem of what to do with this Rube Goldberg mechanism. . . . The Electoral College was neither an exercise in applied Platonism nor an experiment in indirect government based on elitist distrust of the masses. It was merely a jerry-rigged improvisation which has subsequently been endowed with a high theoretical content."[10]

A second reason why the electoral college plan quickly gained support lay in the belief held by most delegates that any problems that might arise in this method of electing the president would not be immediate: they all knew that George Washington was going to be chosen president no matter what the electoral system. In this regard, Felix Morley suggests that "without this assured initial unanimity, it is probable that the electoral system would have been more closely scrutinized, with better anticipation of the troubles that lay ahead."[11] Being the practical men they were, the delegates sought to put off until a later time what could be postponed and considered then.

⌁ A third and particularly important reason for the support the electoral college system received had to do with the arrangements themselves. There was a general belief "that once Washington had finished his tenure as President, the electors would cease to provide majorities and the Chief Executive would usually be chosen in the House."[12] The assumption was that the electors would, in effect, nominate a number of prominent individuals, with no one man— because of diverse state and regional interests—usually receiving the specified absolute majority of electoral votes. At times a George Washington might be the unanimous electoral choice, but, as George Mason of Virginia argued in Philadelphia, nineteen times out of twenty the final choice of president from the top contenders would be made not by the electoral college itself but by the House of Representatives, voting by states with one vote per state. This conception of the electoral arrangements envisioned a mechanism for the selection of the president somewhat similar to today's national nominating conventions and general election procedure, except in this view the electoral college would serve the nominating function and the House the electing function. Implicit in the agreement on the electoral college system was this assumption about how it would work in practice—an assumption that was not to be borne out by events.

The key to acceptance of this two-stage plan for presidential selection lay in the different character of electoral college and House contingent voting. The electoral college, reflecting in a rough way the population of states, would favor the big states at the cost of the small states—or, more accurately, populations rather than equally weighted states. When the contingent House procedure went into effect—as it most often would—the voting would be one vote per state delegation, thus representing equally weighed individual states regardless of population. This mechanism was a compromise between the principle of population and that of equal state interest. As James Madison later described the electoral college, it was "the result of compromise between the larger and smaller states, giving to the latter the advantage of selecting a President from the candidates, in consideration of the former in selecting the candidates from the people."[13]

One of the most common statements about the development of the electoral college is that the apportionment of electors was due to a large-state/small-state compromise. This is, in fact, only partly true. The apportionment did reflect the Connecticut compromise about congressional representation; this feature of the electoral college, however, was due more to expediency than to philosophy. The major large-state/small-state compromise lay in the linkage of electoral college nomination with House election where each state would have only one vote. By itself, the electoral college was not conceived to be a bulwark of small-states' rights; rather, if anything, it was seen as favoring large states—or at least the principle of population.[14]

Five Changes in the Electoral College System

The electoral college system has moved through a series of evolutionary developments during its long and often painful existence.

With the exception of the essentially mechanical changes contained in the Twelfth Amendment, ratified in 1804, these modifications—often massive in impact—have come about through custom, state law, and political necessity, but not by formal constitutional change. These developments, however, have greatly altered the electoral college over the years. As John P. Feerick puts it, "The system which emerged in practice is not the system contemplated by the founding fathers."[15]

Two of the most important of these changes resulted from the rise of political parties out of legislative caucuses about the time of the 1796 election. As these political organizations developed, they began to aggregate national support for their candidates and to recruit electors pledged to them, thus making obsolete both the concept of the free elector who would vote for well-thought-of individuals and the previously anticipated balance expressed as "the electoral college nominates, the House selects."

With national politics emerging out of the era of Washington in dualistic patterns, no party or voter could allow electors to play the role of statesmen—the political stakes were too high. Thus was born the role of the elector as a faceless component of a state-by-state counting device, with predictability rather than wisdom the desired virtue. As a Senate select committee reported in 1826, electors are "usually selected for their devotion to party, their popular manner, and a supposed talent for electioneering."[16] Today, the necessary qualifications of electors are even less exacting: one well-known 1968 elector, for example, forthrightly although modestly reported that he had been selected principally because he had contributed money to his party.[17] In most states even the formal fiction of elector selection has been forsaken: as discussed in Chapter 4, thirty-two states and the District of Columbia do not indicate on the ballot the names of the electors at stake in a presidential election.[18] The body of individuals who are selected every four years to constitute the nation's electoral college are today not only without honor and prestige, they are also largely unknown.

As a direct result of the demise of the free elector even before three national elections had been held, there arose the curious phenomenon of the faithless elector—an elector who votes for president contrary to expectations based on pledge or statement or on the assumption that the elector will support the candidate of the party whose designation as elector has been accepted. The first faithless elector was Samuel Miles, a 1796 Federalist elector in Pennsylvania, who declined to vote for John Adams, the Federalist candidate, and instead cast his vote for Thomas Jefferson. Even at this early point in the evolution of the electoral college, this was rather shocking, leading one outraged Federalist to exclaim in the *United States Gazette,* "What, do I chuse Samuel Miles to determine for me whether John Adams or Thomas Jefferson shall be President? No! I chuse him to *act,* not to *think.*"[19]

Elector Miles established a pattern and opportunity that has been followed by remarkably few later electors. Between 1824 and 1992, 18,995 electoral votes were cast for president. Of these, only 8 can be said to have been cast indisputably "against instructions"— one each in 1820, 1948, 1956, 1960, 1968, 1972, 1976, and 1988.[20] That these men and women have shown so little political independence is certainly due more to their character (or, perhaps, their lack of imagination) than to effective legal restrictions—only sixteen states have laws requiring electors to vote according to their pledges, and these laws themselves are of doubtful constitutionality.[21] The electoral college, then, has changed drastically from that conceived by the founding fathers; in place of a body of statesmen, we have a collection of political nonentities whose actions are justified only to the extent to which they put aside personal values and deliberations and vote automatically in accord with strict party regularity.

A second major change in the electoral college system has been previously identified as also resulting from the emergence of national political parties. With political parties aggregating support for candidates on a national basis, the electoral college soon became not the nomination agency with the House acting as the selection agency—as had been assumed—but rather the final point of decision itself. The House contingency procedure became, conversely, not an integral part of the presidential selection process but an emergency step to be taken when normal procedures break down—as in 1800 and 1824. The assumption of the founding fathers, which had been so important in the acceptance of the electoral college plan, was thus made obsolete by events, while the remnant of the original selection structure—the House contingent procedure—remains, with its inherent chaotic possibilities.[22]

The third major change, besides the development of the bound elector and the emergence of the electoral college as the usual final point of decision, was the development of the popular election of electors. The Constitution gives the states complete freedom concerning the means of elector selection, and in the early elections practices varied widely, including variations on popular election and state legislative election of electors, and often changed in a particular state from election to election. Massachusetts, always in the forefront of political manipulations, changed its system for choosing electors seven different times during the first ten national elections. Political advantage, rather than abstract philosophical principle, was the dominant force in these changes. Over the decades, however, the expansion of the electorate, the popularization of democratic ideals, and unfortunate experiences with legislative politics (as in the case of New York, where a legislative deadlock resulted in the selection of no electors from that state in the 1789 election) combined to create an uneven, uncertain, but inevitable movement to popular selection of electors. Many political leaders found that once popular participation in elector selection had been instituted for one election (often for partisan ends), it was politically difficult to take it away. The last state to resist these trends was South Carolina, which adopted popular selection of electors only after the Civil War.[23]

The fourth change in the electoral college system also arose essentially from political expediency. This was the trend toward deciding all of a state's electoral votes on a unit-rule, or winner-take-all, basis. Generally, division of a state's electoral votes was supported by whatever party was momentarily in eclipse in a state, while the dominant party favored a winner-take-all arrangement. Not very surprisingly, the latter's view usually prevailed. In addition to such internal political pressures favoring a unit-rule approach, another factor tended to force states toward this method. As other states adopted unit-rule selection procedures, it became apparent to state leaders that their state must follow swiftly in order to maintain its relative political position. If another state was going to be able to deliver an entire slate of electoral votes, their state must be able to do so as well.[24] Thus, again, political necessity created another substantial extraconstitutional deviation from the arrangements of the founding fathers.

The fifth change in the electoral college was the direct result of an oversight of the creators of the electoral system and, unlike the other changes, led to a formal constitutional change in the electoral college system. In 1800 the presidential and vice presidential Democratic nominees, Thomas Jefferson and Aaron Burr, both received an identical number of electoral votes, 73, since the Constitution stipulated that each elector would cast two equal votes, undistinguished as to president and vice president. The original conception had been that the strongest candidate would thus become president and the next strongest vice president. This had happened, in fact, in 1796, although the leader, John Adams, and the runner-up, Thomas Jefferson, were of different parties and were strong personal enemies. With national political parties developing an ability to enforce party regularity and electoral faithfulness, the original system now seemed likely to produce hostile presidents and vice presidents at best, and at worst ties between the same party's presidential and vice presidential candidates—as happened in 1800.

Never a man to lose an opportunity (he has often been labeled the "man who could not wait"), vice presidential nominee Burr made no effort to step aside for his presidential running mate, and the House of Representatives was called upon, in 1801, to make one of the most agonizing decisions it has ever faced. After thirty-six ballots between February 11 and 17, marked by the most disreputable deals and maneuvers, Jefferson was elected, partially due to help from his ancient antagonist Alexander Hamilton, who hated only Burr more. The sourness and sordidness of this episode led directly to the adoption of the Twelfth Amendment, which essentially changed the electoral college system only in requiring separate votes by the electors for president and vice president.[25]

The founding fathers showed great wisdom in many of the features of the new Constitution they created in Philadelphia in 1787. In the case of the electoral college system, however, it is difficult to attribute such virtue to them, for this institution never worked as intended by its creators. That the basic electoral college system has continued to exist until today is due not to the wisdom of its creators but to a combination of adaptation and chance.

The Electoral College System Misbehaving

Rather than examining the electoral college system through a chronological review of the fifty-two presidential elections that were held through 1992, this section will instead examine these elections and the operation of the electoral college system in terms of four categories:

1. elections in which there was an electoral college reversal of the popular vote winner
2. elections in which there were an electoral college deadlock and use of the House contingent procedure
3. elections in which the president elected did not have a majority of popular votes
4. elections in which minor vote shifts could have changed the outcome

There have been two, or possibly three, elections where the electoral college itself (as opposed to the House contingent feature, as in 1824) resulted in the candidate with the most popular votes losing

Table 2 Electoral College Reversal of Popular Vote Winners[a]

Year	Candidate	Popular Votes		Electoral Votes	
		Total	Percentage	Total	Percentage
1876[b]	Tilden (D)	4,287,670	50.9	184	50
	Hayes (R)	4,035,924	47.9	185	50

Tilden popular vote margin of 251,746. *Hayes* winner with electoral vote margin of 1.

1888	Cleveland (D)	5,540,365	48.6	168	42
	Harrison (R)	5,445,269	47.8	233	58

Cleveland popular vote margin of 95,096. *Harrison* winner with electoral vote margin of 65.

1960	Nixon (R)	34,108,157	49.3	219	41
	Kennedy (D)	34,049,976	49.2	303	59

Nixon popular vote margin of 48,181. *Kennedy* winner with electoral vote margin of 84.

Source: Adapted from Peirce and Longley, *People's President,* p. 255.
Note: The popular vote totals for 1960 used here are computed by the second method discussed in Chapter 3, which consists of crediting Kennedy with five-elevenths of Alabama's Democratic votes and the unpledged elector slate with six-elevenths.
[a]The election of 1824 also resulted in a reversal of the popular vote winner, but through use of the House contingent procedure.
[b]The electoral vote results in 1876 were arrived at by a bipartisan election commission, voting along party lines, which awarded 20 disputed electoral votes to Hayes.

(see table 2). The first of these elections, in 1876, was a peculiar case in that the electoral college majority for the popular vote loser was based on a partisan verdict at best, and on fraud at worst. Initially, it was assumed that Samuel J. Tilden, with a 250,000-vote margin over Rutherford B. Hayes, had won a comfortable electoral college margin of 39 votes. The day after the election, however, it became apparent that if close races in South Carolina, Florida, and Louisiana could be swung to the Republican side, thus switching 20 electoral votes, Hayes would become president by a single electoral vote. Republican reconstruction state governments in each of these states eagerly cooperated in activities that found "agents of both parties using illegal and corrupt tactics to achieve their ends."[26] The conflict was intensified by the realization that the certification of just one Tilden electoral vote from among the 20 under challenge would suffice to elect him.

The dispute finally resulted in duplicate returns arriving from each of the three states—one certifying Hayes electors, the other Tilden electors. Congress, called upon to decide this fiercely partisan dispute, established a bipartisan election commission made up of seven Republicans and seven Democrats, together with an additional member to be drawn from the United States Supreme Court. It was understood that the crucially important swing member would be Justice David Davis, an appointee of Lincoln, who was widely respected for both his fairness and his nonpartisanship. With him on the commission it appeared likely that at least one of the disputed electoral votes would be awarded to Tilden, thus making the Democrat president.

In probably one of the greatest blunders in American political history, the Illinois Democratic party undid all these plans and destroyed the prospects of the Democratic candidate for president. Within hours of congressional passage of the legislation establishing the election commission, news arrived in Washington that the Illinois legislature, under Democratic control, had the day before named Justice Davis to a vacancy in the United States Senate.[27] With Davis suddenly unable to serve, a substitute had to be found on the Court. He was Justice Joseph P. Bradley, a reputedly independent-leaning Republican. As a member of the election commission, however, Justice Bradley did not exhibit any such independent traits—he joined with the seven other Republicans to constitute an eight-vote majority awarding the disputed electoral votes in every case to Hayes, the Republican.[28]

The result of these events was even more sordid: potential Democratic objections to the commission's recommendations were muted through a Republican deal with southern Democrats, a major element of which involved the carrying out of previously indicated decisions to remove the remaining Reconstruction federal troops from the South in return for acquiescence in the election commission's decisions. This deal—the Compromise of 1877—became a crucial element of a new national willingness to give the South carte blanche to go its own way in its own affairs, including the development of "peculiar" institutions such as Jim Crow segregation. The cost of Hayes's electoral college victory, then, was tremendous in terms of subsequent history—a cost still being paid today.

The election of 1888 had none of the complexities of the earlier election. Very simply, in 1888 the winner in popular votes lost the election, while the candidate who ran second in popular votes won. This came about because of the distortions inherent both in the electoral college apportionment of votes among the states and in its winner-take-all feature. Specifically, in this election Benjamin Harrison, the electoral vote winner, carried a number of large states, such as New York, Ohio, and Pennsylvania, by relatively small popular vote margins, while Grover Cleveland, the popular vote leader, carried a number of states, particularly in the South, by very large margins. Harrison's slender popular vote margins were turned into solid, large blocs of electoral votes, while Cleveland's large popular vote margins in his states were wasted in carrying states he could have carried with far fewer votes. Not one to be daunted by losing a victory, Cleveland ran for president again four years later and defeated Harrison, this time in both the popular vote and the electoral college.

The election of 1960 will be fully discussed in Chapter 3. Suffice it here to say that the third method of counting Alabama's votes—a perfectly reasonable and possibly even preferable method—resulted in an apparent national popular vote plurality for Richard Nixon in that year. Nixon chose not to press this claim because of the complexities of explanation and the likelihood of appearing to be a bad loser.

Table 3 shows the two elections in which there has been a resort to the House contingent procedure. The election of 1800 and the subsequent House action in 1801 were sufficiently painful as to lead to adoption of the Twelfth Amendment, ratified in 1804. The election of 1824 similarly both strained and stained the political system. Without going into great detail here, it can be observed that one crucial component of John Quincy Adams's House victory over Andrew Jackson, the popular vote and electoral vote leader, was the helpful support of Speaker of the House Henry Clay, who had run fourth in electoral votes (although third in popular votes) and was, therefore, eliminated from House consideration, which was limited to the top three contenders.[29] Clay busied himself lining up support for Adams—support that proved both crucial and sufficient. Adams, probably not by coincidence, later appointed Clay secretary of state; this was not, however, to be the only price Adams would have to pay for his "victory." The charges and controversies resulting from the House's election of Adams were to haunt him throughout his single term and would be a decisive issue against him in his rematch with Jackson in 1828—which Adams lost.

—> In 1823 Thomas Jefferson wrote prophetically: "I have ever considered the Constitutional mode of election ultimately by the legislature voting by states as the most dangerous blot on our Constitution, and one which some unlucky chance will some day hit."[30] Chance did hit it within the year, with the dreaded fearful consequences. That chance has missed it in the more than 170 years since 1824 is fortunate, but, as we shall see, not assured.

Table 4 presents a category of elections that probably cannot be generally termed ones in which the electoral college misbehaved. In these sixteen cases no candidate received a popular vote majority (although in every instance except the 1860 election at least one can-

Table 3 Electoral College Deadlock and Use of House Contingent Procedure[a]

Year	Candidate	Popular Votes Total	Percentage	Electoral Votes	House Result
1800	Jefferson (D)			73	*Jefferson* winner
	Burr (D)			73	with 10 states to
	Adams (F)			65	4 for Burr after
	Pinchney (F)			64	36 ballots.
	Jay			1	
1824	Adams (D)	115,696	31.9	84	*Adams* winner
	Jackson (D)	152,933	42.2	99	with 13 states to
	Crawford (D)	46,979	13.0	41	7 for Jackson and
	Clay (D)	47,136	13.0	37	4 for Crawford
					on the first ballot.

Jackson popular vote margin of 37,237.

Source: Adapted from Peirce and Longley, *People's President*, p. 256.
[a]The Senate contingent procedure for selection of the vice president in case of no electoral college majority has been used only once, in 1837, after Democratic electors from Virginia refused to vote for the Democratic vice presidential nominee, Richard M. Johnson. He was subsequently elected by the Senate by a vote of 33 to 16.

didate received over 40 percent, Lincoln falling 0.2 percent below that figure), while in twelve cases there was an electoral college majority for the leading vote-getter. In a thirteenth case, the 1824 election, an electoral college deadlock resulted in a House contingent selection of the second-strongest candidate. The remaining three elections, 1876, 1888, and possibly 1960, each produced an electoral college majority—but for the loser in popular votes.

Table 4 not only summarizes the frequent tendency of voters not to give a clear majority to any one candidate; it also illustrates the feature of the electoral college that usually compensates for these

Table 4 Presidents Elected Without a Majority of Popular Votes

Year	Candidate	Popular Votes		Electoral Votes	
		Total	Percentage	Total	Percentage
1824[a][b]	Adams (D)	115,696	31.9	84	32
	Jackson (D)	152,933	42.2	99	38
	Crawford (D)	46,979	13.0	41	16
	Clay (D)	47,136	13.0	37	14
1844	Polk (D)	1,339,368	49.6	170	62
	Clay (W)	1,300,687	48.1	105	38
	Birney (L)	62,197	2.3	0	0
1848	Taylor (W)	1,362,101	47.3	163	57
	Cass (D)	1,222,674	42.5	127	43
	Van Buren (FS)	291,616	10.1	0	0
	Smith (L)	2,733	0.1	0	0
1856	Buchanan (D)	1,839,237	45.6	174	59
	Frémont (R)	1,341,028	33.3	114	39
	Fillmore (W)	849,872	21.1	8	3
	Smith (LR)	484	0	0	0
1860	Lincoln (R)	1,867,198	39.8	180	50
	Douglas (D)	1,379,434	29.4	12	4
	Breckinridge (D)	854,248	18.2	72	24
	Bell (CU)	591,658	12.6	39	13
	Smith	172	0	0	0
1876[a]	Hayes (R)	4,035,924	47.9	185	50
	Tilden (D)	4,287,670	50.9	184	50
	Others	94,935	1.1	0	0
1880	Garfield (R)	4,454,433	48.3	214	58
	Hancock (D)	4,444,976	48.2	155	42
	Weaver (G)	308,649	3.4	0	0
	Others	11,409	0.1	0	0
1884	Cleveland (D)	4,875,971	48.5	219	55
	Blaine (R)	4,852,234	48.3	182	45
	Butler (G)	175,066	1.7	0	0
	St. John (P)	150,957	1.5	0	0

(continued)

Year	Candidate	Popular Votes		Electoral Votes	
		Total	Percentage	Total	Percentage
1888[a]	Harrison (R)	5,445,269	47.8	233	58
	Cleveland (D)	5,540,365	48.6	168	42
	Fisk (P)	250,122	2.2	0	0
	Others	154,083	1.4	0	0
1892	Cleveland (D)	5,556,982	46.0	277	62
	Harrison (R)	5,191,466	43.0	145	33
	Weaver (PO)	1,029,960	8.5	22	5
	Others	292,672	2.4	0	0
1912	Wilson (D)	6,301,254	41.9	435	82
	Roosevelt (PR)	4,127,788	27.4	88	17
	Taft (R)	3,485,831	23.2	8	2
	Debs (S)	901,255	6.0	0	0
	Others	238,934	1.6	0	0
1916	Wilson (D)	9,131,511	49.3	277	52
	Hughes (R)	8,548,935	46.1	254	48
	Benson (S)	585,974	3.2	0	0
	Others	269,812	1.5	0	0
1948	Truman (D)	24,179,345	49.6	303	57
	Dewey (R)	21,991,291	45.1	189	36
	Thurmond (SR)	1,176,125	2.4	39	7
	Wallace (PR)	1,157,326	2.4	0	0
	Others	289,739	0.6	0	0
1960[c]	Kennedy (D)	34,220,984	49.5	303	56
	Nixon (R)	34,108,157	49.3	219	41
	Unpledged Elector Slates	638,822	0.9	15	3
	Others	188,559	0.3	0	0
1968	Nixon (R)	31,785,480	43.4	301	56
	Humphrey (D)	31,275,165	42.7	191	36
	Wallace (AIP)	9,906,473	13.5	46	9
	Others	244,444	0.3	0	0

(continued)

Table 4 (continued)

Year	Candidate	Popular Votes		Electoral Votes	
		Total	Percentage	Total	Percentage
1992	Clinton (D)	44,909,326	43.0	370	69
	Bush (R)	39,103,882	37.4	168	31
	Perot (Ind.)	19,741,657	18.9	0	0
	Others	670,149	0.6	0	0

Source: Adapted and updated from Peirce and Longley, *People's President,* p. 257.
Note: Number of times a president was elected without a majority of popular votes is 16, or 37 percent of the elections for which popular vote totals are available.
[a]Election where the winner did not have the most number of popular votes as well as lacking a majority of popular votes.
[b]Adams was elected president in 1825 through use of the House contingent procedure, although he lacked both a popular vote majority and a plurality.
[c]Depending on the calculation of returns from Alabama, this election may be one where the winner did not have the most number of popular votes as well as lacking a majority of electoral votes. The popular vote totals used here are computed by the second method discussed in Chapter 3, which consists of crediting Kennedy with all of the popular votes received by the most popular of his pledged Alabama electors.

nonmajorities—the multiplier effect. In the sixteen elections examined, the popular vote leader had an average electoral college percentage 10.1 points greater than his popular vote percentage, in most cases producing an electoral college majority.

Table 5 introduces the concept of the *hairbreadth election*—one where a minor vote shift could have changed the outcome. Twenty-two such elections and twenty-six possibilities are examined—51 percent of the elections for which popular vote totals are available. It is very important to note the qualification at the end of this table that these shifts needed are theoretical minimums, extremely unlikely to occur in precisely these quantities in just these states. The figures do, however, provide a relative measure of closeness more realistic than popular vote margins, which do not take into account

Table 5 Hairbreadth Elections

Year	Shift Needed	In What States	Outcome
1828	11,517	Ohio, Ky., N.Y., La., Ind.	Other candidate elected
1836	14,061	N.Y.	Electoral college deadlock
1840	8,386	N.Y., Pa., Maine, N.J.	Other candidate elected
1844	2,555	N.Y.	Other candidate elected
1848	3,227	Ga., Md., Del.	Other candidate elected
1856	17,427	Ind., Ill., Del.	Electoral college deadlock
1860	18,050	Calif., Oreg., Ill., Ind.	Electoral college deadlock
	25,069	N.Y.	Electoral college deadlock
1864	38,111	N.Y., Pa., Ind., Wis., Md., Conn., Oreg.	Other candidate elected
1868	29,862	Pa., Ind., N.C., Ala., Conn., Calif., Nev.	Other candidate elected
1876	116	S.C.	Other candidate elected
1880	10,517	N.Y.	Other candidate elected
1884	575	N.Y.	Other candidate elected
1888	7,189	N.Y.	Other candidate elected
1892	37,364	N.Y., Ind., Wis., N.J., Calif.	Other candidate elected
1896	20,296	Ind., Ky., Calif., W.Va., Oreg., Del.	Other candidate elected
1900	74,755	Ohio, Ind., Kans., Nebr., Md., Utah, Wyo.	Other candidate elected
1908	75,041	Ohio, Mo., Ind., Kans., W.Va., Del., Mont., Md.	Other candidate elected
1916	1,983	Calif.	Other candidate elected
1948	12,487	Calif., Ohio	Electoral college deadlock
	29,294	Calif., Ohio, Ill.	Other candidate elected
1960	8,971	Ill., Mo.	Electoral college deadlock
	11,424	Ill., Mo., N.Mex., Hawaii, Nev.	Other candidate elected

(continued)

Table 5 (continued)

Year	Shift Needed	In What States	Outcome
1968	53,034	N.J., Mo., N.H.	Electoral college deadlock
1976	11,950	Del., Ohio	Electoral college deadlock
	9,246	Hawaii, Ohio	Other candidate elected

Source: Adapted from Peirce and Longley, *People's President,* pp. 258–63.
Note: Number of hairbreadth elections is 22, or 51% of the elections for which popular vote totals are available. An important qualification to keep in mind concerning this table is that shifts in voting patterns are seldom isolated in individual states, but are usually part of regional or national trends. The changes that would have accomplished the electoral results outlined here most likely would have been part of national or regional shifts not limited to a few states. Or, expressed differently, to swing these key states, there would likely have to be vote switching of considerably greater magnitude than the minimum shown here. This table does serve, however, as a demonstration of the relative closeness of many elections, as an illustration of how mighty results can come from relatively small voting shifts, and as evidence of the real potential for electoral college crisis in many of our past elections.

the crucial factor of the distribution of votes in the separate states. In these terms it can be seen that whole series of elections have been extremely close, such as those of 1836–1868 (with one exception) and 1876–1900 (with one exception)—or, alternatively, of the entire period 1836–1916 (with only five exceptions) and 1960–76 (with one exception). Only from 1920 to 1956 (with the exception of 1948) was there a general absence of hairbreadth elections.

It has previously been argued that the electoral college system has continued to exist for over two centuries through a combination of adaptation and chance. This element of chance is graphically illustrated in table 5. In light of the number of hairbreadth elections there examined, that only two have produced an electoral college deadlock, and only two or three have resulted in an electoral college verdict other than for the popular vote leader, seems remarkable indeed.

chapter three

Recent Crisis Elections

The 1980 presidential election was the quintessence of what Americans call a "landslide" election, an echo of years like 1932 and 1936 (Franklin D. Roosevelt's greatest triumphs), 1952 and 1956 (Dwight D. Eisenhower's massive wins), and 1972 (the reelection of Richard M. Nixon over a Democratic opposition in total disarray).

Although most published national opinion surveys up to election day itself had suggested that the 1980 contest was "too close to call" between Republican challenger Ronald Reagan, incumbent President Jimmy Carter, and independent candidate John B. Anderson, the suspense had drained away by late afternoon. "Exit polls" of voters across the nation, conducted by the CBS, NBC, and ABC television networks, already showed a huge Reagan lead. As NBC signed on with its election night coverage at 7 P.M. (E.S.T.), commentator John Chancellor confidently predicted that "Ronald Reagan will win a very substantial victory tonight, very substantial." And he was right. Over the next hour, television election maps became awash in "Reagan blue" as state after state was called for the Republican.

Just an hour and a quarter into its election night programming, NBC at 8:15:21 flashed "REAGAN WINS" on the nation's screens, followed by ABC at 9:52 and CBS at 10:33. President Carter himself appeared before his election workers (and the nation's television viewers) to concede the election before 10 P.M.—hours before the polls had closed in the West. The shortest election night of the television era was over. The final returns would show Reagan winning 51 percent of the popular vote, Carter 41 percent, and Anderson 7 percent. In electoral votes, it would be an overwhelming 489 votes for Reagan, only 49 for Carter, and none for Anderson.

But the history of U.S. elections demonstrates clearly that it is not always so easy, that the electoral college[1]—that hoary eighteenth-century institution still chugging into the last years of the twentieth—may perform with apparent smoothness in a decisive election but is a faltering and potentially dangerous mechanism when the contest is close or when candidates other than the two major-party nominees complicate the situation.

Six recent presidential elections stand out in terms of their potential for national electoral crisis: those of 1948, 1960, 1968, 1976, 1980, and 1992. It is significant that these crisis elections comprise six of the twelve post–World War II presidential elections, or one-half of the elections in the past fifty-one years. Since 1945, the electoral college has hung on the brink of deadlock or popular mandate reversal as often as it has faithfully recorded the voters' will.

The Election of 1948

Except for President Harry S Truman, virtually everyone in the country expected the Republicans to take over the White House in 1948, thus ending the Democratic dominance that had begun with Franklin D. Roosevelt's first election in 1932. Truman, a Missouri senator until Roosevelt chose him for the vice presidential nomination in 1944, had suddenly been catapulted into the presidency by Roosevelt's death in office in April 1945. But under Truman's leadership the Democrats were thrown for staggering losses in the 1946 midterm elections, relinquishing control of Congress for the first time since the early 1930s.

Truman and the newly elected Republican eightieth Congress were able to work together fairly well on foreign problems and indeed launched such historic programs as the Marshall Plan to aid war-torn Europe. But bitter feuding erupted between president and Congress on domestic issues. In 1947, over the president's veto and the angry protest of organized labor, the eightieth Congress passed the landmark Taft-Hartley Labor-Management Relations Act. Con-

gressional investigation of Communist infiltration of the government in the 1930s further exacerbated White House–Capitol Hill
relations. In his 1948 State of the Union address, Truman shocked a
budget-conscious Congress by simultaneously urging new social
welfare legislation that would cost $10 billion and a $40 tax cut for
every man, woman, and child in the country. Republicans promptly
accused him of gross political opportunism, and that dispute had
scarcely cooled before the president in February advocated a sweeping civil rights program that drew embittered protests from the
southern Democrats. Truman had already won the enmity of the
Democratic left wing by adopting a stiff policy against Soviet
advances in Europe.

By the summer of 1948 the president's popularity had plum-
meted to such depths that many Democrats—conservatives and liberals alike—had cast around for another nominee to head the party's
ticket. In the end, however, Truman was able to exert the massive
political powers of an incumbent president and force his own
renomination by the Democratic National Convention in Philadelphia on July 15. In his acceptance speech, Truman lashed out at the
Republicans as "the party of special interests" that "favors the privi-
leged few and not the common everyday man." Truman used the
occasion to announce that he would call Congress back into special
session on July 26 ("Turnip Day in Missouri") to enact an almost
incredible array of welfare bills. "What the worst 80th Congress does
in its special session will be the test," the president said. Naturally,
the Republican Congress did little that Truman asked, and throughout the campaign Truman could concentrate his fire on the "do-
nothing Republican Congress." The Republicans, Truman declared,
were "predatory animals who don't care if you people are thrown
into a depression." They had "murdered" housing legislation, he said,
and the farmers should oppose the Republicans because "this
Republican Congress has already stuck a pitchfork into the farmer's
back." Truman made a special appeal to minority religious and racial
groups, calling for strong civil rights legislation and condemning

Republicans for passing the Displaced Persons Act, which he said discriminated against Catholics and Jews.[2]

One reason for the near-universal predictions of Truman's defeat was the split-off from the Democratic party of southern segregationists on one side and left-wingers on the other. The southern defection, brewing several months, came to a head at the Democratic National Convention when a tough civil rights plank was adopted at the instigation of Minneapolis mayor Hubert H. Humphrey and other party liberals. The Alabama and Mississippi delegations walked out on the spot, and rebellious southerners from thirteen states subsequently held a rump convention at Birmingham, Alabama, to nominate Gov. Strom Thurmond of South Carolina as the States' Rights (Dixiecrat) party candidate. On the other extreme of the party, former vice president Henry A. Wallace organized a new Progressive party opposed to the United States' Cold War foreign policies. Though few doubted Wallace's own loyalty, his new party was heavily influenced by Communists and others of the extreme left. Both the Dixiecrat and Progressive candidates posed serious dangers for Truman. The former could deprive him of regular southern electoral votes counted on by Democratic presidential candidates ever since 1880, while the latter could cost him enough votes to lose a number of strategic urbanized states of the North.

Regardless of how they personally felt about Truman, most Americans had to admire his courage in launching an exhaustive, 31,000-mile barnstorming whistle-stop tour, crisscrossing the country in the face of almost unanimous predictions from pollsters, reporters, and sundry political "experts" that Thomas E. Dewey would win an overwhelming victory. A Republican of moderate persuasion in his second term as governor of New York, Dewey had emerged as his party's nominee on the third roll call at the Republican National Convention in Philadelphia on June 24. In New York, Dewey had first won fame as a tough and effective district attorney and was respected as an able state administrator. In 1944 he had run a creditable race against Roosevelt for the presidency. These factors helped him outrun Sen. Robert A. Taft of Ohio, leader of the Republican conservative wing, and Harold E. Stassen, a younger liberal leader, in the competition for the nomination. But in the fall campaign, Dewey made the fateful mistake of believing his election was already assured and thus refused to join Truman in a sharp partisan debate on substantive issues. Instead, Dewey concentrated on diffuse calls for "national unity," failed to excite the Republican partisans, and left most of the country indifferent to his fate.

As the first returns came in from the northeastern states the night of November 2, Truman seized the lead in the popular vote. As the night wore on, state after state that observers had marked as "safe Republican" moved into the Truman column. Massachusetts went Democratic, as did the border states. Truman lost only four southern states—Alabama, Louisiana, Mississippi, and South Carolina—to the Dixiecrat ticket. About half the farm belt was Truman's, and he ran ahead in California despite the presence of that state's popular governor, Earl Warren, as the vice presidential nominee on the Republican ticket. Among the larger states, Dewey won only New York, Michigan, and Pennsylvania. When Ohio went conclusively for Truman at eleven o'clock on Wednesday morning, Dewey conceded.

The national popular vote showed that Truman had won by more than two million popular votes and that he ran 114 votes ahead of Dewey in the electoral college. (See table 6.) Truman's electoral vote margin was deceptive, however. A shift from Truman to Dewey of only 29,294 votes in three states (16,807 in Illinois, 8,933 in California, and 3,554 in Ohio) would have made Dewey president instead. The election would have gone into the House of Representatives for final resolution with a shift of only 12,487 votes in California and Ohio.

Even with the hindsight that history affords, it is impossible to determine what might have happened if the House had been called upon to pick a president in the wake of the 1948 election. Control of twenty-five delegations (a majority of the forty-eight states) would have been required to elect a president. Loyalist Democrats would

Table 6 Results of the 1948 Election

	Popular Votes	Electoral Votes
Harry S Truman (D)	24,179,345	303
Thomas E. Dewey (R)	21,991,291	189
Strom Thurmond (SR)	1,176,125	39
Henry A. Wallace (PR)	1,157,326	0
Minor Parties	289,739	0
Truman plurality: 2,188,054		

have controlled twenty-one delegations, Republicans twenty, the Dixiecrats four. Three delegations would have been divided equally between the major parties. In fact, an election by the House was precisely what Thurmond and his Dixiecrats had hoped for. They undoubtedly would have brought pressure on Truman to hold back on civil rights legislation or other steps designed to further racial integration, in return for which the Dixiecrat states would have thrown their support to Truman and made him president. Thus a splinter party that won only 2.4 percent of the national popular vote might have forced its terms on a president. The Dixiecrats probably would have been amenable to a similar deal with the Republicans, but even if their votes had been added to his, Dewey would have been one state short of a majority. These calculations assume, of course, that House members invariably would vote for their own party's presidential candidate or, in the case of southerners from the four Dixiecrat states, would vote the way the people of their states had voted in the fall elections. There might have been "breaks" in this lineup or peculiar types of deals under the pressures of the moment.

One scarcely believable but distinct possibility, if the 1948 election had gone into the House, is that no decision at all would have been made there. Had the House deadlock held from the day of the electoral count, January 6, until inauguration day, January 20, the new vice president would have assumed the presidency under the terms of the Twentieth Amendment. (That amendment, ratified in 1933, provided in part that "if the President elect shall have failed to qualify, then the Vice President elect shall act as President until a President shall have qualified.") But who would have been the new vice president? If Truman had failed to win an electoral majority, his vice presidential running mate, Sen. Alben W. Barkley, also would have failed to win a majority. Under the Constitution the Senate would have had the task of electing the new vice president. The party lineup in the Senate was fifty-four Democrats, forty-two Republicans. The senators would have had only two choices: Barkley or Warren. Barkley was a highly respected senator and member of its inner "club." Thus he could have expected solid backing from all the northern Democrats and probably from all but one or two of his colleagues and long-time associates from Dixiecrat states. The chances are very high that Barkley would have been chosen as vice president. And if the House had failed to break its deadlock by January 20, Barkley would have assumed the powers of the presidency—even though not a single American had voted to elect him to that position.[3] But Barkley would have been only acting president and would have been obliged to relinquish the office at any time in the following four years that the House resolved its deadlock and chose a new president.

The 1948 election did more than demonstrate the dangers of throwing an election into the House. It also provided a striking example of how the electoral college permits splinter parties, which receive only tiny percentages of the national popular vote, to play a decisive role in the ultimate allocation of large blocs of electoral votes. Truman apparently lost a massive bloc of seventy-four electoral votes—those of New York, Michigan, and Maryland—because Henry Wallace was on the ballot in those states. The Wallace vote, liberal and basically Democratic-inclined, accounted for more than the difference between Dewey and Truman in each of those states. Thus the electoral college permits splinter parties in big states to occupy the balance of power in the election of an American president.

The Election of 1960

Dwight D. Eisenhower, the first Republican to win the presidency since the 1920s, was ineligible to seek a third term in 1960 because of the two-term limitation written into the Constitution through the Twenty-second Amendment. The Democrats also felt obliged to come up with a new nominee because Adlai E. Stevenson, their standard bearer in 1952 and 1956, had a record of two successive defeats behind him. For the Republicans, the choice of a presidential candidate was comparatively easy. Vice President Richard M. Nixon had been in the public eye for eight years, had been an exceptionally active vice president, and enjoyed strong support in the Republican organizations throughout the country. New York governor Nelson A. Rockefeller, the only potential opponent to Nixon who might have amassed significant delegate strength, decided the odds against success were too high and declined to make the effort. Nixon was nominated by an almost unanimous vote of the Republican National Convention on July 27 in Chicago.

Four formidable candidates entered the race for the Democratic nomination: Sen. Hubert H. Humphrey of Minnesota, a leading spokesman for the party's liberal wing; Sen. John F. Kennedy of Massachusetts, a liberal, a strong vote-getter, and the first Roman Catholic to be seriously considered for the presidency since Alfred E. Smith in 1928; Sen. Stuart Symington of Missouri, a former secretary of the air force; and Senate Majority Leader Lyndon B. Johnson of Texas, a skilled and powerful Democratic legislative leader since 1953. By winning the most important presidential primaries of the year and obtaining the support of the party's big-city leaders, Kennedy was able to win nomination on the first ballot at the Democratic National Convention in Los Angeles on July 13. In a surprise move, Kennedy picked Johnson as his running mate. Many liberal leaders in the party expressed consternation at the selection of Johnson, but later it became evident that Johnson's presence on the ticket was probably an essential element in holding most of the South

behind Kennedy and effecting Democratic victory in one of the closest elections of U.S. history.

Kennedy promised the voters a "New Frontier" to cope with
"uncharted areas of space and science, unsolved problems of peace
and war, unconquered pockets of ignorance and prejudice, unan-
swered questions of poverty and surplus." The central issue, he
asserted repeatedly, was the need for strong presidential leadership
to reverse the nation's declining prestige abroad and lagging economy at home. Nixon, on the other hand, pledged to "build on" the
achievements of the Eisenhower administration and pictured himself as a man trained for the presidency and its trying problems, especially in the field of international diplomacy. He described Kennedy
as "immature" and "impulsive" and said the Democratic platform
pledges would add $18 billion to the government's annual budget.
As the campaign entered its final weeks, Kennedy was thought to
have gained significantly from an unprecedented series of four face-
to-face encounters between the presidential candidates on national
television.[4]

In some respects, the outcome was similar to that of 1948. The
Democratic candidate won a substantial margin of electoral votes—
303 compared to 219 for his Republican opponent. The substantial
nature of Kennedy's electoral college victory belied the suspense of
election night, November 8, as the nation watched the popular vote
reports in what would prove to be one of the most closely contested
presidential races of the century.

Early in the evening, as the polls began to close across the continent, it had looked like a national sweep for the Democrats. Led by
bellwether Connecticut, the industrial states of the eastern seaboard
had gone for Kennedy—Pennsylvania with its 32 electoral votes,
New York with its gigantic 45-electoral-vote bloc, and Kennedy's
native Massachusetts with 16 electoral votes, the last by a staggering
half-million plurality in the popular vote.

But the East was not all of America, and the later the night grew,
the less certain the result appeared. Kennedy may have been strong

in his native East, but the Republican ticket of Nixon and Henry Cabot Lodge showed remarkable strength as the other regions began to report. To the surprise of virtually every political analyst, Nixon won Ohio with its 25 electoral votes by a decisive margin of a quarter-million votes. The "new South" states of Virginia, Kentucky, Tennessee, and Florida were his. The midwestern Republican heartland delivered Indiana, Wisconsin, and Iowa into Nixon's hands, and as the night progressed it became apparent that virtually every prairie state, from North Dakota to Oklahoma, would be his and that he would capture every one of the western mountain states except Nevada. In addition, he defeated Kennedy in the Pacific states of Washington, Oregon, and Alaska. Several days later it would become official that Nixon had also won his native California, with its 32 electoral votes, by a fragile margin. In all, he would win 26 of the 50 states.

John Kennedy's eastern lead would never be overcome, however. To that solid base, Kennedy added industrial Michigan with its 20 electoral votes; he captured Illinois, too—by a much-disputed margin of 8,858 votes, which brought him 27 electoral votes. Border states like Maryland, West Virginia, and Missouri went for Kennedy, and his victory was clinched by his ability to seize 81 electoral votes from seven states of the old Confederacy—aided in no small part by his vice presidential running mate from Texas.

There was no left-wing splinter party of any consequence in the 1960 balloting, but the southern unpledged elector movement, a successor to the Dixiecrat movement of 1948, won 14 electoral votes in two southern states. The unpledged electors eventually cast their votes for Sen. Harry Flood Byrd in the electoral college. In one major respect, however, the results were markedly different from those of 1948. While Truman had amassed a popular vote plurality of over two million votes, Kennedy's popular vote margin was one of the smallest in the history of presidential elections—apparently just over 100,000 out of a total of 68,738,000 ballots cast in the country.

In fact, it was impossible to determine exactly what Kennedy's popular vote plurality—if it existed at all—really was. With the exception of Alabama, where unprecedented difficulties arose in determining the popular vote, the national count was 33,902,681 for Kennedy and 33,870,176 for Nixon—a Kennedy lead of 32,505. In Alabama, state law provided that the names of the individual candidates for presidential elector would appear separately on the ballot, with the voter allowed to vote for as many or as few members of any electoral slate as he liked. Each elector slate consisted of eleven names—the number of electoral votes to which the state was entitled. All the Republican electors were pledged to vote for Nixon, and the highest Republican elector received 237,981 votes in the general election—establishing a clear Nixon popular vote total in the state.[5] There had been stiff competition in Alabama to determine who would be placed on the ballot as Democratic electors—those pledged to support the party's national nominee or unpledged electors opposed to the national policies of the party. A Democratic primary and runoff held in the spring had resulted in the selection of six unpledged and five loyalist elector candidates to compose the eleven-person Democratic elector slate in the general election. Thus the question arose: For whom should the votes cast for the Democratic elector slate be counted in the national popular vote tally—for Kennedy or for the unpledged elector movement?

On election day the highest unpledged elector on the Democratic slate received 324,050 votes, while the highest loyalist or Kennedy elector received 318,303 votes. It appeared that, with few exceptions, the same people had voted for both the unpledged and the loyalist electors. The national wire services chose to credit Kennedy with the highest vote cast for any Democratic elector in the state—the 324,050 that one of the unpledged members of the Democratic slate received. The wire service accounts made it appear that no unpledged elector votes at all were cast in Alabama. The result, of course, was a gross misstatement of the actual vote in the state, an error that followed over into the wire associations' report that

Kennedy won the national popular vote by some 118,000 votes. The figure was open to criticism on two counts: first, because it included some 6,000 votes that were specifically cast *against* Kennedy by Alabama Democrats who would not support loyalist electors, and second because it totally disregarded the unpledged elector vote, even though it was higher than Kennedy's.

A preferable method of reporting the Alabama vote, adopted by Neal Peirce for the *Congressional Quarterly* and identified as "First Method" in table 7, was to report the vote for the highest Kennedy elector (318,303) as part of his national count and the vote for the highest unpledged elector (324,050) as part of the national unpledged elector vote (eventually credited to Byrd). The result was a Kennedy plurality nationwide of 112,827 votes. In reporting this result, *Congressional Quarterly* took care to note, however, that it was actually reporting the votes of the citizens who supported Democratic electors in Alabama twice—once for Kennedy, once for unpledged electors. The result involved a serious distortion, since the votes of the Democratic voters in Alabama were counted twice, while the Republican voters in the state—and the votes of citizens in every other state—were reported but once.

An alternative method, developed by the *Congressional Quarterly* and identified as "Second Method," was to take the highest vote for any Democratic elector in Alabama—324,050—and divide it proportionately between Kennedy and unpledged electors. Since loyalists held five of the eleven spots on the slate, they were credited with five-elevenths of the party total—147,295 votes. The unpledged electors, holding six elector slots, were credited with six-elevenths of the Democratic vote—176,755. This procedure, while somewhat arbitrary, had the virtue of avoiding any double count of the Democratic votes in Alabama. The state totals would now read: Nixon 237,981; Kennedy 147,295; unpledged electors (Byrd) 176,755. But when these totals were added to the popular vote results from the other forty-nine states, a significant change took place. Kennedy no

Table 7 Results of the 1960 Election

	Popular Votes	Electoral Votes
First Method		
John F. Kennedy (D)	34,220,984	303
Richard M. Nixon (R)	34,108,157	219
Harry F. Byrd*	638,822	15
Minor Parties	188,559	0
Kennedy plurality: 112,827		
Second Method		
Kennedy	34,049,976	303
Nixon	34,108,157	219
Byrd*	491,527	15
Minor Parties	188,559	0
Nixon plurality: 58,181		

First method involves counting split Alabama elector slate for both Kennedy and unpledged electors; *second method* involves dividing vote for Alabama Democratic elector slate proportionately according to its composition. See discussion in text.
*Byrd was accorded the votes of 14 unpledged electors from Alabama and Mississippi, plus one vote by a Republican elector in Oklahoma.

longer led in the national popular vote at all. Instead, Nixon was the popular vote winner by a margin of 58,181.[6]

Interestingly, Nixon never sought to use these figures to argue that he had been the people's choice for president in 1960. Since Kennedy was clearly the electoral college winner, Nixon may have felt that claiming a popular vote victory would simply have made him out as a poor loser. Moreover, the complex issues raised by the Alabama count were not the kind that many people would fully understand. Thus, little public debate took place on the question of how Alabama's votes should be counted, and it seemed likely that the issue would not be raised again.

But in 1964 the problem of determining the 1960 Alabama vote did reappear. The Democratic National Committee, in allocating the number of delegate seats each state would have to the 1964 national convention, employed a formula that rested in part on the number of popular votes the party's nominee—Kennedy—had received in the last presidential election. The northern Democrats in control of the committee were anxious to minimize the weight of the southern states, especially those that had been disloyal to the national ticket in the 1960 election. So when it came to determining the number of Kennedy votes with which Alabama should be credited in determining the delegate apportionment, the national committee used exactly the same formula that the *Congressional Quarterly* had used following the 1960 election. It took the highest vote for a Democratic elector in Alabama, divided it in eleven parts, and credited five parts to Kennedy and six to the unpledged electors. As a result, the size of the Alabama delegation to the 1964 convention was reduced. But by employing this stratagem the committee was accepting the rationale of a counting system under which Nixon was the clear popular vote winner in 1960.

In the weeks following the 1960 election, however, the nation's attention was focused not on the Alabama vote count but rather on the question of fraud. Two days after the election, Republican National Chairman Thurston B. Morton sent telegrams to party leaders in eleven states asking them to look into allegations of voting irregularities. A Republican spokesman said many complaints alleging fraud, payment of money, and other irregularities had been received, most of them from Illinois, Texas, North and South Carolina, Michigan, and New Jersey. Republicans were especially bitter over the outcome in Illinois, which Kennedy had won by 8,858 votes out of 4,757,409 cast, and there were allegations of irregularities in the count in heavily Democratic Cook County (Chicago). The Cook County Republican chairman alleged that 100,000 fraudulent votes had swung Illinois to Kennedy through "systematic" looting of votes in twelve city wards and parts of two others.[7] Republicans laid stress on one precinct, virtually deserted because of highway demolitions, where the vote reported was 79 for Kennedy and 3 for Nixon, although there were fewer than 50 registered voters on election day.[8] Widespread "tombstone" voting and tampering with voting machines were alleged. The Democrats replied angrily that the Republicans had no proof of substantial irregularities and that they were darkening the name of the city before the nation. The recounts in the city soon bogged down in legal maneuvering, and the Republicans were never able to produce hard evidence to show that fraud had been a big enough factor to give the state to Kennedy.[9] (In 1962, however, three Democratic precinct workers in Chicago did plead guilty to "altering, changing, defacing, injuring or destroying ballots" in the 1960 election.[10]) Republicans were even less hopeful of a reversal in Texas, where the Kennedy-Johnson ticket led by 46,233 votes, though Republicans charged that the Democratic-controlled election boards had consistently invalidated Republican ballots with slight defects while counting Democratic ballots with identical deficiencies.

Despite the closeness of the election, the Republicans never publicly claimed that the alleged vote irregularities were sufficient to reverse the outcome. But for a while, between election day on November 8 and December 19 (when the electors met to vote), there was speculation that if Illinois's 27 electoral votes were lost to Kennedy through proof of vote fraud, thus reducing Kennedy's electoral votes to 273—only 4 more than the 269 needed for victory—southern electors might bolt and withhold votes from the Kennedy-Johnson ticket, thus throwing the election into the House of Representatives. This immediate fear was dispelled, however, when the Illinois electoral board, consisting of four Republicans and one Democrat, certified the election of the Kennedy electors from the state on December 14.

The close elections in the northern states had been watched with special interest by conservative southerners who hoped to thwart Kennedy's election. On December 10 Alabama's six unpledged electors met in Birmingham and announced their desire to cast their presidential vote "for an outstanding Southern Democrat who sympathizes with our peculiar problems in the South." They stated that "our position remains fluid so that we can cooperate with other unpledged electors for the preservation of racial and national integrity." The Alabamans specifically deplored the role of southerners who "ally themselves with a candidate [Kennedy] who avowedly would integrate our schools, do away with literacy tests for voting," and "otherwise undermine everything we hold dear in the South."[11]

Two days later a joint meeting was held in Jackson, Mississippi, between the six unpledged electors from Alabama and the eight who had been chosen in Mississippi. The decision was made to throw the unpledged elector support to Senator Byrd of Virginia, and a joint statement was drafted calling on presidential electors from other southern states to join the vote for Byrd in the hope that enough electoral votes might be withheld from Kennedy to throw the election into the House of Representatives. A defection of thirty-five additional southern electors from Kennedy would have been necessary to send the election to the House. Mississippi governor Ross Barnett, one of the South's strongest segregationists, sent letters to six other states asking for support in the move to block Kennedy. In Louisiana, leaders of the White Citizens Council were at the forefront of a move to have the state's Democratic electors withhold their support from Kennedy.[12] The stated hope of the unpledged electors was that if the election reached the House, all southerners would vote for Byrd and that the Republicans, "being fundamentally opposed to the liberalism of Senator Kennedy," would follow suit.[13] The new party lineup in the House would consist of 23 states controlled by northern and border-state Democrats, 6 controlled by Deep South Democrats, and 17 controlled by Republicans. Another 4 delegations were evenly split between the parties. Thus it is highly problematic to guess what would have happened had the election reached the House.

As it turned out, when the electors actually cast their votes on December 19, the only vote Byrd got outside of the anticipated ones from Alabama and Mississippi came not from another southern Democrat but from a Republican. He was Henry D. Irwin, who had been elected as a member of the winning Republican elector slate pledged to Nixon in Oklahoma. Irwin subsequently stated on a nationwide television program that he had performed "his constitutional duty" as a "free elector." The next July, subpoenaed to appear before a U.S. Senate Judiciary subcommittee, Irwin said he had never planned to vote for Nixon, whom he "could not stomach." Irwin revealed that he had worked in concert with R. Lea Harris, a Montgomery, Alabama, attorney, in a national movement to get the members of the electoral college to desert Nixon and Kennedy in favor of a strongly conservative candidate. An alternative was to support a plan, reportedly considered by some conservatives in the Louisiana legislature, to call a meeting of conservative southern governors in Baton Rouge, to which Kennedy would have been invited and presented with the following conditions for receiving the southern electoral votes he needed for election: "(1) Eliminate the present sizable foreign aid we presently give to the Communist economy; (2) adhere to the spirit of the 10th Amendment [reserving powers not specified in the Constitution to the states]; and (3) appoint one of these Southern Governors Attorney General."[14]

On November 20 Irwin had telegraphed all Republican electors in the country, saying, "I am Oklahoma Republican elector. The Republican electors cannot deny the election to Kennedy. Sufficient conservative Democratic electors available to deny labor Socialist nominee. Would you consider Byrd President, [Barry] Goldwater Vice President, or wire any acceptable substitute. All replies strict confidence." Irwin received approximately forty replies, some of them favorable, but most of the electors indicated that they had a moral obligation to vote for Nixon. Irwin subsequently asked the Republican national committee members and state chairpersons to free Republican electors from any obligation to vote for Nixon, but received only three sympathetic replies. Republican National Committeeman Albert K. Mitchell of New Mexico wired Irwin that he had taken up the idea "with some of the leaders of the Republican National Committee level and found that while everyone was in favor of the move, they felt it should not be sponsored by the Republican organization." Mitchell, however, encouraged Irwin to take further steps "to eliminate Kennedy from the Presidency." Later, Republican National Chairman Morton said that if Irwin "had the support of the Republican National Committee, I knew nothing about it." Not a single additional Republican elector in the country followed Irwin's lead.[15]

Thus every move to upset the results of the 1960 election—from a Republican challenge of vote returns to the efforts of the southern unpledged electors and the machinations of Henry Irwin of Oklahoma—was to prove fruitless. But it was only by chance that the country was spared weeks or months of indecision following the 1960 contest. A shift of only 8,971 popular votes—4,480 in Illinois and 4,491 in Missouri—would have thrown the election into the House. If an additional 1,148 votes had shifted from Kennedy to Nixon in New Mexico, along with 58 in Hawaii and 1,247 in Nevada, Nixon would have become president. Whether that would have violated the popular will one cannot say, because there is no obviously fair way to count the popular vote for the 1960 election. Had it not been for the electoral college, each candidate might have conducted his campaign somewhat differently, and one candidate or the other might have won a clear-cut popular vote victory.*

*Kennedy's strategy was to carry the Midwest and the eastern industrial states, plus California, while counting on the normal Democratic vote from the majority of southern states. The Nixon strategy was to carry the normally Republican farm areas, run strongly in the far West, and make sufficient inroads in the major industrial states and normally Democratic South to win a majority of the electoral votes. Perhaps one reason Kennedy won was that since 1956 he and his advisers had shown an extraordinarily keen perception of the workings of the electoral college and understood how an appeal centered on the major industrial states might win for a Democratic candidate. Nixon, on the other hand, pledged to visit every one of the fifty states in his campaign, a pledge that would bedevil him on the final weekend before the election as he spent valuable hours in a visit to Alaska (a state with 3 electoral votes) instead of concentrating on big, doubtful states like Michigan and Illinois (with 20 and 27 electoral votes, respectively). In retrospect, neither candidate could say his strategy had been

In many ways, the 1960 election summed up the evils of the electoral college in our times. First, it showed once again the irrational, chance factors that decide a close election, when the shift of a few votes can throw huge blocs of electoral votes in one direction or the other. Second, it underscored the danger of fraud deciding a presidential election, because Illinois, where the most ballot disputes arose, was the state that almost determined the outcome of the entire election. Third, it showed the potentially decisive role that a narrowly based regional or splinter party can play in the choice of a president and how the system actually encourages independent elector blocs. Fourth, the election showed how a faithless elector, chosen to carry out a specific function, could suddenly break his or her trust and try to determine the choice of the chief executive for 180 million Americans. (What if Henry Irwin's vote had been the deciding vote in the electoral college in 1960?) Last, the election showed that as long as individual states have carte blanche in deciding how presidential electors will be chosen, it may be difficult and sometimes impossible to compile accurate national popular vote totals (as in Alabama in 1960) and to learn whom the majority of Americans really wanted to be their president.

We have not, so far, paid attention to the *real* election—the moment when the electoral votes are counted before a joint session of Congress and the next president and vice president of the United States are officially proclaimed. The scene following the 1960 election was one such occasion of particular interest.

At 12:55 P.M. on January 6, 1961, the doorkeeper of the House of Representatives announced the arrival of the vice president and

---

completely effective. Kennedy, to be sure, did carry most of the big states. But he lost Ohio and California and, by his failure to win the prairie or mountain states, came perilously close to defeat. Nixon did win a majority of the states, a fitting conclusion for his campaign. But he had diffused his effort and fell short of victory. Without the electoral college, the campaigns probably would have been less oriented to specific states or blocs of states and more focused on the nation as a whole.

the members of the Senate for the purpose of counting the electoral votes. Two handsome boxes of inlaid wood, holding the electoral votes submitted from all the states, had been brought by pages from the Senate chamber and were now taken down the center aisle of the House and placed on the desk of the Speaker's podium. For the Democrats it was a happy occasion, and their side of the chamber was almost filled, while only a few of the seats on the Republican side were taken.

As the presiding officer of the Senate, Vice President Richard M. Nixon had the constitutional duty to preside at this joint session of Congress. It was the first time in a century that a vice president had been called upon to preside over an electoral vote tally that would certify the election as president of the man he had run against. The last occasion had been on February 13, 1861, when Vice President John C. Breckinridge, who had run unsuccessfully for president the previous autumn, certified the election of Abraham Lincoln.

Before ordering that the ballot count begin, Nixon threw his arm around the shoulder of the Speaker of the House, Sam Rayburn of Texas, and, as applause mounted, offered the congratulations of the Senate to the venerable Speaker on his seventy-ninth birthday. Then the official business of the joint session got underway. Four tellers had been appointed—a Republican and a Democrat from both the Senate and the House. The senior man among them was Arizona senator Carl Hayden, whose congressional service had begun forty-eight years before, when his state entered the Union. Representing the Senate Republicans was Carl Curtis of Nebraska, while Representatives Edna F. Kelly of New York and Frances P. Bolton of Ohio had been designated from the Democratic and Republican sides of the House, respectively.

The returns from Alabama, the first state by alphabetical order, were withdrawn from the boxes and handed to Nixon, who opened the certification and then handed it to the tellers, who announced the result. The count for Alabama showed 6 electoral votes for Sen. Harry Flood Byrd of Virginia and 5 for Sen. John F. Kennedy of

Massachusetts. Nixon nodded to Senator Byrd and said it seemed that "the gentleman from Virginia is now in the lead." The count proceeded uninterrupted until Nixon announced that three certificates had been received from Hawaii—one certifying the election of Republican electors, one certifying the election of Democratic electors, and a third, from the governor of the state, certifying the proper election of the Democratic electors. The first official count in Hawaii had shown a Republican electoral victory by a margin of 141 votes, but on a recount the Democrats forged ahead by 115 votes. Nixon suggested that the governor's certification of the Democratic electors be accepted, and there being no objection, it was so ordered.

The count then proceeded through the last state on the list—Wyoming. Nixon had sought, more or less successfully, to maintain a cheerful demeanor through the long ballot tally, but now he fidgeted as the tellers assembled the documents that showed the final results. The count, reported to him by the tellers, showed:

For president: John F. Kennedy, 303 electoral votes; Richard M. Nixon, 219 electoral votes; Harry F. Byrd, 15 electoral votes.

For vice president: Lyndon B. Johnson, 303 electoral votes; Henry Cabot Lodge, 219 electoral votes; Strom Thurmond, 14 electoral votes; Barry Goldwater, 1 electoral vote.[16]

The Election of 1968

The tumultuous events surrounding the presidential election of 1968 included massive riots and demonstrations—on college campuses because of the nation's involvement with the war in Vietnam, in the cities because of race tensions that culminated with the springtime assassination of civil rights leader Martin Luther King, Jr., in Memphis, Tennessee.[17] President Lyndon B. Johnson, who had succeeded to the presidency on the death of John F. Kennedy in 1963 and won an overwhelming election victory in 1964, found himself under such heavy challenge for renomination that he withdrew shortly before the crucial Wisconsin primary. The majority Democratic party was wracked by dissension and disunity, culminating in a nightmarish convention in Chicago that ended with bloody street confrontations between antiwar protesters and Mayor Richard Daley's police. Robert F. Kennedy, former attorney general and brother of the late president, had entered the primaries, only to be cut down by an assassin's bullets in Los Angeles on the night the returns from the California primary were being counted.

The final nominees of the major parties were Vice President Hubert H. Humphrey for the Democrats and Richard M. Nixon—the vice president who had retired eight years before, now returned to political life—for the Republicans. But if there was an interesting figure in the 1968 elections, particularly for observing the workings of the electoral college, it was former Gov. George C. Wallace of Alabama, whose candidacy on the ticket of the party of his own creation—the American Independent party—presented America with the most formidable third-party candidacy of many decades.

In a sense, Wallace was simply a Dixiecrat—a direct descendant of the brand of anti–civil rights southern politics that had propelled Strom Thurmond into the 1948 election and motivated the group of electors that eventually supported Harry F. Byrd in 1960. But Wallace had a much broader appeal. He had demonstrated that by strong runs in the 1964 Democratic presidential primaries and now proved it again by galvanizing supporters to place elector slates pledged to him on the ballots of all fifty states—an organizational miracle in modern-day politics. (Up to that time, it had been assumed that it would be virtually impossible for an independent candidate to qualify so broadly; after Wallace, it would be clear that with sufficient planning and effort, candidates could indeed qualify without a major-party nomination.)

Nor was racism the only motivating factor of Wallace supporters. True, the Alabaman had declared in his 1963 inaugural address: "Segregation now—segregation tomorrow—segregation forever." Later he had "stood in the schoolhouse door" trying to prevent integration at the University of Alabama. But one needed to attend only one or two of his 1968 rallies to detect the broader attraction. They were half revival, half political meetings, with Wallace appealing to the plain folks present—those steelworkers and beauticians and cab drivers decked out in red, white, and blue—with his hot rhetoric about pseudo-intellectual government and long-haired students, bussin' and lenient judges, welfare loafers, and the fate that awaited any anarchist "scum" who "lies down in front of our car when we get to be President." (The line that always brought down the house, reflecting the quintessential violence of the Wallace appeal: "It'll be the *last* car he'll ever lie down in front of.")

Wallace's southernism worked both for and against him. He played strongly on the region's lingering sense of inferiority, telling southerners that they were tired of being looked down upon and repeating a sure-applause line: "Folks down here in Alabama are just as refined and cultured as folks anywhere!" But the provinciality doubtless hurt him in the North. When the election returns were in, Wallace had carried only five states, and all in the Deep South— Alabama itself, Mississippi, Louisiana, Georgia, and Arkansas. It was not much different from 1948, when Thurmond had won three of those states—Alabama, Mississippi, and Louisiana—and his own South Carolina. Ironically, South Carolina was denied Wallace in 1968 because Thurmond went all-out for Richard Nixon.

Opinions differ on whether Wallace ever believed he had a chance to win in 1968, but in addition to the build-up it gave him for future runs, he counted it a solid success. "I think my movement defeated Hubert Humphrey, which was something the majority of the people of my region wanted done," Wallace told Neal Peirce.[18] "My running took away enough labor vote from Humphrey in California, in Ohio, in Illinois, in New Jersey, and Missouri, so that those states went for Nixon." (Independent analysts think Wallace hurt Nixon much more than Humphrey, especially in the South, but the interesting point is his own analysis.) Wallace also thought he had changed the whole tone of the campaign, especially on issues like "law and order and tax exemptions for the multirich such as foundations and otherwise. Before it was over it sounded as if both national parties' speeches were written in Clayton, Alabama."

Wallace's 1968 campaign probably marked the high-water point of southern-based third-party politics in the twentieth century, and one of those tantalizing historical "ifs" is what would have happened if Nixon had received a few less electoral votes, so that he would have lacked a majority and George Wallace would have held the power to choose the next president through his 45 electors (eventually to total 46 due to a faithless elector).

Asked how he would have handled the situation, Wallace first made it very clear to Peirce that he would have instructed his electors how they should vote in the electoral college, which convenes in mid-December, and would never have permitted the choice of a president to remain unresolved there so that the House of Representatives would have chosen the following January. "Why," he said, "would I want to lose control of the matter by throwing the election into the House where we would have no control whatsoever? No, the matter would have been settled in the electoral college." And his own electors, Wallace said, "were pledged to go along with me in the matter, and they would have gone with me."

How would he have instructed his electors? "The chances are the votes probably would have gone to Mr. Nixon, because we were violently opposed to Mr. Humphrey's philosophy and ideology." Would he have demanded concessions, in advance, from Nixon? "We would probably have asked Mr. Nixon to reiterate some of his campaign statements he'd already made . . . just to restate what he had already said in substance: 'I want to work for world peace, I want tax reduction, tax reform. I want the neighborhood school concept protected. I'm in substance for freedom of choice in the public school system and against busing.'" Wallace on other occasions talked of a "solemn covenant" to stop foreign aid to Communist nations and left-leaning neutrals, of a revamping of the U.S. Supreme Court, and of a halt to federal civil rights enforcement. In other words, Wallace might well have forced on Nixon the same kind of "hands-off" attitude toward the South that Rutherford B. Hayes had agreed to in 1877 in exchange for the electoral votes he needed to be elected. The South's price then had been termination of the first Reconstruction, a decision that would be followed by three-quarters of a century of impingement on black people's rights in the South. The net result of Wallace's demands would have been to end the second Reconstruction—the civil rights advances of the 1960s.

It does seem unlikely that there could have been any secret deal between Wallace and one of the major-party contenders—some kind of selling off of the highest office to the highest bidder.[19] For the participants there would be the disastrous consequences of the almost inevitable disclosure—such a deal would involve too many people to be kept secret; and it is unlikely that Wallace would have wished to do so—a kingmaker enjoys real advantage from his actions only if he is recognized as being one. Given leaks about such arrangements, a major-party nominee would suffer the stigma of having bought the presidency by a deal, face possible threat of impeachment if the nonenforcement of existing laws were part of the understanding, and very likely find at least a few of his own electors in revolt and threatening to block the deal by abstaining on December 16.[20] This would be a very effective action on their part, since the needed majority of 270 electoral votes remains the same no matter how many electors might abstain.

The three-candidate nature of the 1968 election underscores other anomalies of the electoral college. It serves as a reminder that, under the winner-take-all or unit-rule procedure, a plurality of votes determines the entire electoral vote for a state, even if it is a distinct minority of the vote cast. The results of this feature can be clearly seen in the state-by-state returns. North Carolina, South Carolina, and Tennessee all exhibited similar patterns in which one candidate—Nixon—received 100 percent of the state's electoral votes by obtaining only 39.5 percent, 38.1 percent, and 37.8 percent, respectively, of the popular vote. Although Nixon did carry 17 of his 32 states with less than a majority of the votes cast, these three-way divisions did not always help him.[21] In some states such as Arkansas, the major-party candidates, Nixon and Humphrey, divided the popular vote and Wallace received all of the state's bloc of electoral votes.

Of course, in most states outside the South, Wallace was not likely to receive a plurality—although to do so he might need as little as 34 percent of the popular vote. His real impact came through his ability to draw off votes from the two major parties and possibly tilt a large state's bloc of 26 or 40 or 43 electoral votes one way or the other. In other words, it was the magnifying tendency of the unit rule, with its winner-take-all feature, that constituted Wallace's impact outside the South.

As election day approached, Wallace's popular vote strength and, more important, his electoral vote strength (at one point he had been expected to sweep the entire old Confederacy) had shrunk. Humphrey's popular and electoral vote strength, low during the early autumn, had rebounded—a not coincidental relationship. With Nixon and Humphrey running neck and neck, the potential of an electoral college deadlock seemed very real.

The results on election day, November 5, 1968, finally laid these fears to rest for the next four years. Wallace, with a national popular vote of 13.5 percent, received 45 electoral votes from his five Deep South states,[22] only 8.4 percent of the total electoral vote. Although Nixon, with a popular vote of 43.4 percent, led Humphrey by 0.7 percent nationally, the vicissitudes of the electoral college resulted in Nixon receiving 302 electoral votes, or 56 percent of the total—a seeming comfortable 32 electoral votes over the 270 required.[23]

How close Wallace came to being the pivotal figure was illustrated by the fact that a shift of 53,034 votes from Nixon to Humphrey in New Jersey, Missouri, and New Hampshire[24] would have reduced the Nixon electoral vote to 269, one less than the needed majority, with Humphrey then receiving 224 and Wallace 45. A shift of 111,674 popular votes in California alone—1.5 percent of the vote cast in that state—would have had the same result.

Table 8 Results of the 1968 Election

	Popular Votes	Electoral Votes
Richard M. Nixon (R)	31,785,148	301
Hubert H. Humphrey (D)	31,274,503	191
George C. Wallace (AIP)	9,901,151	46
Minor Parties	242,568	0
Nixon plurality: 510,645		

One factor could have affected the preceding analysis: a faithless elector who would cast his vote for president contrary to expectations. In fact, the 1968 election, like the 1960 election, did give rise to such an individual—the fifth in the history of the electoral college and the fourth in the postwar elections to vote clearly contrary to the expectations of those who had elected him. Not as colorful as Henry Irwin, the 1960 defecting elector, the 1968 individual was Dr. Lloyd W. Bailey of North Carolina, a Nixon elector. A member of the John Birch Society, Dr. Bailey finally decided that he could not vote for Nixon because of his concern over alleged leftist tendencies in the early Nixon appointments of presidential advisers and Nixon's decision to ask Chief Justice Earl Warren to continue on the Supreme Court for an additional six months. When the electoral college met on December 16, Dr. Bailey therefore gave his electoral vote to Wallace, thus increasing Wallace's final count to 46 electoral votes.[25] (See table 8.)

The danger shown here is less in the action of one isolated individual—although voters of a state might wonder what their vote is really worth in such a situation—than in the possibility of electors deviating from their pledges on a multiple basis should an electoral vote majority rest on one or two votes, a very real possibility in both 1960 and 1968. One thing is certain: if Nixon had lost the three close states previously mentioned and thus had had only 269 electoral votes, one short of a majority, it would not have been Dr. Bailey who would have saved the day. He was a Nixon-pledged elector—and in fact, if he had still switched, Nixon's revised total would have been 268, two short of a majority.

In analyzing elections as close and precarious as that of 1968, it is important to remember that even if the general election did not produce a majority electoral vote winner, or even if it produced a winner who clearly had lost in the popular vote, there might well be what has been termed the "legitimacy of the popular vote majority"[26]—the demand that the electoral college choose the winner in terms of the popular vote. These pressures would undoubtedly be exceptionally strong if the winner of the popular vote had fallen just a few votes shy of an electoral college majority. Along these lines, author James Michener, the president of the 1968 Pennsylvania electoral college and a Democrat, tells how he had resolved that if this were the case, with Nixon leading, he would seek to swing enough electoral votes to Nixon so as to decide the election in the electoral college. He reports that he was both pleased and surprised to discover, on December 16, that Thomas Minehart, the Pennsylvania Democratic state chairman, had had the same resolve.[27]

The candidates' knowledge of the prospective party lineup of the House of Representatives, indicating their chances in a contingent election there, could also have played a heavy role.[28] Only nineteen House delegations were controlled by Republicans, so that Nixon, if he had trailed Humphrey in the popular vote and there was no electoral college majority, might well have seen that he had no hope of election and released some of his electors to Humphrey. Had the situation been reversed, with Nixon leading in popular votes but still short of an electoral majority, the "bargaining" with Wallace to obtain elector support, and prevent the contingent election altogether, would have been quite active.

But what if the election were not settled in the elector college by explicit or implicit deals, or through the switch of a few electors to prevent a deadlock? In this case, the electoral college meetings on December 16 would have resulted in a deadlock, with no candidate receiving 270 electoral votes, and the action would now shift to the newly elected House of Representatives, meeting at noon on January 6, 1969, only fourteen days before the constitutionally scheduled inauguration of the new president.[29]

The difficult and dangerous circumstances likely to attend any contingent election will be discussed in the following chapter. In 1968 it was widely assumed that the House, if it received the decision, would have elected Humphrey. Twenty-six state delegations were controlled by Democrats, nineteen by Republicans, and five were evenly divided and consequently would cast no vote.[30] However, this belief is based on one very questionable assumption: that each representative would have voted along party lines. A closer analysis shows that the complexity of the election in the House would have been much greater.[31]

The first complicating factor is that in many cases House delegations that were split, and thus could cast no vote, or that had a narrow majority for one party or another, could be swung through the actions of a single House member seeking to express independence or maverick tendencies, to raise his or her price, or just to seek mammoth publicity.

This problem, however, pales in comparison with another: How would the House delegations from the five Deep South states carried by Wallace, with percentages up to 66 percent, vote? While at least normally Democratic and thus counted in the twenty-six-state Democratic total, the representatives from these states would likely feel compelled to recognize and support Wallace in the House voting. On the other hand, if they broke party rank and failed to support the Democratic nominee at this critical moment, they would be subject to terrible retribution, including loss of patronage, party seniority, and committee chairmanships. The dilemma of these representatives would be intense, and its resolution uncertain, although a likely pattern would be to support Wallace for a couple of ballots and then to switch to Humphrey. The problem here, then, would not be manipulation by Wallace, for his direct control over these unhappy representatives would be comparatively weak, but the possibility that sufficient Democratic leadership pressure would lead to an eventual Democratic House majority.[32]

One last factor in the actual 1968 election might have given severe problems in reaching a twenty-six-state majority—and possibly have resulted in a House deadlock. This factor was the 1968 election-time pledges of a number of members of Congress—mainly Southern Democrats in Wallace- or Nixon-leaning districts—that if elected, and if the election came to the House, they would not automatically vote for Humphrey but would vote however their district had voted. In many states, this pledge would not have made a difference, but in several it would have.

Among at least thirty candidates for the House who had make such pledges prior to the election[33] were the six men who were elected to the House from South Carolina. All six were Democrats, but three of their districts went for Nixon, two for Wallace, and one for Humphrey.[34] If these candidates had honored their pledges, South Carolina's vote would have gone to Nixon, despite its solid Democratic representation.

The Virginia delegation would have been evenly divided between Republicans and Democrats. However, two Democratic representatives, David E. Satterfield III and John O. Marsh, Jr., had made the pledge; their districts were carried by Nixon. A third Virginia Democrat, W. C. Daniel, would have been pledged to Wallace. Thus Virginia's vote might have gone to Nixon.[35] Finally, Nevada's lone congressman, Walter S. Baring, a Democrat, would have been publicly pledged to cast his state's vote for Nixon.[36]

The results of these publicly recorded pledges, alone, would be—assuming complete party loyalty otherwise and no Wallace defections—a House vote not of 26 to 19 and 5 states split but of 24 to 22 and 4 states split. No majority of 26 states would have been immediately forthcoming, and political chaos could have resulted as the nation approached inauguration day with the question of who was to be president unresolved.[37]

The 1968 election did not put the electoral college system to its greatest test; Richard Nixon did receive a majority of the electoral votes, and the nation was spared the opportunity of observing the dark nooks and crannies of the contingent election procedure in action. The 1968 election, however, did illustrate a broad range of electoral college perils: (1) the uncertainty of state winner-take-all results with a three-way split of popular votes; (2) the incentive given to regional third parties and the handicaps conferred upon nationally based third parties; (3) the likelihood of electoral college deadlock if a third-party movement coincides with an evenness of major party strength; (4) the possibilities that shifts of relatively few votes could deadlock an election; (5) the dangers of one or a few faithless electors affecting the electoral college results; (6) the opportunity for a third-party candidate to throw his or her electors one way or the other, with or without a deal; and (7) the likelihood of uncertainty, confusion, and even deadlock in the House contingent selection of the president.

The Election of 1976

Virtually every presidential election brings its share of surprises and "firsts," and the 1976 contest was clearly no exception.[38] Out of a crowded Democratic field, a man virtually unknown to most of the country when he started his campaign—Georgia's former governor, Jimmy Carter—emerged victorious, winning enough primaries to arrive at the party's national convention with sufficient votes to ensure his nomination on the first ballot. Carter, a moderate and an alien figure to the powerful national Democrat liberal establishment, made a bow to his adversaries by selecting as his running mate Sen. Walter F. Mondale of Minnesota, a liberal and a close associate of Senator and former vice president Hubert H. Humphrey.

On the Republican side, Gerald R. Ford, Jr., had assumed the presidency following the resignation, under threat of impeachment for his involvement with the Watergate affair, of Richard M. Nixon in August 1974. A party moderate, Ford was actually the first appointed president of the United States. He had been selected for the vice presidency by President Nixon following the resignation of Vice President Spiro Agnew in 1973. (Agnew had been forced to resign and pleaded *nolo contendere* to income tax evasion following an investigation by the U.S. attorney in Baltimore, who had proven a widespread pattern of Agnew acceptances of payments—some clearly kickbacks—from contractors and others doing business with the Maryland government during the time he was governor. Some of the payments had continued while he was vice president.) Under the Twenty-fifth Amendment regarding presidential succession, ratified in 1967, Nixon was empowered to appoint a successor to Agnew, subject to congressional approval.

Ford, who had spent most of a long political career as a Grand Rapids, Michigan congressman, rising to the post of minority leader in 1965, had previously had no higher ambition than one day becoming Speaker of the House if the Republicans gained control. As president, he proved to be a less-than-dynamic leader. And he made what was to prove a fatal error: he pardoned Richard Nixon, to the great resentment of millions of citizens, for any and all crimes he might have committed during his presidency. In the primaries, Ford was vigorously challenged by former California Gov. Ronald Reagan, a favorite of the party's right wing, and barely repulsed the Reagan onslaught. In the general election he consented to a series of nationally televised debates with Carter; though neither performed brilliantly, Carter probably emerged as the net winner.

But Carter, from a broad lead in the national polls at the time of his nomination, sank rapidly through the autumn months—partly because of a number of fumbled campaign issues. As election day approached, the outcome was very much in doubt. As in all close elections, the functioning of the electoral college again became a crucial—and worrisome—factor in the selection of the next president.

The most obvious manifestation of the importance of the electoral college could be observed in the obsession of Carter and Ford strategists, in the closing weeks of the campaign, with the nine big electoral states, which together had 245 of the 270 electoral votes necessary to win an election. These campaign managers knew well what all campaign strategists realize: when a large-electoral-vote state is marginal, it is crucially important to commit an enormous amount of campaign resources to that state. A candidate's visit, additional advertising expenditures, more key campaign workers—any of these *might* be enough to win the few thousand popular votes sufficient to swing that state's *entire* bloc of 41 or 45 electoral votes—more than 15 percent of the total needed to win—to your side.

As a result, Ford and Carter campaign managers targeted these large states with an enormous commitment of resources in the closing weeks of the 1976 campaign.[39] In fact, this strategy proved to be wise: the contest in seven of these nine states turned out, in the final count, to be exceedingly close, with both candidates receiving at least 48 percent of each state's vote.

Because of this obsession in the campaigns with large pivotal states, the electoral college does not treat voters alike—a thousand voters in Scranton, Pennsylvania, are far more strategically important than a similar number of voters in Wilmington, Delaware. This also places a premium on the support of key political leaders in large-electoral-vote states. This could be observed in Carter's desperate wooing of Mayors Frank Rizzo of Philadelphia and Richard Daley of Chicago because of the major roles these political leaders *might* have in determining the outcome in Pennsylvania and Illinois. The electoral college treats political leaders as well as voters unequally—those in large marginal states are vigorously courted.[40] (This point will be analyzed empirically, using computer-based data, in Chapter 5.)

The electoral college also encourages fraud—or at least fear and rumor of fraud. New York, with more than enough electoral votes to elect Ford, would eventually go to Carter by 288,767 popular votes. Claims of voting irregularities and calls for a recount would be made on election night but later withdrawn because of Carter's clear national popular vote win. *If* there was fraud in New York, only

288,767 votes determined the election; under direct election, at least 1.7 million votes, Carter's national plurality, would have had to have been irregular to determine the outcome.

Another impact of the electoral college on the campaign arose from the independent candidacy of Eugene McCarthy, former Democratic senator from Minnesota. No one thought it at all likely that McCarthy would gather enough popular votes anywhere to win any electoral votes—or even that he would receive a significant total of popular votes nationally. Yet there was considerable alarm over the impact of his candidacy. This was directly due to the fact that McCarthy had the possibility of drawing a few percent of usually Democratic votes in those very same large states that were judged to be pivotal between Carter and Ford. Concern was expressed that McCarthy had found another loophole avenue to electoral influence, complementing the Wallace electoral college strategy of 1968. While Wallace had sought power by winning enough electoral votes to deadlock the electoral college, McCarthy sought kingmaker influence by determining the election outcome. This potential power did not come because of McCarthy's strong electoral appeal but solely because of where his limited electoral appeal was: in pivotal states where small numbers might determine a winner-take-all bloc of electoral votes. In other words, the electoral college was threatening to provide yet another minor-movement candidate with inordinate influence over who would be president.

In the final outcome, McCarthy received less than 1 percent of the national popular vote and in no state exceeded 4 percent (Oregon, at 3.9 percent, and Arizona and Massachusetts, both at 2.6 percent, were his top states). Yet in four states (Iowa, Maine, Oklahoma, and Oregon), totaling 26 electoral votes, McCarthy's vote exceeded the margin by which Ford defeated Carter. In those states, McCarthy's candidacy *may* have swung those states to Ford. Even more significant, had McCarthy been on the New York ballot, it is likely that his votes would have been sufficient to tip that state, with its micro-thin Democratic margin, from Carter to Ford. With that switch would have gone New York's entire bloc of 41 electoral votes, and with it the presidential election victory would have gone from Carter to Ford—despite Carter's clear national vote margin of nearly 1.7 million votes. Only by the dubious means of denying Eugene McCarthy a place on the New York ballot was he denied his goal: being the maker of the president in 1976.

On election night, its polling completed, a curious nation waits to see whether Jimmy Carter will become president or whether Gerald Ford will retain the job he first won by luck of appointment to the vice presidency. In most Americans' minds, the real race is in the popular votes. Since early evening, Carter has led by a rather comfortable margin; when the final returns are reported a few weeks later, the election night trend will be confirmed and Jimmy Carter will enjoy a popular vote margin of 1,682,790 votes. It is not a stupendous plurality; in fact, it is a pale shadow of the margin for Carter suggested in polls just after the two parties' nominating conventions. But it is an unambiguous, clear, unchallengeable margin. The people have spoken. Jimmy Carter is to be their next president.

But will he? Even as November 2 fades at midnight into November 3 on the East Coast, a sliver of doubt lingers in the minds of the professional politicians, the political aficionados, the political journalists. Regardless of that substantial popular vote margin, they know there is still a doubt, perhaps mostly theoretical but still not to be entirely dismissed, that Jimmy Carter will become president. The reason, of course, is the electoral college. In any close election, there is a chance that the electoral college may choose a candidate the people have rejected. In this election, Carter's heavy vote is in his native South; his popular vote is not well distributed throughout other regions. Indeed, political commentators have already reported on the possibility of a misfire in 1976. Among them is Neal Peirce, who wrote in a syndicated column on October 10, 1976: "The nation may face the greatest threat in this century that the antiquated electoral college system will elect the President who lost the popular vote." According to Peirce, campaign strategists on both sides were aware "that Jimmy Carter, bolstered by strong majorities in his native South, could lead by as much as 1.0 to 2.5 million votes in the national popular vote, but still lose in the electoral college because of narrow margins for President Ford in big Northern states with heavy electoral vote blocs." Independently, Lawrence Longley took the opportunity of an appearance on NBC's *Today* show on the very morning of election day to offer the similar prediction that 1976 might well see a divided-verdict election, with the winner of the popular vote losing the presidency in the electoral college and the presidency going instead to the loser of the popular vote.

The scorekeepers everyone is watching as election night 1976 rolls along are a group of totally self-appointed persons, occupying positions beyond the farthest stretch of the imagination when the electoral college was first conceived. They are the staffs of the three national television networks, each with millions of dollars invested in the election coverage, reporting from their studios in New York City. An army of thousands of poll watchers has been phoning in election returns from selected precincts across the nation, permitting the networks to declare on the basis of clear trends from representative voting areas, even when the computed vote is quite incomplete, just which candidate will carry each state. They use complex formulas involving several cross-checking computations to decide whether a state can be "called" for one candidate or the other. There have been known instances of "goofs"—when a network has called a state and then had to withdraw its projection. But these cases are rare. And it is virtually unthinkable that a network would risk calling the entire presidential election for a candidate without being convinced, beyond reasonable doubt, that it was right.

At midnight Carter is comfortably ahead in every network's electoral vote calls. If one is watching CBS News, Carter's score over Ford is 208–62. NBC viewers see a 156–76 Carter lead, those viewing ABC, 224–113. Carter has won his electoral vote lead by sweeping most of the South and New England and winning a good share of the mid-Atlantic regions plus Minnesota and Wisconsin. Two of the three networks have already credited Pennsylvania, with a hefty 27-vote bloc of electoral votes, to Carter; as early as 9:31 P.M., taking a flyer on the basis of what must have been quite fragmentary reports, ABC has credited New York, with its 41 electoral votes, to Carter.

But at midnight it is still not impossible to construct a scenario for a Ford win. CBS and NBC still consider New York too close to call; Ford has won Connecticut, Vermont, and New Hampshire and seems on his way to winning the lion's share of the Midwest and virtually all of the mountain West. If the Pacific Coast and a handful of doubtful southern states all go for him, Ford might still be elected, Carter's popular vote plurality notwithstanding.

By forty-three minutes after midnight, Carter has added New York to both the CBS and NBC projections. CBS also credits Carter with Missouri (12 electoral votes) and Oregon (6 votes) in the hour after midnight, for a total of 267—only 3 votes short of the 270 required for election. But then, for almost two hours—until 2:58 A.M.—Carter remains frozen at 267 in the CBS count. And it is not a firm 267: at 2:58 CBS rescinds its Oregon call, bringing Carter back down to 261 electoral votes. At the same hour NBC decides that Hawaii will be a Carter state (the Hawaiian call has taken so long because none of the networks had thought it worthwhile to establish sample precincts in the island state, so they had only raw vote returns to go on). At 3:28 A.M. CBS also decides to call Hawaii for Carter; now both CBS and NBC counts stand at 265 Carter electoral votes— 5 short of the magic number.

In earlier decades, there would have been no doubt about the vote of Mississippi: for a century it had been one of the states in which the Democratic nomination was tantamount to election. But now, hours after the closing of the last polls, Mississippi has moved to center stage. It is the only uncertain state at the moment that (1) clearly leans toward Carter and (2) has enough electoral votes—7— to put him over the top. ABC called Mississippi for Carter at 1:37 A.M., but both CBS and NBC are extremely leery, and with good reason. For one thing, the vote is reported as exceptionally close. Second, Mississippi election law incorporates a provision one could well consider a relic in modern America: separate votes for the individual candidates for elector. (The only other states with similar provisions are Louisiana and South Carolina.) This feature means that in a close race it would be possible for the elector slate to split, some electors of one party being elected, some of another. The News Election Service, which the networks and wire services depend on for raw vote returns, is counting in Mississippi only the vote for the front-running Carter and Ford elector candidates, county by county. There is no way to look behind these returns to determine whether there is a major differential in the vote for various electors.

Finally, at 3:31 A.M., NBC decides to call Mississippi's 7 electoral votes for Carter. With that, the Carter vote is 2 over the 270 required for election, and the network declares him president-elect. ABC moves simultaneously to make a late call of Hawaii, also putting Carter over the top with 272 electoral votes. And fifteen minutes later, finally convinced of the soundness of the Mississippi returns, CBS follows suit. Most of America has already gone to sleep. Yet it is only now, hours after Carter's popular vote victory has been unequivocally established, that the networks dare confirm that the electoral college will follow the lead of the people. (See table 9.)

And in fact 1976 went down in the history books as another election in which the college barely did its work. After most television sets had gone dark, enough returns came in to confirm that several more states—California, Alaska, Maine, Illinois, Oregon, and South Dakota—had gone for Ford. Days later, it was confirmed that Carter had won Ohio by a razor-thin margin of 11,116 votes out of 4,111,873 cast. The final electoral vote was 297 for Carter, 241 for Ford (later reduced to 240 because of one "faithless" Ford elector in Washington state). Had an exceedingly small number of votes shifted from Carter to Ford—5,559 in Ohio and 3,687 in Hawaii—Ford would have had 270 electoral votes to Carter's 268 and won the election. But if the same faithless elector had then withheld his support

Table 9 Results of the 1976 Election

	Popular Votes	Electoral Votes
Jimmy Carter (D)	40,830,763	297
Gerald R. Ford (R)	39,147,793	240
Eugene J. McCarthy (Ind.)	756,691	0
Roger MacBride (Libert.)	173,011	0
Others	647,631	1
Carter plurality: 1,682,970		

from Ford, the Ford total would have been only 269—one fewer than the constitutionally required majority of the 538-member electoral college—and thus neither candidate would have had an electoral college majority. The presidency finally would have been decided either in informal bargaining among or breaking of pledges by electors or, in a cumbersome contingent election procedure, by the U.S. House of Representatives. But at what cost to the stability of the American government and the legitimacy of the presidency, no one can know.

Curiously enough, the 1976 faithless elector, as in the previous three occurrences, once again was a deviant *Republican* elector. Washington elector Mike Padden decided, six weeks after the November election, that Republican nominee Gerald Ford was insufficiently forthright in opposition to abortion and thereby unsuitable to be president. Padden instead cast his vote for Ronald Reagan. As we note elsewhere, similar defections from voter expectations have occurred in 1948, 1956, 1960, 1968, 1972,[41] and 1988—in other words, a total of seven of the twelve postwar elections. Even more important is that the likelihood of this occurring on a multiple basis would be greatly heightened in the case of an electoral vote majority resting on one or two votes—a very real possibility in 1976 and other recent elections.

In fact, when one looks at the election returns for the 1976 election, one can observe that if about 5,560 votes had switched from

Carter to Ford in the single state of Ohio, Carter would have lost that state and had only 272 electoral votes, two more than the absolute minimum needed of 270. In that case, two or three individual electors seeking personal recognition or attention to a pet cause could withhold their electoral votes and thus make the election outcome very uncertain.

A startling reminder of the possibilities inherent in such a close electoral vote election as 1976 has been provided by that year's Republican vice presidential nominee, Robert Dole. Testifying before the Senate Judiciary Committee on January 27, 1977, in favor of abolishing the electoral college, Senator Dole remarked that during the election count, "we were looking around on the theory that maybe Ohio might turn around because they had an automatic recount. We were shopping—not shopping, excuse me. Looking around for electors. Some took a look at Missouri, some were looking at Louisiana, some in Mississippi, because their laws are a little bit different. And we might have picked up one or two in Louisiana. There were allegations of fraud maybe in Mississippi, and something else in Missouri. We need to pick up three or four after Ohio. So that may happen in any event. But it just seems to me that the temptation is there for that elector in a very tight race to really negotiate quite a bunch."[42]

In a less ominous vein, the 1976 election gave rise to another fascinating event. Following this election, Robert L. Brewster of Albuquerque sent a letter to all members of the electoral college, urging them to elect him as president in order to save the country from earthquakes and tidal waves. Nevertheless, Brewster received no electoral votes for president. There are no data available reporting unusual earthquakes and tidal waves.[43]

Besides the possibility of electors negotiating "quite a bunch" or being intimidated by imminent natural disaster, the electoral college in the 1976 election also held at least a possibility of electoral uncertainty—even in the absence of a significant third-party candidate or any faithless elector. If 11,950 popular votes in Delaware and Ohio had shifted from Carter to Ford, Ford would have carried these two states. The result would then have been: *an exact tie in electoral votes—269–269!* The presidency would have been decided not on election night but through deals or switches at the electoral college meetings on December 13, or through the later uncertainties of the House of Representatives.

What specifically might happen in the case of an apparent electoral college deadlock? A first possibility, of course, is that a faithless elector or two, pledged to one candidate or another, might subsequently switch at the time of the actual meetings of the electoral college so as to create a majority for one of the candidates. This might resolve the crisis, although it would be sad to think of the presidency as being mandated on such a thin reed of legitimacy.

If, however, no deals or actions at the time of the December 13 meetings of the electoral college were successful in forming a majority, then the action would have shifted to the House of Representatives for a contingent election—with all the possibility of political and social upheaval during the time between the November election and the January presidential vote in the House, as well as of the other dangers to the stability of the body politic we have previously reviewed in connection with the contingent election.

One final—and most definitely major—problem of the electoral college was demonstrated anew in the election of 1976. This is that under the present system there is no assurance that the winner of the popular vote will win the election. This problem is a fundamental one—can an American president operate effectively in our democracy if he or she has received fewer votes than the loser? An analysis of the election shows that if 9,246 votes had shifted to Ford solely in Ohio and Hawaii, Ford would have become president with 270 electoral votes, the absolute minimum,[44] despite Carter's 50 percent of the popular vote and victorious margin of nearly 1.7 million votes.

One hesitates to contemplate the consequences of a nonelected president being inaugurated for four more years after being rejected by a majority of the voters in his or her only presidential election.

What, then, are the electoral college evils illustrated by the election of 1976? They are: (1) the distortions of campaign strategy resulting from candidates focusing on certain large, pivotal states; (2) the resulting inequities in candidate attention to voters and political leaders—some are viewed as vastly more important than others; (3) the fear of fraud or electoral accident tilting a large state's entire bloc of electoral votes, and with it possibly the election; (4) the possibilities of a relatively insignificant minor candidate being able to determine the election outcome if his or her limited support occurs in large, pivotal states; (5) the occurrence of yet another faithless elector and the probable incentive for others should the electoral vote count be close; (6) the possibility of electoral college deadlock, even in an essentially two-candidate race, through an exact tie; and (7) the very real chance in a close election that the electoral college will elect the candidate who has run second in popular preference.

The Election of 1980

The contest of 1980, in which Republican nominee Ronald Reagan swamped incumbent President Jimmy Carter with a 10-percentage-point lead in the popular vote and an overwhelming 90 percent of the electoral votes cast, scarcely ranks with the preceding "years of controversy" in which the electoral college system was put to severe test.

There was, however, a wild card in the 1980 contest: the independent candidacy of John B. Anderson, a lifelong Republican and veteran member of the U.S. House. Anderson initially sought the Republican nomination, only to find his brand of moderate Republicanism quite out of tune with the resurgent conservatism dominant in his party. In April 1980 he withdrew from the remaining Republican primary contests and announced his candidacy as an independent, calling on Americans of all political allegiances to join his "National Unity Campaign." Later he selected former Wisconsin governor Patrick J. Lucey (a Democrat) as his vice presidential running mate.

The Anderson campaign, though bedeviled by fundraising problems, ultimately succeeded in qualifying for the ballot in all fifty states and the District of Columbia. Public opinion surveys showed discontent with both major party nominees. Carter had to battle Sen. Edward M. Kennedy of Massachusetts for his party's nomination and was gravely weakened by the nation's economic and foreign policy reversals of the preceding four years. Reagan appeared—especially at the campaign's outset—to represent a rigid conservatism outside the "winning" mainstream of American politics. At one point in early summer, Anderson was the expressed preference of almost 25 percent in voter surveys.

But from that point, his support gradually evaporated. Reagan, in the general election campaign, was able to present himself as far more moderate than he had appeared in the early primary season. And Carter, although he would eventually lose by a huge margin, drew many one-time Anderson supporters who feared the prospect of a Reagan presidency. By early September Anderson's poll readings had declined to the 15 percent range; by early October they were in single digits. Millions of Americans were clearly drifting back to the major-party nominees. This illustrated the continuing difficulty, despite the decline of party allegiance in the nation, of any independent candidate being considered a likely enough winner to maintain and build support during a general election campaign. The vast preponderance of Americans apparently still consider it a wasted vote to support a maverick candidacy. This is a phenomenon essentially unrelated to the electoral college. It is the reason that, with rare exceptions, third-party or independent candidates are unable to win, or even score substantial support, in the direct vote that Americans cast for governors, U.S. senators, and other major officials. Even if the nation were to abolish the electoral college and substitute direct popular election, the "go with a winner" phenomenon would likely remain. Under the electoral college system, however, it is exaggerated in states reported to be close, where people are particularly anxious to cast meaningful votes that might shift a bloc of electoral votes one way or another.

Had the 1980 election been close, however, the Anderson vote, even if small, could have thrown crucial states to one or the other of the major party contenders—and to a much greater extent than Eugene McCarthy, in fact, appeared to do in 1976. But in only four-teen states with a total of 159 electoral votes did the Anderson vote exceed the margin of difference between the winning Reagan total and the trailing Carter count;[45] even in the unlikely event that Carter would have received all the Anderson votes if Anderson had not run, Reagan would still have won by a margin of 330 electoral votes to 208. (See table 10.)

Had Anderson's support remained high enough to permit him to win some states in the three-way contest, he could have ended up—strategically though certainly not ideologically—in much the same swing position in electoral votes that George Wallace, running as a chiefly regional candidate, had striven for in 1968. This eventu-ality evoked considerable media comment in the early stages of the campaign, as commentators speculated on what Anderson and his electors might do if they held the balance of power or what would result if there were no final electoral majority, throwing the election into the House of Representatives. (One fundamental difference between the Anderson and Wallace candidacies, of course, was the more national nature of Anderson's support compared to Wallace's special regional appeal.)

A final feature of the 1980 election, similarly present in all con-temporary presidential elections, was the potential for a faithless elector casting a vote contrary to expectations. Reagan was suffi-ciently concerned about this possibility to send a letter to each of his 538 elector candidates days before the election reminding them that he would expect them to fulfill their "obligation" to vote for him,

Table 10   Results of the 1980 Election

	Popular Votes	Electoral Votes
Ronald Reagan (R)	43,904,153	489
Jimmy Carter (D)	35,483,883	49
John B. Anderson (NUC)	5,720,060	0
Ed Clark (Libert.)	921,299	0
Others	485,826	0
Reagan plurality: 8,420,270		

even if President Carter should win the national popular vote.[46] In fact, no such faithless elector did appear when the electors convened in the various state capitals on December 15, 1980, making this presidential election the first since 1964 and only the third among the preceding nine in which no elector sought to act independently of the will of the American people in expressing a preference for president.

The Election of 1992

A year or more before the 1992 presidential election, it seemed clear that incumbent president George Bush was likely to repeat his 1988 success in defeating whomever the Democratic party might put up against him. The aftermath of the United States success over Iraq in the Persian Gulf War and exhilaration over the collapse of the Iron Curtain had put Bush in a strong position for the upcoming election. Indeed, in March 1991 fully 91 percent of respondents reported that they generally approved of his performance as president. This popularity, as fragile as it would prove to be, was sufficient to lead a number of prominent Democratic officeholders—most notably New York Gov. Mario Cuomo of New York, Senators Bill Bradley of New Jersey, Al Gore of Tennessee, and Jay Rockefeller of West Virginia, and Rep. Richard Gephardt of Missouri—to decide to forgo a run against a seemingly invincible incumbent.

A few Democrats, however, were still willing to take on the effort. First of these was former Massachusetts senator Paul Tsongas; in time he was joined by fiery liberal Sen. Tom Harkin of Iowa, centrist Sen. Robert Kerrey of Nebraska, Gov. L. Douglas Wilder of Virginia (that state's first black governor), former Gov. Edmund G. "Jerry" Brown of California (making his third quixotic race for the presidency), and a relatively little-known governor from the small border state of Arkansas, Bill Clinton. Unkindly, the Democratic field of candidates, as it emerged, was termed the "six dwarfs."

The strength of President Bush, however, was more illusionary than real. Americans appreciate international successes, but what really counts to the average voter are "pocketbook" issues involving jobs, taxes, and, in general, the economy. The preoccupation of Bush with global issues would make him politically vulnerable on these immediate domestic issues. Further, Bush's presidency was in substantial degree an inherited office, won by him in 1988 after eight long years as vice presidential understudy to Ronald Reagan. As *Congressional Quarterly* points out, "Presidents who gain their office by carrying the legacy of their mentors have a hard time developing their own program or strategy."[47] Such was the case with Bush as he fumbled countless efforts to define his presidency and to describe a vision to which he would direct the energies of a second administration.

Bush also would be plagued by a feisty conservative primary opponent, television commentator and former White House aide Patrick J. Buchanan, who never tired of reminding voters of Bush's 1989 promise of "no new taxes"—and of his subsequent betrayal of that pledge.

Meanwhile, the Democratic field of "dwarfs" was dwindling as first Wilder, then Harkin and Kerrey, dropped out, leaving the field to two relatively weak candidates (Tsongas and Brown) and the de facto front-runner, Bill Clinton. Although he would eventually win his party's nomination, Clinton's progression through the primaries was not smooth. Losing the New Hampshire primary after stories appeared about alleged womanizing and adultery, he subsequently recovered to win key contests in Georgia, on "Super Tuesday," and in New York in early April. By late spring the struggle in both parties for the nomination was over—Clinton and Bush would be the undisputed, if wounded, choices.

The 1992 election, however, would not be limited to the Republican and Democratic nominees. In every presidential campaign there are countless additional candidates, often narrow in their appeal or even frivolous in their quest. This one, however, was marked by the most significant—and certainly the best-financed—independent candidacy in seventy years. As early as February 1992, wealthy businessman Ross Perot suggested, in a cable television interview on CNN's *Larry King Live*, that he might run for president if volunteers were able to get him on the ballot in all fifty states. In that case, he stated, he would be willing to commit up to $100 million of his huge resources to create a "world-class campaign."

Although at first Perot was generally discounted as a serious candidate, his volunteers (often "paid volunteers") quickly achieved the fifty-state ballot goal. During the spring of 1992, as Clinton locked up the Democratic nomination and Bush confirmed his Republican designation, media, and then voter, attention swung to the Perot candidacy. To the national media, Perot was a new political face, in refreshing contrast to the two major-party nominees of which so much had been said and resaid over the preceding months. To many voters, unenthusiastic about a choice between Clinton and Bush, Perot appeared appealingly outspoken and folksy.

The Perot candidacy surged throughout the spring months. In May, national polls found him, astonishingly, in second place, ahead of Democrat Clinton and close behind President Bush. Even more important, state-by-state polls showed him a major factor in most states and even winning some states in the South and West. Some commentators began to hint of the unthinkable—that Ross Perot, in a three-way division of popular votes, might conceivably win the presidency.

More thoughtful analyses, however, pointed to two more likely consequences of the Perot phenomenon. The first of these was the unpredictability of state outcomes in a three-way division of popular votes. In many states, any three of the contenders could aspire to win the minimum of 34 to 45 percent of the popular vote, which might be sufficient to carry the state and to win its entire bloc of electoral votes. Strategists for all of the campaigns hunkered down with their polls and issues to devise a "34 percent solution" in the various states.[48]

An even more serious concern was also coming to the fore in the late spring of 1992. With three candidates dividing not only the national popular vote but also the electoral vote, it was looking increasingly unlikely that any candidate would be able to win the constitutionally required absolute majority of electoral votes—270. The probable outcome of the three-candidate contest was now appearing to be an electoral college deadlock, with the election being decided after the voters had spoken, either in the electoral college itself or in the House of Representatives.

Anticipating the former contingency, state parties began to give close attention to the selection of their electors. Should an electoral tally be close or unresolved, the parties and campaigns must be confident of the absolute loyalty of their electors.[49] Mavericks and independent thinkers need not apply.

In the House of Representatives, nervous inquiries were launched (and immediately denied as existing) to prepare for the possibility that the House might be faced, for the first time in nearly 170 years, with electing a president. The precedents of 1801 and 1825 were dusted off and carefully examined.[50] (The House Rules adopted for the election of the president in 1825 are reprinted in Appendix F.) Academic advisers (including a coauthor of this book) were recruited as consultants to the House Judiciary Committee as efforts were made to determine what procedures could and should be used to elect the president in the context of the 1990s.

Many matters were unclear. How binding would House members find party loyalty—or, alternatively, the pledges that some had already taken to honor the electoral outcome in their congressional districts (echoing similar commitments that some thirty members had made in 1968)? Was a plurality sufficient to commit the vote of a state delegation, or was an outright majority needed in the delegation in order for that delegation to be able to vote? If the latter, how would abstentions count in constituting that delegation majority? How continuous must House efforts to elect the president be during the fourteen days prior to inauguration day? Could other business be transacted during this period, or was the House limited to repeated electoral roll calls? Under what conditions, and by whose authority, would the electoral proceedings be suspended—or even abandoned? On one matter there was easy agreement: contrary to the precedent of 1825, House proceedings to elect a president would *not* be closed-door, secret sessions. Rather, House sessions would be open, nationally televised events very much in public view.[51]

The panic in the House over being confronted with such weighty questions and constitutional responsibilities was well expressed in the title of an earlier 1968 survey reporting member attitudes toward the opportunity to elect a president: "Let This Cup Pass." And it did pass. As spring turned to summer, Perot's campaign increasingly ran into difficulties. Reporters and columnists began to inquire into his sweeping promises to eliminate the budget deficit, to resolve U.S. trade and foreign affairs issues, and to deal with governmental inefficiency. His grasp of complex issues was questioned, and often he seemed irritable as well as ill-informed. Those who saw him unfavorably grew to exceed those who viewed him favorably.

In a dramatic step, on July 13 Perot announced the suspension of his presidential campaign. He cited two reasons for his action. First, the Democrats, in the form of Clinton and his running mate Al Gore, were "getting their act together." Further, he stressed, a continuation of his independent candidacy would split the popular vote and throw the presidential election into the House of Representatives. (The latter observation, grasped by Perot only after many months, is perhaps a unique instance of a third-party or independent candidate claiming a reluctance to do what so many had been so eager to accomplish!) When Perot announced his campaign's suspension, House members were reported to be sighing in relief.[52]

Meanwhile, major-party candidates Clinton and Bush, relieved by the disappearance of the Perot wild card, reset their strategies along the lines of a more familiar two-way race. Increasingly, however, this two-way contest was shifting to the disadvantage of President Bush. The Democratic convention that confirmed the nomination of Clinton was a harmonious affair which favorably showcased the candidate while launching his fall campaign. The Republican convention in August in Houston, in contrast, was marked by harsh right-wing rhetoric; and major speeches by Patrick Buchanan and Pat Robertson "questioning the Democrats' patriotism and raising the specter of a rollback of civil rights, played badly."[53] Following the conventions, the Democratic ticket took a significant lead in the polls, an advantage that it would not lose for the duration of the campaign.

As the fall campaign was moving toward its final weeks, however, the wild card returned to the deck when Perot announced that he was reactivating his dormant campaign. He explained that his earlier July campaign exit had resulted from several factors, including a "dirty tricks" effort by Republican operatives to smear his family. Despite much negative comment on his erratic behavior, Perot's fall campaign proved to be significant. Spending a total of $60 million of his own money, Perot was able to hold the support of almost 20 percent of the voters throughout the last month of the election campaign. There was now little chance of electoral college deadlock—the lead of Clinton was too great and the likelihood of Perot receiving any state's electoral votes too low. It was, however, surprising that so many Americans were willing to give their presidential vote to a candidate who had little if any chance of winning

Table 11 Results of the 1992 Election

	Popular Votes	Electoral Votes
Bill Clinton (D)	44,909,326	370
George Bush (R)	39,103,882	168
Ross Perot (Ind.)	19,741,657	0
Minor Parties	670,149	0
Clinton plurality: 5,805,444		

the presidency—or even carrying a single state. It is reasonable to speculate that the Perot candidacy in 1992 was relatively immune to the "wasted vote" argument (which had so devastated the effort of John B. Anderson in 1980) precisely because many of Perot's supporters were casting a protest vote against the two major parties and their nominees. Little did they care whether they were wasting their votes in the choice between Clinton and Bush.

The final election tally for the presidential election of 1992 reflected few of the uncertainties of the past year. Clinton won a decisive victory *in the electoral college* with a total of 370 electoral votes, fully 100 more than needed. (See table 11.) His 69 percent of the electoral vote, however, was obtained on the basis of a very low 43 percent of the popular vote. He thus achieved the dubious distinction of being the third least popular candidate in the history of the Republic to achieve an election-night electoral college majority.[54]

Nevertheless, Clinton *did* win the presidency, a prize certainly sufficient to make up for any embarrassment over a low popular vote tally. More striking was what happened to the nearly 18 percent of the popular vote won by Perot, when translated into electoral votes. The more than 19 million citizens who voted for Perot—by far the greatest number to support an independent or third-party candidate in American history—could only wonder about the strange electoral system for president, as their efforts resulted in not one electoral vote for their candidate.

Other anomalies in the electoral college system were also evident in 1992 (but not the curiosity of the faithless elector). Three-way divisions of popular votes resulted in surprising state outcomes. Florida's 25-electoral-vote slate went as a bloc to Bush on the basis of his popular vote of 2,173,310, just 40.9 percent of the state total; the 58.8 percent of Florida's voters who preferred Clinton or Perot received no electoral votes for their trouble in voting. Meanwhile, in California, Clinton, with 46 percent of the state popular vote, received 100 percent of that state's huge bloc of 54 electoral votes. In the most dramatic example of the consequences of a three-way popular vote division, Arizona's 8 electoral votes went as a bloc to Bush in 1992 on the basis of his state popular vote of only 38.5 percent—far less than a majority and a total only 29,036 popular votes greater than the 36.5 percent won by Clinton.

The electoral college did not deadlock in 1992, as had been widely anticipated. Although the American people were saved in 1992 from the dubious pleasures of electoral college deals or House of Representatives machinations, it could so easily have worked out differently, with crisis being the result.[55]

Reviewing the perils and close calls of all six of these elections, one recalls with amusement Alexander's Hamilton's assertion in *The Federalist* concerning the method the Constitutional Convention decided upon for choosing the president: "I . . . hesitate not to affirm that if the manner of it be not perfect, it is at least excellent."[56] In the light of the history of these six postwar elections, the inevitable conclusion is that the electoral college system is far from perfect and hardly appears to be excellent.

chapter four
How Today's Electoral College Works

The process by which the American people select their chief executive has two distinct aspects: the highly visible, popular campaign, which is seen, experienced, and participated in by millions of citizens, and the almost invisible workings of the constitutional mechanism for presidential elections, which goes unnoticed by the vast majority of Americans. In most elections the electoral college mirrors the popular will, so that the two systems coincide in their results. But there are always the dangers that the electoral system may go awry and that the popular choice for president will be rejected by the electoral college. The interplay between these two systems—popular and constitutional—defines presidential elections in America today.

The Popular Campaign

Early in the year preceding a presidential election, the would-be candidates of each party begin their preliminary soundings across the nation, wooing influential party leaders and trying to establish a public image that will help them win the greatest prize the American electoral system has to offer. The first objective is to win the presidential nomination of one of the dominant national political parties, for under the country's prevailing two-party system no other road leads to the presidency.

The National Nominating Conventions

The historian Carl Becker has written:

> The national nominating convention is something unknown to the Constitution and undreamed of by the founding fathers. It

is an American invention, as native to the U.S.A. as corn pone or apple pie. A Democratic or a Republican nominating convention, once it gets going, emits sounds and lights that never were on land or sea. Superficially observed, it has all the variety of a Slithy Tove. At different hours of the day or night, it has something of the painted and tinseled and tired gaiety of a four-ring circus, something of the juvenile inebriety and synthetic fraternal sentiment of a class reunion, something of the tub-thumping frenzy of a backwoods meeting.

This is only the semblance, the picture to the outer world, however. "What goes on beneath the surface and behind locked doors," Becker adds, "is something both realistic and important. For it is here, unexposed to the public eye, that deals and bargains, the necessary compromises are arranged—compromises designed to satisfy as well as possible all the divergent elements within the party.... What really goes on in a national nominating convention is the attempt, by the party leaders, to forecast the intangible and uncertain will of the people, as it will be registered in the state pluralities, and to shape the party policies in conformity with it."[1] Thus in many important respects the national conventions perform the task for the people that the Constitution's framers thought would be performed by the electors. But instead of settling on one candidate, the nominating conventions—and only those of the two dominant parties are usually of any lasting importance—propose the two presidential candidates from which the people and their agents, the electors, will choose the following November.

The Constitution's framers never contemplated national conventions for two reasons: because nationally organized political parties were unknown at the time, and because they dreaded the idea of partisan coalition and sought in the charter of government they wrote to isolate the presidential election from any pressures of faction or party.

By the early 1800s, however, national political parties were a fact of life in the United States. Institutions had to be developed by which each party could decide on its candidates for president and vice president rather than fragmenting its support in the election. The congressional caucus, operating from 1796 until 1824, was the first answer to this problem. In the era before the railroad, when travel from one part of the country to another was arduous and time-consuming, the congressional caucus provided the only logical national forum for a political party. Ironically, the caucus placed the nomination of the president precisely where the Constitutional Convention had been determined not to place it: in Congress. Significantly, it was the supporters of frontier democracy and egalitarianism, grouped around Andrew Jackson, who effectively killed the caucus system in 1824. The caucus (or King Caucus, as it opponents derisively called it) could not survive an era of expanding democracy because its power base was too narrow: congressmen were chosen by the people to make laws, not presidents.

In 1828, Andrew Jackson and John Quincy Adams were nominated by a combination of state legislatures, public meetings, and irregular conventions scattered throughout the Union. The time was ripe for national nominating conventions to appear; the first was held by the Anti-Mason party in Baltimore in September 1831. The short-lived coalition called the National Republican party met in Baltimore in December 1831 to nominate Henry Clay for the presidency, and the Democrats held their first national convention in the same city in May 1832, nominating Jackson for a second term. The first Whig Convention was in 1839, its last in 1852. The first Republican National Convention was held in Philadelphia in 1856, nominating John C. Frémont for the presidency.

The delegates to each national convention come from every state and thus represent a broad geographic cross-section of party and political activists. Some are governors, congressmen, and other prominent leaders from political as well as nonpolitical professions;

some are simply party hacks who come to vote as party leaders tell them to; but most are individuals primarily loyal to their preferred candidate or to a particular cause or issue. Some are chosen by state party conventions, but the vast majority are elected in popular presidential primaries. Collectively, the delegates to a national convention constitute the continuing entity of the national political party, a continental alliance that will continue to function and flourish only as long as it represents a significant cross-section of American people and reflects the major issues of the day.[2]

The rapid growth of presidential primaries from the 1960s to the 1990s had the effect of transferring, more than ever, the decisive role in the selection of presidential nominees from the party powers of the day directly to the electorate. It became increasingly rare for a convention to be the arena of final decision; in most cases a clear decision had already emerged from the primaries. This tended to have a debilitating effect on the prestige and authority of the conventions—and thus of the established political parties.

The Presidential Campaign

In the early days of the Republic, the candidates for president remained quietly in their home cities and awaited the decision of the people. Today, through massive media coverage, every American is aware of the whirlwind of activity surrounding a presidential campaign. The candidates for president and vice president cover the face of the continent again and again, by air, rail, and motorcade, visiting every major population center at least once and even the smallest states of the Union. With the advent of radio, and especially of television in the years since World War II, the presidential campaign has been carried into the homes of all but a handful of the people. Whether the issues brought forth by the candidates be great or petty, the battle is distinctively national in character and is recognized by all as the decisive plebiscite on the course of the nation for four years to come.

Election Day

The grand climax of the race for the presidency comes as the people register their votes, starting with the stroke of midnight in a few early-voting hamlets in New England and ending some twenty-six hours later with the close of the last polling place in Alaska, four thousand miles to the west. In early American elections, it was days or weeks until the result was known; now, with quick reporting through the News Election Service, a cooperative ballot-counting operation of the major television networks and wire services, and rapid computer calculations by the national television networks, the result is generally known by midevening. A few hours later, except in the closest of contests, the losing candidate will concede, wishing her or his opponent all success in office and urging the nation to unify behind the winner. The drama seems to be closed for another four years.

The Constitutional System

As far as the Constitution is concerned, the popular election every fourth November is only the first step in a complex procedure that should culminate in the declaration of a winner a full two months later. In fact, under the Constitution, the November election is not for the presidential candidates themselves but for the electors who subsequently choose a president. And all the Constitution says of this stage of the election process is that "each state shall appoint, in such manner as the legislature thereof may direct, a number of electors, equal to the whole number of Senators and Representatives to which the state may be entitled in Congress." (The constitutional provisions relating to presidential election are reprinted in Appendix D at the end of this volume.) Thus the major controversies over the way the president is elected have centered on the presidential elector.

How Many Electors Are There?

Since each state's representation in the electoral college is equal to its representation in Congress, a state is guaranteed three electoral

votes: two corresponding to the number of its United States Senators, and one (or more) corresponding to the minimum of one seat
in the U.S. House that the Constitution assures each state. In the
1990s, with fifty states in the Union, the electoral college consists of
538 persons—435 corresponding to the number of representatives,
100 to the number of senators, and an additional three for the District of Columbia under the Twenty-third Amendment to the Constitution.[3]

The relative power of various states in the electoral college has
risen and fallen dramatically in the course of U.S. history. Virginia,
the early "mother of Presidents," swung the heaviest weight in the
first years of the nation with 21 out of a total of 138 electors in the
last decade of the eighteenth century. Today Virginia contributes
only 13 electors to a vastly enlarged college. New York had 12 of the
138 electors in the 1791–1800 period, rose to a high of 47 electors
between 1931 and 1950, but has 33 votes today. California, starting
with only four electors when it entered the Union in 1850, had 47
electoral votes in the 1980s, and now controls an all-time high of 54
of the 538 electoral positions—over 10 percent of the total, and more
than 20 percent of the total electoral votes a candidate needs to win.

A state's congressional apportionment—and thus its electoral
vote—tends to lag behind actual population shifts. Since each census
takes place in the first year of a decade (1790, 1800, 1900, 1990, and
so on), a new apportionment cannot take effect, at the earliest, until
two years later. If a presidential election falls in the same year as a census, the initial election of the new decade is governed by the apportionment based on the census of a full decade before, and the new
census figures will not go into effect until the presidential election
four years subsequent. Thus, the first presidential election under a
new apportionment will take place either two years after the apportionment (as in 1972 and 1992) or a full four years later (as in 1984 and
2004), depending on the quadrennial cycle. Any increase or decrease
in a state's population since 1990, for example, will not be reflected
in that state's electoral vote apportionment until the year 2004!

Who Picks the Electors?

In practice, the people of the states have been given the power to choose the electors in statewide elections since the 1830s. The last scattered instances in which a legislature chose the electors directly were in South Carolina until 1860, in the newly reconstructed state of Florida in 1868, and in the newly admitted state of Colorado in 1876. With these minor exceptions, the people have chosen the electors.

If any state legislature should wish, however, it would have the right under the Constitution to take the choice of the electors away from the people and do the job itself or deputize some other body to make the selection. In the words of a Senate committee in 1874, "The appointment of these electors is thus placed absolutely and wholly within the legislatures of the several states. They may be chosen by the legislature, or the legislature may provide that they shall be elected by the people of the state at large, or in district; . . . and it is, no doubt, competent for the legislature to authorize the Governor, or the supreme court of the state, or any other agent of its will, to appoint these electors." The language was quoted approvingly by the U.S. Supreme Court in a landmark 1892 case, *McPherson v. Blacker,* in which a group of Michigan citizens challenged the right of that state's legislature to shift to a district system for the 1892 elections.[4] The Court rejected the appeal, saying that the word "appoint" in the Constitution conveys the "broadest power of determination" to the legislatures. "There is no color for the contention," said the Court, that "every male inhabitant of a state being a citizen of the United States has from the time of his majority a right to vote for Presidential electors." The Court said the state legislatures have "plenary power" over appointing electors, and could even refuse to provide for appointment of any electors at all if they so chose. This court opinion echoed a statement made years earlier, during a debate in the House in 1826, by Rep. Henry R. Storms of New York. He asserted that nothing in the Constitution prevented a state legislature from vesting the power to choose presidential electors "in a board of bank directors—a turnpike commission—or a synagogue."[5]

Despite such sweeping language, there are some limitations on the discretion of state legislatures in setting the mechanism for presidential election in their respective states. Even *McPherson v. Blacker* recognized that *if* a state permits the people to choose the electors, then the Fourteenth Amendment protects citizens from having their vote denied or abridged. Congressional enactments designed to prevent fraud or regulate campaign expenditures in connection with presidential elections have been upheld by the Supreme Court.[6] The governor of a state, moreover, might well veto a legislative act abolishing popular election for presidential electors. In referendum states, a law abolishing popular election could be referred to the people, where it would almost certainly be defeated. Initiative measures could be used in a similar way.[7]

For the most part, however, it is not state or federal constitutional guarantees that assure the people the right to choose presidential electors. First of all, it would probably never occur to modern-day state legislatures to take the power of appointment of presidential electors directly unto themselves. And even if the temptation presented itself, fear of retribution at the polls would restrain them. After the 1960 election, for example, segregationist forces in the Louisiana legislature suggested revoking the choice of the regular Democratic electors already elected by the people and substituting a new slate of electors that would oppose Kennedy's election. But despite the strong conservative sentiment in the legislature, the motion was withdrawn before it could come to a vote. Even if the motion had passed, it could probably have been subjected to successful challenge in the courts because it would have violated the congressional requirement that the electors be chosen on a uniform date—which had already passed. But a move by a legislature to take the appointment of the electors into its own hands *before* the nationally established date for choosing the electors would not be open to similar challenge.

Who Are the Electors?

The Constitution merely says that "no Senator or Representative, or person holding an office of trust or profit under the United States, shall be appointed an elector." The probable intent of the founding fathers was that the electors would be distinguished citizens, and such they were in some early elections. As early as 1826, however, a Senate select committee observed that electors were "usually selected for their devotion to party, their popular manners, and a supposed talent for electioneering";[8] in contrast, in 1855 it was asserted that the electors in Alabama and Mississippi were among the state's ablest men and went among the people to instruct, excite, and arouse them on the issues of the campaign.[9] Today, it is probable that no one voter in thousands knows who a state's electors are. Persons are usually nominated for elector on the basis of their long service to their party, because of their financial donations to party or candidate, or out of a wish to have an ethically or politically balanced elector slate. Since the only payment is normally a small per diem allowance (if even that) on the day they cast their votes, some small measure of fleeting prestige is about all that electors can hope for from their selection.[10]

Based on an entirely unscientific perusal of the pictures of electoral colleges convened in several states, it appears that such "rewards" are often reserved for women and party workers in the twilight of their lives. Many octogenarians are apparent. Thomas O'Connor, for example, was ninety-three years of age when he was elected president of the Massachusetts electoral college in 1960. Besides often being aged party workers, electors are frequently rewarded with the office because of their past financial generosity. As one well-known 1968 elector, best-selling author James Michener, candidly put it, "My finest credentials were that every year I contributed what money I could to the party."[11] An example of an effort to utilize the elector list for political purposes occurred in New York State in 1936, when the Democratic party put several prominent trade unionists, including Ladies' Garment Workers' chief David

Dubinsky, on its electoral slate in an effort to attract the labor vote to Franklin D. Roosevelt. At the time, some fears were expressed that a "Tammanyizing" of electoral slates might occur, with the introduction of class, racial, and religious appeals through giving each of these groups some of the electoral nominations.[12] But these fears may largely be illusory, for fewer and fewer states actually list the names of the electors on their ballots. In short, the electoral college is far from being the assembly of wise and learned elders assumed by its creators; it is rather little more than a state-by-state collection of political hacks and fat cats. (This harsh judgment is offered here despite the fact that one of this book's authors has twice been a presidential elector!)

Nomination and Election of the Electors

Presidential electors for each party are today nominated by a variety of methods. The most widely used procedure—in effect in thirty-four states—is for state conventions of the parties to nominate the electors. In ten other states and the District of Columbia, nominations are made by the state political committees. One state, Arizona, authorizes nomination of the electors in primary elections. The remaining five states use a combination of methods. The most unusual nomination law is Pennsylvania's, which authorizes the presidential nominee of each political party directly to select electors on his or her behalf in the state.

Before 1845, Congress refrained from setting any specific day for the actual election of the electors. The Act of 1792, spelling out procedures for presidential election, stipulated only that the electors must be chosen within thirty-four days preceding the first Wednesday in December every fourth year.[13] A uniform national election date, however, was established in 1845: the first Tuesday after the first Monday in November.[14] The date was especially appropriate for an agrarian society, for it fell after most of the autumn harvest had been gathered but before the rigors of winter set in. This date has been observed in every subsequent presidential election.

Since the advent of Jacksonian democracy, the states have almost exclusively used the winner-take-all method for choosing electors. Under this system, electors are chosen "at large" (on a statewide basis) and the party with the most votes receives all the state's electoral votes. Since 1832, only three states have reverted to the district system that several states used in the first years. The first instance occurred in 1892 in Michigan, where Democrats were temporarily in control of the legislature and sought to divide the state's electoral votes so that they would not go en bloc to the Republicans, who normally had a voting majority in the state. Each of the state's twelve congressional districts became a separate elector district, and two additional "at large" districts, one eastern and one western, were established for the votes corresponding to Michigan's two senators. The plan was successful in dividing the Michigan electoral vote: nine electoral votes went for the Republican presidential ticket and five for the Democratic ticket in that year's election, but the national outcome was not close enough to be influenced by the Michigan return. It was this Michigan plan that the Supreme Court refused to invalidate in *McPherson v. Blacker*.

Two more recent experiments with the district plan continue today. In 1969, Maine resurrected the district division of electoral votes by adopting a plan, which went into effect as of the presidential election of 1972, allowing for the determination of two of its four votes on the basis of the presidential popular vote in its two congressional districts. As of the 1996 election, however, after twenty years of use of the district plan, an actual division of Maine's electoral votes three to one (the only division possible) has not yet occurred. In 1992 Nebraska followed the lead of Maine and adopted a similar district determination of three of its five electoral votes, to go into effect with the 1992 presidential election. In that election, however, Nebraska's electoral vote went solidly for George Bush—this because of his pluralities in each of the state's three congressional districts as well his solid strength in the state overall. Such unanimity of outcome in Nebraska, however, is less likely in a future closely balanced election because of significant compositional differences among its three congressional districts.

During 1992 a number of additional states, including the important megastate of Florida, contemplated comparable changes in their winner-take-all arrangement for electoral votes, although all these efforts eventually failed. Should Florida or other states adopt such changes in the future, divided electoral vote state tallies could become a common feature of presidential elections.

The virtual anonymity of the presidential elector has been rein-forced in recent years by the marked trend, apparently spurred by the desire to simplify the vote count and by the spread of voting machines, toward the use of the presidential elector "short ballot" in the November election. Instead of facing a ballot or voting machine with long lists of elector candidates, the voter sees the names of the parties' presidential candidates printed in large type, sometimes pre-ceded (in small type) by the words "Presidential electors for . . . ." Many states even omit the wording about presidential electors alto-gether, so that voters, unless they are well versed politically, have no way of knowing that they are actually voting for presidential electors rather than directly for president and vice president. The presiden-tial short ballot was employed by fifteen states in 1940, by twenty-six in 1948, and was prescribed by the laws of thirty-eight states by 1980. The names of both the presidential candidates and the electors appear on the ballots in only eleven states. Most of these states require that the voter choose one slate or another as a unit, although three—Mississippi, Louisiana, and South Carolina—permit the voter to pick and choose among electors on various slates and fur-ther permit write-ins. One state—Mississippi—uniquely prints the names of the electors but makes no mention of the presidential can-didates they favor—unless the electors are pledged and wish to indi-cate their preference.

One beneficial result of the short ballot is to cut down the chances for voter confusion in marking ballots. History abounds with examples of spoiled ballots resulting from voter confusion over how to vote for electors. In the 1904 presidential election in Florida, the names of the twenty candidates for elector, five from each of the four parties that qualified, were printed in a close column, one name below the other, with no line or space separating the party nominees. Nor did the ballot carry any emblem or name to indicate which party each candidate for elector represented. The Democratic voter had to mark the first five electoral candidates, the Republican numbers six through ten, the Populist numbers eleven through fifteen, and so on. Naturally, a large number of voters were muddled, and 4,300 out of the 39,300 voters in the state failed to mark all the electors of their parties.[15] Similarly, in Maryland in 1904, some 2,000 Republican voters marked only the square for the first Republican elector, thinking that that square represented a vote for all eight Republican elector nominees. The result was that the Republicans received only one instead of all eight Maryland electoral voters.[16] One of the most serious voter mix-ups of modern times occurred in Ohio in 1948. The state normally employs the short ballot, with the names of the Republican and Democratic electors not appearing on the ballot. Henry Wallace's Progressive party was unable to qualify as a regular party for the general election ballot, however, so that the Wallace electors appeared on the ballot as individual names. Thousands of voters were confused by the double system and voted for some Wallace electors as well as marking ballots for Dewey or Truman. It has been estimated that more than 100,000 Ohio presidential ballots were invalidated for this reason. The confusion may well have determined the outcome in the state, which Truman won by a margin of only 7,105 votes.[17]

Under the general ticket ballot as employed by most states, the voter chooses one entire elector slate as a unit, and there is no chance for a split result: some electors elected from one slate and some from another. But where an elector can split his or her ticket, there is a chance for a divided result, as happened in Maryland in 1904. It also occurred in California in 1912, when two Democratic electors and eleven Progressive electors were victorious because of slight differences in the vote cast for the various elector candidates on those two slates.[18] The spreading use of the short ballot has minimized the chances for such split results.

Electors: Bound or Not?

Since the first election, there has been controversy about the proper role of presidential electors. Are they to think and act independently, or are they merely agents of the people who choose them? History records that in 1792 the electors chosen in North Carolina met and debated the respective merits of John Adams and George Clinton and finally decided to support Clinton.[19] Debates among the Virginia electors in the same year were reported to have shifted six votes from Adams to Clinton.[20] But even in the first elections, few electors really acted as independent evaluators. The newspaper *Aurora* said in 1796: "The President must not be merely the creature of a spirit of accommodation or intrigue among the electors. The electors should be faithful agents of the people in this very important business; act in their behalf as the people would act were the President and Vice President elected immediately by them. . . . Let the people then choose their electors with a view to the ultimate choice."[21]

With the passage of the Twelfth Amendment in 1804, any semblance of the electors as independent statesmen faded. In an 1826 Senate committee report, Thomas Hart Benton of Missouri said that the founding fathers had intended electors to be men of "superior discernment, virtue and information," who would select the president "according to their own will" and without reference to the immediate wishes of the people. "That this invention has failed of its objective in every election," Benton said, "is a fact of such universal notoriety, that no one can dispute it. That it ought to have failed," he concluded, "is equally uncontestable; for such independence in the electors was wholly incompatible with the safety of the people. [It] was, in fact, a chimerical and impractical idea in any community."[22]

Thus, even by the early nineteenth century, the function of the electors had come to be little more than ministerial. Benton said the electors had "degenerated into mere agents"; and Justice Bradley, the famed "fifteenth man" on the Electoral Commission of 1877, characterized electors as mere instruments of party—"party puppets" who are to carry out a function which an automaton without volition or intelligence might as well perform.[23] Sen. John J. Ingalls of Kansas commented in the same era that electors are like "the marionettes in a Punch and Judy show."[24] Reviewing the historical failure of the electors to be free agents, as had been contemplated by the founding fathers, Supreme Court Justice Robert H. Jackson wrote in 1952: "Electors, although often personally eminent, independent and respectable, officially become voluntary party lackeys and intellectual nonentities to whose memory we might justly paraphrase a tuneful satire: 'They always voted at their party's call / And never thought of thinking for themselves at all.'"[25] Jackson concluded that "as an institution, the electoral college suffered atrophy almost indistinguishable from *rigor mortis*."[26] Sen. Henry Cabot Lodge of Massachusetts said in 1949 that electors "are mere rubber stamps—and inaccurate rubber stamps at that. The people know the candidates for President and Vice President; rarely do they know the identity of the electors for whom they actually vote. Such 'go-betweens' are like the appendix in the human body. While it does no good and ordinarily causes no trouble, it continually exposes the body to the danger of political peritonitis."[27]

Nevertheless, under the Constitution, electors remain free agents and, if they choose, can vote in any way they like. At least as far as the law is concerned, Senator Benton warned, the elector "may give or sell his vote to the adverse candidate, in violation of all the pledges that have been taken of him. The crime is easily committed, for he votes by ballot; detection is difficult, because he does not sign it; prevention is impossible, for he cannot be coerced; the injury irreparable, for the vote cannot be vacated; legal punishment is unknown and would be inadequate. . . . That these mischiefs have not yet happened, is no answer to an objection that they may happen."[28] Since Benton's day, some efforts have been made to restrict the elector's independence, but his basic point still holds: electors are free agents subject only to their own consciences, lack of imagination, and, perhaps, some degree of public opinion. In regard to the latter, former President Benjamin Harrison warned in 1898 that "an elector who failed to vote for the nominee of his party would be the object of execration, and in times of high excitement might be the subject of a lynching."[29]

In fact, there have been a number of instances where presidential electors have broken their pledges. The first known case was recorded in Pennsylvania in 1796, when Samuel Miles, chosen as a Federalist, voted for Thomas Jefferson, prompting the much-quoted voter's remark that Miles had been chosen "to act, not to think." In 1820 former Sen. William Plumer of New Hampshire cast his electoral vote for John Quincy Adams rather than James Monroe, to whom he was pledged. Accounts vary about Plumer's motivation; he is reported to have said he felt that only George Washington "deserved a unanimous election"; but biographers also report that he wanted to draw attention to his friend Adams as a potential president and to "protest against the wasteful extravagance of the Monroe administration."[30] In 1824 North Carolina's fifteen electors voted en bloc for Andrew Jackson despite a reported agreement to divide their votes according to the result of a presidential preference vote, which the voters were allowed to make by writing on the ballot the name of the man they preferred. Adams's name was written in by about a third of the state's voters, according to the historian J. B. McMaster, so that he should have received about five electoral votes. Other authorities maintain, however, that it was understood that all of the state's votes would go to the most popular candidate.[31] In the same election the New York legislature picked a mixed slate of electors, including seven electors expected to back Henry Clay (from the state total of thirty-six in that election). One of the Clay electors was elected to Congress, however, and the man who replaced him voted for Adams. By the time the New York electors actually cast their ballots, they already knew that Clay would not even qualify for the runoff in the House. Two of the remaining six Clay electors from the state then deserted him—one to vote for William H. Crawford, one to support Jackson.[32]

In recent times, seven presidential electors have broken their pledges or otherwise voted differently than expected. The first of these was Preston Parks, who was nominated on two elector slates in Tennessee in 1948—the regular Democratic (pledged to Harry S Truman) and the States' Rights (pledged to Dixiecrat candidate Strom Thurmond). The regular Democratic slate, including Parks, was elected, but he voted for Thurmond anyway. In 1956 W. F. Turner of Alabama, a Democratic elector, voted for a local circuit judge, Walter E. Jones, for president instead of supporting the regular Democratic nominee, Adlai E. Stevenson, to whom he was pledged. Turner subsequently commented: "I have fulfilled my obligations to the people of Alabama. I'm talking about the white people."[33] Henry D. Irwin, the renegade Republican elector in Oklahoma who voted for Harry Byrd in 1960 despite his pledge to vote for Nixon, is another example. Irwin, who listed his occupation as "slave labor for the federal government," explained his action on a national television program: "I was prompted to act as I did for fear of the future of our republic form of government. I feared the immediate future of our government under the control of the socialist-labor leadership. . . . I executed my constitutional right . . . as a free elector." Irwin went on to say that the founding fathers were landowners and propertied people who never intended "that the indigent, the nonproperty owners should have a vote in such a momentous decision" as election of the president.[34]

In 1968 Dr. Lloyd W. Bailey, Republican of North Carolina, declined to abide by his pledge to support his party's nominee, Richard Nixon, and in 1972 Republican elector Roger MacBride of Virginia also deserted Nixon. The defection in 1972 made Nixon the only man in history to suffer elector defections on three separate occasions. The 1976 election saw yet another faithless Republican elector. (We are at a loss for any theory that could explain why every faithless elector for thirty years was a Republican.) Mike Padden of the state of Washington cast his vote for Ronald Reagan instead of for Republican party candidate Gerald Ford. This defection was the third occurrence of a faithless elector in successive presidential elections and the sixth such action in eight successive elections (as of 1976) since World War II.

To the surprise of most observers, the presidential elections of 1980 and 1984 failed to produce new faithless electors; however, another such occurrence marked the electoral vote in 1988. A Democratic presidential elector in West Virginia, for reasons best understood by her, cast her presidential electoral vote for Democratic vice presidential nominee Lloyd Bentsen and her vice presidential electoral vote for Democratic presidential candidate Michael S. Dukakis. Her action thus provided the seventh such instance of deviant electoral voting in the twelve most recent president elections (no faithless elector appeared in 1992).

Fortunately for the nation, Henry Irwin, Dr. Lloyd W. Bailey, Roger MacBride, Mike Padden, and the other self-willed men who broke electoral pledges before them were not able to change the outcome of the elections. Statistically, the changes are not very high that they could have. In the nearly 170 years between 1824 and 1992, only 8 of the 18,995 electoral votes for president were indisputably cast "against instructions." If one also includes the disputed 1824 votes in New York and North Carolina, the total of bolting electors rises to sixteen. It should be noted, however, that the incentives for elector defections occurring on a multiple basis would be much greater in the case of a very close election. Should an electoral college majority rest on a margin of only one or two votes, then we might well witness faithless electors appearing in order to gain personal fame or draw attention to some favorite case or issue.

Most electors consider themselves irrevocably bound to support the presidential candidate on whose party ticket they were elected.

In the disputed Hayes-Tilden election of 1876, James Russell Lowell, who had been chosen as a Republican elector in Massachusetts, was urged to switch his vote from Hayes to Tilden—a move that would have given Tilden the election, since only one vote divided the candidates in the national count. Lowell refused to take the step, however. "In my own judgment I have no choice, and am bound in honor to vote for Hayes, as the people who chose me expected me to do," Lowell wrote to a friend. "They did not choose me because they have confidence in my judgment but because they thought they knew what the judgment would be. If I had told them that I should vote for Tilden, they would never have nominated me. It is a plain question of trust."[35] At the meeting of the California electoral college in Sacramento in 1960, former Gov. Goodwin Knight told his fellow Republican electors: "Before coming here today, many of us received messages by mail and wire urging that we cast our ballots for prominent Americans other than Richard Nixon and Henry Cabot Lodge. Among those mentioned were former Governor Allan Shivers of Texas, Senator Barry Goldwater of Arizona, and Senator Harry Byrd of Virginia. Conceding that these gentlemen have merit as statesmen, the fact remains it is our solemn duty, in my humble judgment, to vote for those men the people selected on November the eighth."[36]

In an effort to prevent the phenomenon of runaway electors, the party organizations in a few states require specific pledges by electors that they will support the national nominees of their party in electoral college balloting, although these pledges are of dubious constitutionality (see below). Electors must now make such pledges in Alaska, Oregon, Oklahoma, and Florida—in the latter two states by formal oath.[37] In a number of other southern states, the party committees are given sufficient discretion by state law to demand party loyalty pledges. Alabama has done so in several elections (but not when the party machinery was supporting unpledged electors). In 1944 some Texas Democratic electors indicated that they might bolt the national ticket. A special party committee was convened. One of its members, Rep. Wright Patman, later said that the committee had "tried the proposed electors for disloyalty" and "put most of them off the ticket and put loyal ones on." In 1972 an already chosen Democratic-Farmer-Labor party elector in Minnesota indicated that he would be unlikely to vote for Democratic nominee George McGovern. That elector was promptly replaced by the state party. Twenty years later, the independent presidential campaign of Ross Perot was plagued by doubts about the loyalty of some of its elector-nominees, as the independent candidacy of John B. Anderson had been in 1980.[38]

A number of states have specific statutory provisions directing electors to vote for the presidential–vice presidential ticket of the party that nominated them. Only five states had such laws in the 1940s, but in the next four decades the list expanded to fifteen, including the nation's two most populous states, California and New York. In the wake of the defection by Republican elector Irwin in 1960, for example, the Oklahoma legislature added a section to its election code stipulating that each elector candidate must take an oath to support his or her party's presidential and vice presidential candidates, and that any elector who voted for another person would be guilty of a misdemeanor and fined up to $1,000.[39]

Serious constitutional questions are raised by any such effort to bind or control electors. Custom may have made electors into little more than instruments of party, but the Constitution provides that they shall vote by a procedure which would seem to imply that they are free agents. In 1952 the U.S. Supreme Court was called upon to judge the constitutionality of a requirement laid down by the Democratic Executive Committee of Alabama that candidates for elector pledge to support the presidential and vice presidential candidates of the party's national convention as a condition to being certified as an elector candidate in the Democratic primary. The Court, in a 5 to 2 opinion, held that the pledge requirement represented a legitimate exercise of the state's right to appoint electors under Article II of the U.S. Constitution. The majority opinion noted the popular expectation that electors would vote for the party nominees and implied that the states' power to control electors was supported by the traditional practice of elector pledges. Even if a loyalty pledge were unenforceable, the Court said, it would not follow that a party pledge as a requisite for running in a primary was unconstitutional, since any person not wishing to take the oath could run independently of party.[40] But the Court did not rule on the constitutionality of state laws that require electors to vote for their party's candidates, or indicate whether elector pledges, even if given, could be enforced.

The preponderance of legal opinion seems to be that statutes binding electors, or pledges that they may give, are unenforceable. "If an elector chooses to incur party and community wrath by violating his trust and voting for some one other than his party's candidate, it is doubtful if there is any practical remedy," writes James C. Kirby, Jr., an expert on electoral college law. Once the elector is appointed, Kirby points out, "he is to vote. Legal proceedings which extended beyond the date when the electors must meet and vote would be of no avail. If mandamus were issued and he disobeyed the order, no one could change his vote or cast it differently. If he were enjoined from voting for anyone else, he could still abstain and deprive the candidate of his electoral vote."[41]

Conditionally Pledged or Unpledged Electors

Quite separate from the problem of elector fidelity is that of electors who either announce before the election that in certain circumstances they may support an alternative candidate or who simply refuse to be pledged in any way. An example of electors announcing alternatives came in 1912, when South Dakota electors, nominally pledged to Theodore Roosevelt, let it be known before the election that if the returns from the rest of the country made it clear that Roosevelt could not be elected and the contest was between Woodrow Wilson and William Howard Taft, they would vote for Taft. The voters apparently found this assurance satisfactory, for the Roosevelt slate was victorious on election day in South Dakota. But Taft had run so far behind across the country that the state's electors stuck with Roosevelt anyway.

The concept of totally unpledged electors disappeared from the political scene around the time of the adoption of the Twelfth Amendment early in the nineteenth century, only to reappear in the mid-twentieth century as a device by conservative, segregationist-minded southerners to force the major parties to pay more heed to southern views. The genesis of the movement can be traced to the abortive States' Rights (Dixiecrat) third-party movement in the 1948 election. The Dixiecrat goal of 1948 was revived in the form of the unpledged elector movement of 1960 with the same goal: to prevent either of the major-party nominees from receiving a majority of the electoral votes. With the power to dictate the result of the election in their hands, the southerners could extract pledges from one of the major-party candidates with respect to southern positions on segregation and other issues, in return for the swing-elector support from the South. If that strategy failed, the election would be thrown into the House of Representatives, where the southern states and their powerful congressional representatives might also find themselves in a crucial bargaining position.

In 1948 the Dixiecrat nominees for president and vice president, Strom Thurmond (South Carolina) and Fielding Wright (Mississippi), won the elector votes of the four states where they actually appeared on the ballot as the Democratic nominees: Alabama, Louisiana, Mississippi, and South Carolina. Presumably, Thurmond and Wright would have released their electors to vote for one of the national-party nominees had they achieved enough votes to occupy a balance of power and could have struck a bargain with Harry S Truman or Thomas E. Dewey. Thus the Dixiecrat electors were technically pledged but would quickly have become unpledged had such an action suited political purposes. A similar strategy had been contemplated for the George Wallace electors in 1968 in the event they should hold the balance of power between the major-party candidates in that election.

In 1960 the unpledged electors chosen in Alabama and Mississippi decided to cast their votes for Harry Byrd when it appeared they had been unable to achieve a balance-of-power position. Major preparations were made to launch another unpledged-elector movement in 1964, but they were discarded when the Republicans nominated Barry Goldwater for president.[42] Goldwater's general conservatism and stand against civil rights legislation satisfied most of the segregationist southerners; of the six states he carried, four were the same ones that had gone Dixiecrat in 1948.

The Electors Cast Their Votes

The Constitution, in Article II and the Twelfth Amendment, provides that the electors shall meet in their respective states to vote by ballot for president and vice president. Congress is given the power to determine the day of voting, "which day shall be the same throughout the United States." This system of simultaneous elections in each state was adopted, according to one of the delegates to the Constitutional Convention, in the hope that "by apportioning, limiting and confining the electors within their respective states, . . . intrigue, combination and corruption would be effectively shut out, and a free and pure election of the President of the United States made perpetual."[43] The founding fathers had apparently hoped that the electors would be unaware of, and thus not influenced by, the action of their counterparts in the other states.

Even in the first election, of course, the curiously naive hope for absolutely independent action by the electors in the various states was not fulfilled. But the form of election that the Constitution's framers prescribed has remained unchanged for almost two centuries, and on a specified day every fourth year a separate group, or "college," of electors meets in each state capital to vote for president.

In 1792 Congress decreed that the day should be the first Wednesday in December. This provision remained in effect until 1877, when Congress shifted the date to the second Monday in January, reportedly to allow a state more time to settle any election disputes.[44] The final adjustment, to the first Monday after the second Wednesday in December—still the law today—was set by Congress in 1934 following ratification of the Twentieth Amendment, which shifted inauguration day forward from March 4 to January 20.[45]

On the appointed day in December, the electors convene, in most states at noon. The meeting usually takes place in the state legislative chambers, the executive chambers, or the office of the secretary of state. Under federal law, the governor of the state must by this time have sent to the administrator of General Services in Washington a certificate reporting the names of the electors elected and the number of popular votes cast for them. Copies of these certificates are presented to the electors when they convene, and the governor or secretary of state generally makes a short speech welcoming the electors to their august duty.[46]

Frequently, however, some of the electors fail to appear for their great day. Congress, in a law first passed 1845, has authorized the states to provide for filling of elector vacancies. In almost all the states today, the electors themselves are authorized to choose replacements. Sometimes the replacements are found by scouring the hallways of the state capitol for likely candidates. This process was followed by the Michigan electoral college in 1948, when only thirteen of the nineteen chosen electors—all pledged to Dewey and Warren—appeared. But one of the substitutes recruited on the spot, a J. J. Levy of Royal Oak, had to be restrained by his colleagues from voting for Truman and Barkely. "I thought we had to vote for the winning candidate," Levy was quoted as saying.[47] Substitute electors must frequently be designated because federal office holders have been improperly chosen as electors, in violation of the Constitution.

While they have but one function—to vote for president and vice president—the electors in many states go through an elaborate procedure of prayers, election of temporary and permanent chairmen, speeches by state officials, appointment of committees, and the like. Robert G. Dixon, in an interesting review of electoral college procedures, points out that the secretary of state is the "shepherd and guiding spirit of the electoral college in all states . . . the high priest who knows the ritual prescribed by laws and usages, federal and state, and under his prompting the electors go through their paces like obedient children."[48] In a speech accepting the chairmanship of the Ohio electoral college (for the fifth time) in 1948, Alfred M. Cohen said: "Our task is purely perfunctory if we are faithful to the trust confided in us." Cohen had apparently developed little love of the institution he often headed, however, because he told his colleagues that he favored abolishing the system altogether in favor of direct popular voting for president.[49]

In 1976, while Wisconsin's electoral votes were being collected and tabulated, Wisconsin governor and electoral college chairman Patrick Lucey invited a political scientist in the audience to speak to the electoral college. The resulting remarks were severely critical of the electoral college as an institution, described as "little more than a state by state collection of political hacks and fat cats." Instead of being insulted by these words, the Wisconsin electors instead immediately proceeded to adopt a resolution calling for abolition of their office as well as the entire electoral college system.[50]

The Constitution provides specifically that the electors shall vote "by ballot" for president and vice president, which would seem to require a secret vote. In reality, the voting is not at all secret in many states. A survey of electoral college practices showed that in seventeen of the forty states from which responses were received, the electors voted either by signed ballot, by oral announcement only (with no ballot whatever!), or by unsigned ballot accompanied by a public announcement of how each of them was voting. Fourteen states used paper ballots, twelve typewritten ballots, eight printed ballots, two engraved ballots, and five the obviously unconstitutional practice of oral voting. Many of the printed ballots, in fact, actually listed only the names of the presidential and vice presidential candidates of the party that had carried the state, thus destroying even the semblance of a free vote.[51] Sometimes such loss of confidentiality is resisted: in 1800 one New York elector, Anthony Lispenard, insisted on his right to cast a secret ballot. It was reported, however, that Lispenard intended to forsake Thomas Jefferson and cast his double vote for Aaron Burr and someone else—a maneuver that would have given Burr the presidency. The prestigious De Witt Clinton was then brought into the meeting, and his presence had such an impact that the participants showed each other their ballots before placing them in the ballot box. Lispenard hesitated but finally exhibited his ballot, marked properly for Jefferson and Burr.[52] Thus, by common practice since the earliest days, the ballot is not secret and sometimes is not even a ballot at all. Actual use of the secret written ballot, as one observer has noted, "is an anti-democratic provision which may cause a blunder, and could be easily used to cover a crime. An agent of the people should never be permitted to act secretly in transacting their business, except in cases where the public safety may require."[53]

After balloting separately for president and vice president, as required by the Constitution, the electors send lists of their votes by registered mail to the president of the Senate in Washington. This constitutional requirement has been amplified by statute to safeguard against loss of the first copy. Two copies are kept by the secretary of state of the state, two go to the General Services administrator, and one to the judge of the local federal district court.[54]

The Count in Congress: Disputed Votes

Once the electors have balloted and the certificates of their votes have been forwarded to Washington, the scene shifts to Congress, where the votes are to be counted. The Twelfth Amendment to the U.S. Constitution provides simply that "the President of the Senate shall, in the presence of the Senate and House of Representatives, open all the certificates and the votes shall then be counted." In 1792 Congress provided that the joint session for counting the votes should take place on the second Wednesday in February; since passage of the Twentieth Amendment, the date has been January 6. The count takes place in the chamber of the House of Representatives, with the president of the Senate (the vice president of the United States) presiding.

Throughout the nineteenth century, major controversies regarding the electoral college procedure centered on the technicalities of the vote count in Congress. By one theory, the president of the Senate has authority to count the votes; by another, the two houses present in joint session have the responsibility for counting; by still another theory, the Constitution is silent on who actually should do the counting.[55] The question was of great importance because of a number of disputed electoral votes. Obviously, the officer (or officers) responsible for the actual count enjoyed tremendous power, because he could disqualify disputed electoral votes or decide in the event of double returns from a state. During the first two decades of the nineteenth century it was the unquestioned custom for the president of the Senate "to declare the votes." But from 1821 onward, his authority was undercut, and in the Reconstruction period, Congress itself exercised the power to judge disputed returns.

Major nineteenth-century ballot controversies centered on whether a state was fully admitted to the Union at the time its electoral ballots were cast (Indiana in 1817, Missouri in 1821, Michigan in 1837); whether certain southern states were properly readmitted to the Union when they sought to cast electoral votes immediately following the Civil War; and which ballots should be counted when two sets of returns were submitted by a state. Some of the objections raised during the century seem to have bordered on the trivial. In 1846 Wisconsin's electors met and voted one day later than the date set by Congress because of a blizzard that prevented their assembling on the proper date. The certificate of their vote was transmitted to the president of the Senate with an explanation of the circumstances that precluded their meeting on the appointed day. But although Wisconsin's vote would not have changed the national result, spirited argument began when the presiding officer in the joint session of Congress announced the count of the tellers "including the vote of Wisconsin." The arguments were ruled out of order, but the two houses withdrew to their own chambers for two days of bitter and inconclusive argument over whether the Constitution was inexorable in its requirement of the casting of the electoral vote on a single day. Among the most arbitrary actions of Congress was its vote in 1873 to exclude the electoral vote of Arkansas because the certificate of returns bore the seal of the secretary of state instead of the state's great seal—an article that the state did not possess at the time.[56]

In 1877 Congress finally enacted a law covering procedure in all disputed vote cases—a law still largely in force today. It shifts the onus of decision in disputed-vote cases back onto the states by providing that if a state has established a mechanism to resolve disputes, the decisions of the state officials will be binding on Congress. Congress may refuse to count votes from a state only if the two houses decide concurrently that the certification is invalid or that the electoral votes were not "regularly given" by the certified electors (for the text of existing statutes on the electoral count, see Appendix E).

Over the years the role of the president of the Senate with regard to the electoral college has been reduced to little more than presiding at the joint session and breaking the seals on the ballots. The ballots are then given to tellers—two from each house—who actually announce each state's votes and add up the national tally. The president of the Senate then has the honor of announcing the names of the new president and vice president of the United States—assuming that there has been a majority electoral vote.

The counting and certification of electoral votes has become an entirely ceremonial act since the celebrated battle over the returns of the 1876 election—with the sole and important exception of the election of 1968. When the House and Senate met in joint session on January 6, 1969, to count the 1968 electoral votes, objection was made to a vote for George Wallace of Alabama cast by Republican elector Dr. Lloyd W. Bailey. Those objecting included Sen. Edmund Muskie of Maine, the Democratic vice presidential nominee, along with Rep. James G. O'Hara (D., Mich.) and six other senators and thirty-seven other representatives. Under the terms of an 1887 statute, the two bodies then moved to separate deliberations on the disputed electoral vote, with a rejection of the vote by both House and Senate necessary to invalidate it.

The House debate was marked by the feeling of many members that elector Bailey had violated his trust, but Congress lacked any power to remedy the matter without a constitutional amendment. In contrast, the Senate debate explored some of the issues more fully. Senator Muskie, ironically fighting to preserve an electoral vote for the opposing Nixon-Agnew ticket, argued (1) that electors, in effect, bind themselves when they agree to be part of a slate of electors in a state using the short ballot not listing individual electors; (2) that the Supreme Court, in placing Wallace on the ballot in Ohio in 1968, had spoken of the need to ensure citizens an effective voice in the selection of the president—a concept violated by Bailey's action; and (3) that to allow his act to stand unchallenged would establish a precedent encouraging future electors to unpredictable actions. To this, Sen. Birch Bayh (D., Ind.), soon to be the Senate champion of electoral reform, added the observation that he hoped this debate would "galvanize this Congress to find an equitable way of electing the President."

The dangers in congressional challenges to properly certified electoral votes, however, were stressed by Sen. Howard H. Baker, Jr. (R., Tenn.), who also pointed out that this challenge, if successful, might "diminish pressures" for more basic electoral reform. Sen. Sam J. Ervin, Jr. (D., N.C.) asserted that Congress has no power to control or review electors. Sen. Karl E. Mundt (R., S.Dak.), long a district-plan supporter, irrelevantly observed that the congressional district in which Dr. Bailey lived had favored Wallace. Sen. James B. Allen (D., Ala.) declared his belief in the "free elector system" and declared that "the Senator from Maine would expect to make of the electors robots."

Throughout the debate in both houses, there was general dismay about the possibility of electors casting unexpected votes; there was also a feeling, however, that after-the-fact congressional challenges were not the appropriate mechanism for eliminating this evil. The challenge to Dr. Bailey's vote was rejected by both the House (229 to 160) and the Senate (58 to 33). The result of the debates in both houses on January 6, 1969, however, was to give considerable new impetus in 1969 and 1970 to intense but ultimately stymied congressional attempts to abolish or modify the electoral college through the constitutional amendment process.[57]

Contingent Election

If no presidential candidate receives a majority of the electoral votes, the task of choosing a new chief executive is transferred to the House. This phenomenon has occurred only twice in our history, following the elections of 1800 and 1824, but a minor shift of popular votes in the nation would have sent a number of other elections—including those of 1860, 1892, 1948, 1960, 1968, and 1976—into the House for decision. Under the Twelfth Amendment, the House must choose among the three leading electoral vote recipients, rather than the top five originally stipulated in the Constitution. The original system giving each state one vote in the House, regardless of its size, remains in effect, and any state whose delegation is evenly divided loses its vote altogether. (For the 1825 rules of the House in a contingent election, see Appendix F.)

Few Americans have found much commendable in the system of presidential contingent election in the House. Martin Van Buren in 1826 declared that "there is no point on which the people of the United States were more perfectly united than upon the propriety, not to say the absolute necessity, of taking the election away from the House of Representatives."[58] Sen. Oliver P. Morton of Indiana said in 1873 in a Senate speech: "The objections to this constitutional provision for the election of a President need only to be stated, not argued. First, its manifest injustice. In such an election each state is to have but one vote. Nevada, with its 42,000 population, has an equal vote with New York, having 104 times as great a population. It is a mockery to call such an election just, fair or republican." Morton showed that under the apportionment then in effect, 45 members of the House, drawn from 19 states, could control an election in a House then consisting of 292 members representing 37 states. The 19 states with an aggregate 1870 population of a fraction over 8 million people would be able to outvote 18 states with an aggregate population of 30 million. Morton declared that "the rotten borough system was a mild and very small bagatelle" in comparison.[59]

These distortions in the popular will, in the case of an election of a president by the House, continue unabated in the twentieth century. Under the 1960 census, for example, 76 members of the House, drawn from 26 states with an aggregate population of 30.7 million people, could outvote representatives from 24 states with a total population of 148.6 million. In the 1990s the inequities which the nation would face should the House need to elect a president are equally intolerable. Under the congressional apportionments currently in effect until the year 2002, seven states are represented by only one congressman. These seven House members, representing a total of 4,366,426 citizens, in casting their states' one vote for president, would be able to outvote 177 members of the House from the six largest states with a total population of 100,987,157—twenty-five times greater. And, of course, the 606,900 citizens residing in the District of Columbia, lacking any congressional representation at all, would be totally disenfranchised in the election of the president of all the American people.

A number of other objections to election by the House are also apparent. First, representatives are elected not with an eye to their preference for president but for very different reasons. Many districts and states elect congressmen of one party and vote for the presidential candidate of another. Second, the choice of the president by Congress could place the chief executive under heavy obligations to the legislative branch. Third, the whole presidential election could swing on one or two people from one or two key states, as it did in 1825. Fourth, the Constitution does not explain the procedure if a tie for third place should occur in the electoral balloting. Would the House consider just the top two, or in reality the top four candidates? After extensive research on these questions, one political scientist noted, somewhat wryly, "A certain amount of perseverance is needed in order to discover something good to say about the possibility of an election of the President in the House of Preventatives."[60]

The existing rules of the House (left over from the 1825 process) provide for continuous House balloting for president until a winner is declared. The balloting would not start until January 6, leaving only fourteen days until the scheduled presidential inauguration. In most cases, a speedy resolution could be hoped for. But a prolonged deadlock could occur, so that no president would be chosen by January 20. In that event the new vice president would become acting president under the specific mandate of the Twentieth Amendment. If, as would be likely, there had also been no majority in the electoral college vote for vice president, he or she would have been chosen by the Senate. Since only the top two vice presidential elector candidates could be considered by the Senate, with each member having a single vote, a choice would probably have occurred—unless an exact tie resulted!

Only once in history has the Senate been called on to choose a vice president. In 1836 Martin Van Buren won 170 of the 294 electoral votes in a split field. But his vice presidential running mate, Col. Richard M. Johnson of Kentucky, had only 147 electoral votes—one less than a majority. Johnson, who had been hailed as the man who personally killed the Indian leader Tecumseh in the Battle of the

Thames during the War of 1812, was boycotted by the Virginia electors, who voted for Van Buren for president but reportedly wanted to register disapproval of Johnson's social behavior.[61] The Senate proceeded to elect Johnson by a vote of 33 to 16 over Francis Granger of New York, the runner-up in the electoral vote for vice president.[62]

If a presidential election should ever be thrown into Congress again, at least the decision would not be made by hold-over, lame-duck legislators, as it was in 1801 and 1825. Under the Twentieth Amendment, ratified in 1933, a new Congress—elected the same day as the presidential electors—takes office on January 3, three days before the official count of the electoral votes.

Death of a Presidential Candidate or President-Elect

Under the United States' multistage process of electing a president— stretching from the day that the national party conventions nominate candidates to the day in January that a new chief executive is inaugurated—a number of contingencies can arise through the death, disability, or withdrawal of a prospective president or vice president.[63]

The first contingency may arise through the death of one of the nominees between the adjournment of the convention and the day in November when the electors are officially chosen. No law covers this contingency, though both the Democratic and Republican parties have adopted procedures to cover the eventuality. The rules of the Democratic party, approved by its National Committee most recently on March 23, 1991, provide that the approximately 410 members of the Democratic National Committee shall have the power to fill the vacancy. A resolution adopted by each Republican National Convention similarly authorizes the Republican National Committee to fill any vacancy, but in the Republican case with each state's or territory's representatives empowered to cast the same number of votes that the state or territory had at the original nominating convention. Alternatively, the Republican National Committee is authorized to call a new convention, a step it might well take if the election was not imminent.[64] Should they be called on to fill a vacancy caused by the death of a presidential candidate, the national committees might in most instances select the vice presidential nominee as the candidate for president and substitute a new candidate for vice president, but this would be by no means certain. If the death of a candidate took place just before election day—especially if she or he were one of the major presidential candidates—Congress might decide to postpone the day of the election, allowing the national party time to name a substitute contender and the new candidate at least a few days to campaign among the people.

At no time in our history has a presidential candidate died before election day. In 1912, however, Vice President James S. Sherman, who had been nominated for reelection on the Republican ticket with President William H. Taft, died on October 30. No replacement was made before election day, but thereafter the Republican National Committee met and instructed the Republican electors (only eight had been elected) to cast their vice presidential votes for Nicholas Murray Butler.[65] In 1860 the man nominated for vice president by the Democratic National Convention, Benjamin Fitzpatrick of Alabama, declined the nomination after the convention had adjourned. By a unanimous vote, the Democratic National Committee named Herschel V. Johnson of Georgia to fill the vacancy.[66] The Democratic vice presidential nominee in 1972, Sen. Thomas F. Eagleton, resigned a few weeks after being nominated after it had been revealed that he had twice been hospitalized and had received electroshock therapy for depression. The Democratic National Committee hastily assembled and selected Sargent Shriver of Massachusetts as his replacement.

The second major contingency may arise if a presidential or vice presidential candidate dies between election day and the day that the electors actually meet—under current law, a period of approximately five weeks. Theoretically, the electors would be free to vote for anyone they pleased. But the national party rules for the filling of vacancies by the national committees would still be in effect, and the electors would probably respect the decision of their national committee on a new nominee. Again, the elevation of the vice presidential candidate to the presidential slot would be likely but not certain.

The only time a candidate died during this period was when the defeated Democratic presidential nominee, Horace Greeley, died on November 29, 1872—three weeks after the election and a week before the electors were to meet. Sixty-six electors pledged to Greeley had been elected, and they met to vote on the very day Greeley was laid in his grave. Sixty-three of them scattered their votes among a variety of other eminent Democrats, but three Greeley electors in Georgia insisted on marking their ballots for him despite his demise. Congress refused to count these votes in the official national tally.[67]

The third contingency may occur through the death of a president- or vice president–elect between the day the electors vote in mid-December and January 6, when the electoral votes are counted in Congress. There would likely be debate about whether the votes cast for a dead man could be counted, but most constitutional experts believe that the language of the Twelfth Amendment gives Congress no choice but to count all the electoral votes cast, providing the "person" voted for was alive when the ballots were cast.[68] The U.S. House committee report endorsing the Twentieth Amendment sustains this view. Congress, the report said, would have "no discretion" in the matter and "would declare that the deceased candidate had received a majority of the votes." The operative law would then be section 3 of the amendment, which states: "If, at the time fixed for the beginning of the term of the President, the President elect shall have died, the Vice President elect shall become President."[69] And when the vice president–elect took office as president, he or she would be authorized under the Twenty-fifth Amendment to nominate a new vice president.

Similarly, if the vice president–elect should die before the count in Congress, she or he would still be declared the winner, and the new president would be able to nominate a replacement.

A fourth contingency may be caused by the death of either the president- or the vice president–elect between the day the votes are counted in Congress and inauguration day, January 20. If the president-elect died, the foregoing provisions of the Twentieth Amendment would elevate the vice president–elect to the presidency. In the event of the death of the vice president–elect, the Twenty-fifth Amendment would similarly authorize the new president to nominate a vice president, subject to the approval of Congress.

No president-elect has ever died in this period. But on February 15, 1933, a week after his election had been declared in joint session of Congress and three weeks before his inauguration, President-elect Franklin D. Roosevelt barely escaped a would-be assassin's bullets in Miami.

In the event that neither a president nor a vice president qualified on inauguration day, then the Automatic Succession Act of 1947 would go into effect, placing the Speaker of the House, the president pro tempore of the Senate, and then the various Cabinet officials in line for the presidency. (For an exploration of this possibility, see the fable of the 1996 election in Chapter 1.)

"A More Perfect Union"

The importance of the presidency in American life can scarcely be underestimated, and thus the way that office is filled must be a matter of major national concern. In 1961 Senator and former vice presidential candidate Estes Kefauver commented, "Every four years the electoral college is a loaded pistol aimed at our system of government. Its continued existence is a game of Russian roulette. Once its antiquated procedures trigger a loaded cylinder, it may be too late for the needed corrections."[70]

Of course, it is possible that even if the electoral college sent the popular vote loser to the White House (an all too real possibility further examined in the next chapter), the people would find a way to live with the situation—even though the authority of the presidency and the quality of American democracy certainly would be undermined. But even if one assumes that the country *could* somehow exist with a president the people had rejected, the question still remains: What good reason is there to continue such an irrational voting system in an advanced democratic nation, where the ideal of popular choice is the most deeply ingrained of governmental principles?

Democratic elections do not always guarantee that the best candidate will win. Even when we finally scrape the barnacles of the electoral college from the ship of state, there is no guarantee that we or our descendants may not one day elect a charlatan or an ideologue to the presidency. For all our talk of great American presidents, we have elected some pretty grim mediocrities to that office, and we could again—although we would like to believe that the levels of education and political sophistication in the United States today make it less likely. But even when one admits that the *vox populi* may err, the fact remains that through our entire national experience we have learned that there is no safer, no better way to elect our public officials than by the choice of the people, with the candidate who wins the most votes being awarded the office. This is the essence of the "consent of the governed." And no matter how wisely or foolishly the American people choose their president, he or she *is* their president. No one has been able to show how the preservation of a quaint eighteenth-century voting device, the electoral college, with all its anomalies and potential wild cards, can serve to protect the Republic. The choice of the chief executive must be the people's, and it should rest with none other than them.

The framers of the Constitution sought to embody the essence of American nationality in the opening words of the Preamble: "We the People of the United States, in order to form a more perfect Union . . . ." Yet the perfection of the Union has more than once been marred by the workings of the electoral college, and every four years the nation runs the risk that a malfunction of the presidential voting system could disrupt the "domestic tranquility" and threaten the "general welfare" of which the Preamble also spoke. By amending the Constitution to provide a direct vote of all the people for their president, the nation would strike a serious defect from its charter of government and lay a sound foundation for a fuller realization of that "more perfect Union" in the times to come.

chapter five

Popular Votes Do Not Equal
Electoral Votes

A popular misconception is that electoral votes are simple aggregates of popular votes. In reality, the electoral vote regularly deviates from the popular will as expressed in the popular vote— sometimes merely in curious ways, usually strengthening the electoral edge of the popular vote leader, but at times in such a way as to deny the presidency to the popular preference. Popular votes do not equal electoral votes; the former express the people's will, while the latter determine who is to be the people's president.

Popular Votes Versus Electoral Votes

The term *popular vote* would seem to be simple and self-explanatory, but its calculation can be quite complicated. As reported and generally understood in the United States, it is determined by taking the number of votes cast by the people on election day for each slate of electors in each state—Republican, Democratic, or minor-party— and then adding up the totals on a national basis. If a state requires that an elector slate be chosen as a unit, then the popular vote represents the number of ballots cast for that slate.[1] In the 1992 election, for example, 11,131,721 Californians voted for president. Of that total, 5,121,325 cast their ballots for the Democratic elector slate, and Bill Clinton was thus credited with that number of popular votes. The Republican slate pledged to George Bush received 3,630,574 votes and he was seen as receiving that total in California. Similarly, Ross Perot electors received 2,296,006 popular votes in that state in 1992 and Perot was credited with these popular votes.

Minor-party elector slates received 83,816 votes and were credited appropriately in the national count. If a state permits its voters to ballot separately for presidential electors, however, each elector is likely to have a slightly different total vote. In this case, the modern practice is to credit the presidential candidate with the number of votes received by the highest-polling elector pledged to him in that state.[2] The national popular vote total for any particular candidate thus consists of the total of the votes cast for the most popular elector pledged to him in the various states.

With rare exceptions, this gives an accurate picture of the national will. There have been instances, however, in which a candidate's national vote was unnaturally reduced when state party rules or state laws prevented a slate of electors pledged to the candidate from qualifying. In 1860 no electoral slate was pledged to Lincoln in ten of the thirty-three states then in the Union. In 1912 the only way for California voters to cast ballots for President Taft was to write in the names of thirteen elector candidates, since the Republican slot had been seized by Theodore Roosevelt's Progressives. In 1948 and again in 1964 the Dixiecrat and unpledged elector movements controlled the Alabama Democratic party machinery and appropriated the Democratic electoral slate for their own purposes. The Alabama voter had no way to register a vote for the national Democratic nominees in those years.

The percentage of electoral votes received by a candidate on a nationwide basis rarely coincides with his or her percentage of the popular vote because of three factors: (1) the winner-take-all (or unit-vote) system, in which all the electoral votes of a state are credited to whichever elector slate receives a plurality of the state vote (minority votes in a state are washed out completely in the electoral vote count); (2) the distortions caused by the existence of the two electoral votes in each state corresponding to the two U.S. senators; (3) the fact that each state has the number of electoral votes accorded it in the national apportionment, regardless of how few or how many citizens actually go to the polls.

Disparities Due to the Winner-Take-All
(Unit-Vote) System

The operation of the winner-take-all system results in effective massive disenfranchisement of voters who support losing candidates. This effect is perhaps unusually well expressed in Matthew 13:12: "For whosoever hath, to him shall be given, and he shall have more abundance; but whosoever hath not, from him shall be taken away even that he hath."

In 1992, for example, 2,072,698, or 39.0 percent, of Florida's voters cast their ballots for Clinton and another 1,053,067 voters, or 19.8 percent, chose Perot, but Florida's 25-elector slate went as a bloc to Bush on the basis of his popular vote plurality of 2,173,310, just 40.9 percent of the state total. The 58.8 percent of Florida's voters who preferred Clinton or Perot received no electoral votes for their trouble in voting. Conversely, in California in 1992, Bush won 3,630,574 votes, or 32.6 percent of the state total, and Perot 2,296,006, or 20.6 percent; nevertheless, Clinton, with 46 percent of the state popular vote, received 100 percent of the state's 54 electoral votes.[3]

Adjacent states can be in sharp contrast: North Carolina in 1992 went to Bush by only 20,619 popular votes (less than 0.8 percent of the total), but its unified bloc of 14 electoral votes thus won for Bush reflected no such state division. Next door, Georgia in the same election was narrowly carried by Clinton by a popular vote margin of only 13,714 (less than 0.6 percent of the total—the closest significantly sized state in 1992); this paper-thin margin, however, was sufficient to give Clinton all 13 of Georgia's electors.[4] At times the results of the winner-take-all determination of a state's bloc of electoral votes can be breathtaking. In 1992 Arizona's electoral votes went to Bush on the basis of his state popular vote of only 38.5 percent—far less than a majority (in fact, 61.8 percent voted for other candidates). In a three-way division, however, this 38.5 percent of the vote was still sufficient for Bush to win all eight electoral votes at stake. Reviewing the operation of the winner-take-all system some ninety years ago, one observer wrote: "A plurality or majority in one section may, it is true, at times be counteracted by one in another section, and thus the net result be a rude approximation to fairness, taking the country as a whole; but this theory of averages may not work constantly, and the steady suppression of minority conviction in a state is an undisputed evil."[5] To this should be added the observation that in a multiple-candidate contest what may be suppressed by the winner-take-all determination of state electoral votes often is is not just minority conviction but even the convictions of the *majority*.

Effect of Two Additional Electoral Votes Corresponding to the Number of Senators

The significance of the population factor is further diminished in the electoral vote count by the two senatorial "counterpart" electoral votes that each state enjoys, no matter how few inhabitants it has.[6] As a result of the 1990 census, for example, an electoral vote in Wyoming corresponds to only 151,196 persons, while one in California corresponds to 551,112 persons. On this basis, small states having two bonus electoral votes regardless of their population are technically "overrepresented" in the electoral college in contrast with large states where the two additional electoral votes proportionally have far less weight. In short, the "constant two" senatorial votes in the electoral college introduces yet another deviation from voter equity into the election of the American president.

Voter Turnout Disparities

Since each state has a set number of electoral votes, the actual vote total in a state has no relevance to its electoral votes. The electoral votes of a state will all be determined, whether one person or all eligible persons go to the polls.[7] The net result of these distorting factors is that there is a gross disparity in almost all elections between

Table 12 The Election of 1860

	Lincoln	Douglas	Breckinridge	Bell
Popular Votes	1,867,198	1,379,434	854,248	591,658
Electoral Votes	180	12	72	39
Percentage of Popular Votes	39.8	29.4	18.2	12.6
Percentage of Electoral Votes	59.1	3.9	24.0	13.0

the national popular vote a candidate receives and her or his percentage of the electoral vote. Tables 12–17 illustrate six elections in which these disparities were most noteworthy.[8]

The Election of 1860

Although Stephen A. Douglas was second in popular votes, he was fourth in the electoral college in this contest. And although he won 74 percent as many popular votes as were cast for Abraham Lincoln, his electoral vote was only 6.7 percent of Lincoln's. Douglas's popular vote was 162 percent of John C. Breckinridge's, but he received only 16.7 percent of the number of electoral votes for Breckinridge. Douglas's popular vote exceeded John Bell's by more than two times, but Bell had three times as many votes in the electoral college.

The Election of 1912

William H. Taft had 85 percent as many popular votes as Theodore Roosevelt, but he carried only two small states, Vermont and Utah, with a total of eight electoral votes, or exactly one-eleventh of the Roosevelt electoral vote. Woodrow Wilson, the winner in this three-way contest, saw his popular vote of nearly 42 percent magnified by the electoral college system into 82 percent of the electoral votes.

Table 13 The Election of 1912

	Wilson	Roosevelt	Taft	Debs
Popular Votes	6,301,254	4,127,788	3,485,831	901,255
Electoral Votes	435	88	8	0
Percentage of Popular Votes	41.9	27.4	23.2	6.0
Percentage of Electoral Votes	82.0	16.5	1.5	0

This 40-percentage-point discrepancy between popular and electoral vote was by far the greatest to that date in the history of the Republic.

The Election of 1936

In 1936 Alfred M. Landon received 36.5 percent of the total popular vote but won only 1.5 percent of the electoral vote. Franklin D. Roosevelt's magnification of electoral votes over popular votes was a strong 37 percentage points—the second greatest in history.

Table 14 The Election of 1936

	Roosevelt	Landon	Others
Popular Votes	27,757,333	16,684,231	1,213,199
Electoral Votes	523	8	0
Percentage of Popular Votes	60.8	36.5	2.7
Percentage of Electoral Votes	98.5	1.5	0

Table 15 The Election of 1972

	Nixon	McGovern	Other
Popular Votes	47,170,179	29,171,791	1,385,622
Electoral Votes	520	17	1
Percentage of Popular Votes	60.7	37.5	1.8
Percentage of Electoral Votes	96.7	3.2	0.2

The Election of 1972

An equally great instance of a disparity between electoral votes and popular votes occurred in the landslide election of 1972. Richard M. Nixon received over 60 percent of the popular vote and over 96 percent of the electoral vote. George S. McGovern saw his 37 percent of the popular vote transformed into a humiliating 3 percent of the electoral vote. The "multiplier effect" of the electoral vote percentage exceeding the popular vote percentage was a very high 36 percent—far above the twentieth-century average (through 1992) of 23 percent and less only than in the elections of 1912, 1936, and 1980.

The Election of 1980

The first presidential election of the 1980s produced the greatest disparity between electoral votes and popular votes in the history of American presidential elections, before or since. In a three-way division of popular votes somewhat parallel to 1912, Ronald Reagan saw his winning popular vote margin of 50.7 percent swell into a landslide 90.9 percent of all electoral votes. The disparity between Reagan's popular vote and electoral vote percentages was 40.2—a new record for the forty-three elections for which popular vote totals are available.

Table 16 The Election of 1980

	Reagan	Carter	Anderson	Others
Popular Votes	43,904,153	35,483,883	5,720,060	1,407,125
Electoral Votes	489	49	0	0
Percentage of Popular Votes	50.7	41.0	6.6	1.7
Percentage of Electoral Votes	90.9	9.1	0	0

The Election of 1992

The three-way contest between Bill Clinton, George Bush, and Ross Perot in 1992 was also marked by noteworthy discrepancies between popular and electoral votes. Winner Clinton received his solid 68.8 percent of the total electoral votes on the basis of a strikingly low 43 percent of the national popular vote, while Bush enjoyed no such electoral college bonus: his 37.4 percent of the popular votes was diminished by the electoral system to 31.2 percent of the electoral votes. This diminution was minor, however, in contrast to the electoral annihilation suffered by independent candidate Perot. In his personally financed, quixotic campaign, Perot won nearly 18 percent of the popular vote. Despite receiving more than 19 million votes—the greatest number polled by any third-party candidate in the history of the Republic—Perot received precisely zero electoral votes. For Clinton, the electoral magnification of electoral votes over popular votes was 26 percentage points—placing 1992 among the top half of U.S. elections in terms of electoral vote magnification (see Appendixes A and C).

Indeed, in few elections have the percentages of electoral votes received by the candidates shown any reasonable semblance to the popular vote breakdown. Since 1916 there have been only two elections—those of 1948 and 1976—in which the winning presidential

Table 17 The Election of 1992

	Clinton	Bush	Perot	Others
Popular Votes	44,909,326	39,103,882	19,741,657	670,149
Electoral Votes	370	168	0	0
Percentage of				
Popular Votes	43.0	37.4	18.9	0.7
Percentage of				
Electoral Votes	68.8	31.2	0	0

candidate failed to run at least 10 percentage points better in the electoral college than in the popular vote. Electoral votes are indeed not the same as popular votes—the popular vote leader usually enjoys a greater proportion of electoral votes than in the popular vote tally.

Chances of a Misfire

Despite the apparent tendency of the electoral vote count to inflate a winner's margin of victory, the fact is that in any close election the disparity between popular and electoral votes can easily cause the candidate who has lost the popular vote to win in the electoral college. In fact, in the nine presidential elections in which the leading candidate had a popular vote lead of less than 3 percentage points over his closest competitor, the electoral college has elected the "wrong man"—the popular-vote loser—in three instances.*

Careful analysis shows that the danger of an electoral college misfire is not just historical but immediate in any close contest. In fact, only sheer luck in several recent elections has saved the nation

*The elections included in this category are 1844, 1876, 1880, 1884, 1888, 1916, 1960, 1968, and 1976. The two that clearly misfired were those of 1876 and 1888, along with the less certain case of 1960. The count excludes the election of 1824, when Andrew Jackson ran 10.3 points ahead of John Quincy Adams in the rather incomplete national popular vote count yet lost in the House of Representatives.

from the electoral college victory of the popular vote loser. The danger lurking in the dual-count system emerges clearly from a statistical analysis of presidential voting patterns commissioned in the late 1960s for an earlier book of ours, *The People's President.* Charles W. Bischoff of the Department of Economics, Massachusetts Institute of Technology, concluded that the experience of the preceding fifty years had shown that in an election as close as that between Kennedy and Nixon in 1960, or between Carter and Ford in 1976, there is no better than a 50–50 chance that the electoral vote will agree with the popular vote as to the winner. When the leading candidate has a plurality of about 500,000 (or 0.57 percent, based on a turnout of 70 million voters), the verdict will still be reversed about one time in three. Even a plurality of 1 to 1.5 million votes (a percentage point lead of 1.1 to 1.7) will provide not quite three chances out of four of winning the election, and a plurality of 2 million votes might not suffice one time out of eight. Projected twelve years hence (to the election of 2008), when the voter turnout will probably be at least 140 million, even a plurality of 1 million votes will fail to elect the popular vote winner in one election out of three. A plurality of 2 to 3 million votes will not quite provide three chances out of four of winning the election. A plurality of 4 million votes still might fail to elect the winner in one election out of eight.*

---

*An alternative analysis of the misfire question by mathematician Samuel Merrill III utilizes an empirical model based on state-by-state presidential election results since 1900 as a means of estimating the likelihood of a divided verdict. Merrill's estimates are that in an election as close as 1960, there is a 0.23 probability of an electoral reversal by the electoral college; in the case of a vote as close as in 1976, there is a 0.5 probability of a misfire.

Merrill's conclusions are a valuable extension and substantiation of the Bischoff analysis utilized here; both analyses are in substantive agreement. As Merrill concludes: "The likelihood of a divided verdict is significant when the winner's proportion of the major party popular vote does not exceed 52 or 53 percent and is most significant (rising to a probability of about .5) when that proportion falls below 51 percent" ("Empirical Estimates for the Likelihood of a Divided Verdict in a Presidential Election," *Public Choice* 33, no. 2 [1978]: 130).

Bischoff counsels that it is not possible to make precise probability statements because the chance of a reversal depends in substantial measure on the particular candidate and the particular political context in which an election takes place. For instance, when the South voted solidly Democratic, the Democratic party almost invariably needed more than 50 percent of the national major-party popular vote to win an election—a result of large Democratic pluralities in southern voting which in effect were wasted because they could not increase the region's electoral votes. (Today the situation is reversed: Republican presidential candidates with inflated margins in the contemporary South are unable to have those excess votes effectively enhance their electoral prospects.)

But Bischoff was able to arrive at some fascinating conclusions about presidential elections by assuming various shifts in the popular votes between the two leading candidates in each contest. These conclusions, in turn, cast light on the possible problems of the next decades, regardless of what the exact political conditions of the time may be.

Bischoff's method postulated a range of uniform shifts in the percentage of popular votes received by major-party candidates in each election. The impact of these assumed shifts on the electoral vote results was then calculated for each election. In 1948, for example, Truman received 52.4 percent of the major-party vote. If his vote had been reduced by 1 percent, he would have received 51.9 percent of the major-party vote (52.4 percent less 1 percent of 52.4 percent, or 0.524, = 51.9 percent). The method further assumes that the percentage reduction occurred uniformly in each state, with a corresponding increase in the popular vote for the opposing major-party candidate—in this example, Dewey—in each state.*

---

*Bischoff notes that some assumption about the distribution of the reduced vote is needed and that this symmetrical assumption seems to be the *most reasonable* one to make.

Minor-party votes in each election were assumed to remain unchanged. In the 1948 example, the question may then be asked, would Truman still have won in the electoral college? The answer is no, for with a reduction of 1 percent of his vote total in all states, Truman would have lost Ohio, California, and Illinois—three of the states he carried by the narrowest margins. This would have left him with only 225 electoral votes and would have given Dewey 267 electoral votes and the election. By repeating this experiment with different percentages, Bischoff was able to estimate the minimum percentage of the major-party vote needed by each party to win an electoral college majority in the twelve elections between 1920 and 1964 (see table 18).

It is interesting to note that with growing two-party competition in the South in the 1960s and 1970s, the Republicans lost the advantage they had enjoyed up to the early 1950s. The year 1960 may be taken as a watershed when the parties seemed to be on a fairly even footing in terms of the percentage of the vote they needed to win election.

But it would be incorrect to assume that the haphazardness of the system depends only on phenomena like solid-party voting in one region. Bischoff concludes that the more important, and perhaps more permanent, feature of the system depends on the existence of strong two-party systems in large states like New York, California, and Illinois. As long as these states are likely to swing either way, thus throwing large blocs of electoral votes into one column or the other, the electoral college often will fail to reflect the popular vote in a close election. By rearranging and summarizing the data in table 18, Bischoff developed a chart showing the number of electoral vote victories each party would have enjoyed at set percentages of the national vote in the twelve elections between 1920 and 1964 (see table 19)—data that can, with a fair degree of confidence, be extended into assessing the relative discontinuities between popular and electoral votes in any set of contemporary elections.

Table 18 Minimum Percentage of Major-Party Popular Vote Needed to Carry the Electoral College

Year	Needed by Democrats	Needed by Republicans
1920	51.34	48.66
1924	50.36	49.64
1928	48.75	51.25
1932	50.14	49.86
1936	52.25	47.75
1940	51.71	48.29
1944	51.36	48.64
1948	52.24	47.99
1952	50.32	49.68
1956	49.71	50.29
1960	49.82	50.31
1964	48.67	51.33

The dangers of electoral defeat the Democrats faced in every close election in the years surveyed, even when they won the most votes, are clear from the figures. But even with the advantage the Republicans generally enjoyed at the time because of the Democrats' wasted popular votes in the one-party South, it is noteworthy that the Republicans would have lost one-third to one-fifth of the elections in which they received between 50.2 and 51.0 percent of the total popular vote.[9]

The American public may have failed to notice the haphazard nature of the electoral college because of the runaway nature of many recent elections. Almost any halfway reasonable electoral system can elect the right person in a landslide election. The times in which a good electoral system is needed are precisely those times in which it *does* make a difference—in close elections. With spirited two-party competition today in most regions of the country, there is every possibility that the nation may again experience a string of

Table 19 Elections Won by Each Major Party, 1920–1964, Assuming the Specified Division of Major-Party Popular Votes*

Division of Major-Party Vote	Democratic Victories	Republican Victories
Democratic 52.5% (5-point lead)	12	0
Democratic 52.0% (4-point lead)	10	2
Democratic 51.5% (3-point lead)	9	3
Democratic 51.0% (2-point lead)	7	5
Democratic 50.5% (1-point lead)	7	5
Democratic 50.4% (0.8-point lead)	7	5
Democratic 50.2% (0.4-point lead)	5	7
Tie Vote	4	8
Republican 50.2% (0.4-point lead)	3†	8†
Republican 50.4% (0.8-point lead)	2	10
Republican 50.5% (1-point lead)	2	10
Republican 51.0% (2-point lead)	2	10
Republican 51.5% (3-point lead) (or greater)	0	12

*This chart, which was developed by applying uniform percentage shifts to the votes of each party, shows the percentage of the popular vote that would have given it a bare majority in the electoral college in each election. This chart simply adds up the number of elections either party would have won at any set percentage of the national popular vote. For instance, there were seven elections when the Democrats needed 51.0 percent *or less* of the popular vote to win the election—1924 (when they needed only 50.36 percent), 1928 (48.75 percent), 1932 (50.14 percent), 1952 (50.32 percent), 1956 (49.71 percent), 1960 (49.82 percent), and 1964 (48.67 percent). But in five other elections, the Democrats needed *more* than 51.0 percent of the popular vote to win and thus would have lost even if they had polled that much—1920 (when they needed 51.34 percent), 1936 (52.25 percent), 1940 (51.71 percent), 1944 (51.36 percent), and 1948 (52.24 percent). Therefore, the fourth line on this chart, which assumes that the Democrats had received 51.0 percent in all elections between 1920 and 1964, shows that in that event the Democrats would have won seven elections and the Republicans five. The notation of a percentage-point lead on the chart is simply a translation of the absolute percentage-point figure. If a party has 51.0 percent of the major-party vote, the other party has 49.0 percent—2.0 points less.

†One election would have gone to the House of Representatives for decision.

close elections like those of the 1870s and 1880s. And if history and mathematics can be our guide, the country will run a high chance of electoral disaster in every such election.

The Biases of the Electoral College

Thus far we have been stressing the disparities between popular votes and electoral votes in terms of overall electoral outcomes. As noted in preceding chapters, the electoral college can reverse the lead of the popular vote winner and elect the popular vote loser as president (three times in our history), deadlock an election and force the utilization of House contingent procedures (twice, in the elections of 1800 and 1824), choose a president who did not receive a majority of the popular vote (16 elections, or 37 percent of the elections for which popular vote totals are available), and produce a hairbreadth election where relatively tiny popular vote shifts can have enormous consequences (22 elections, or 51 percent of the elections for which popular vote totals are available). (For tables summarizing all instances of these categories of electoral outcomes, see Chapter 2.) Now we turn to a different aspect of the electoral college system—the way it makes some citizens' votes for president worth more than others. In short, we are interested in evaluating the biases of the electoral college in regard to individual votes. What advantages—or disadvantages—do voters have in electing a president as a direct result of the state in which they cast their vote? Because of the electoral college, a voter casting a ballot for president in California has a different probability of affecting the electoral outcome than a voter in Delaware. How can these voter irregularities be best measured?

Measuring State Biases of the Electoral College

Major efforts have been made over the years to measure the biases of the electoral college in terms of the ability of a voter to affect decisions through voting.[10] Methodologies based on the mathematical theory of games and utilizing computer simulations of thousands of elections have been developed to estimate the relative differences in the voting power of citizens of the different states. Additionally, some studies have sought to determine the voting power of various categories of voters, including residency, regional, ethnic, and occupational groups.[11]

The purpose of this research in every case is the same: to discover the advantage or disadvantage the electoral college gives to voters *solely according to where they chance to reside and vote*. Essentially, the "voting power" approach to the evaluation of the electoral college involves three distinct steps.

> 1. A determination is made of the chance that each state has in a "fifty-one-person" game (the fifty states plus the District of Columbia) of casting the pivotal bloc of electoral votes in the electoral college.
>
> 2. An evaluation is made of the proportion of voting combinations in which a given citizen can, by changing his or her vote, alter the way in which his or her state's electoral votes are cast.
>
> 3. The results of the first step are combined with the results of the second to determine the chance that any voter has of affecting the election of the president through the medium of his or her state's electoral votes.

These calculations are normalized with the power index of the state whose citizens have the least voting power set at 1; all other states have voting powers greater than 1; the result is an index of *relative voting power* of each citizen vis-à-vis voters residing in other states.

Table 20 reports relative voting power figures under the electoral college for the electoral college apportionments of the 1990s for citizens of the fifty states and the District of Columbia. The voting power figures are normalized on the power index of the state with the least voting power (Montana). Citizens of the seven most populous

Table 20 Voting Power per Citizen-Voter Under the Electoral
College in the 1990s, Based on State Populations

State	Population (1990 Census)	Electoral Votes	Relative Voting Power†	Percent Deviation from Average Voting Power‡
Wyoming	453,588	3	1.327	−14.3
Alaska	550,043	3	1.205	−22.1
Vermont	562,758	3	1.192	−23.0
Dist. of Columbia	606,900	3	1.147	−25.9
North Dakota	638,800	3	1.118	−27.7
Delaware	666,168	3	1.095	−29.2
South Dakota	696,004	3	1.071	−30.8
Montana	799,065	3	1.000	−35.4
Rhode Island	1,003,464	4	1.141	−26.3
Idaho	1,006,749	4	1.139	−26.4
Hawaii	1,108,229	4	1.086	−29.9
New Hampshire	1,109,252	4	1.085	−29.9
Nevada	1,201,833	4	1.043	−32.6
Maine	1,227,928	4	1.031	−33.4
New Mexico	1,515,069	5	1.111	−28.2
Nebraska	1,578,385	5	1.088	−29.7
Utah	1,722,850	5	1.042	−32.7
West Virginia	1,793,477	5	1.021	−34.0
Arkansas	2,350,725	6	1.040	−32.8
Kansas	2,477,574	6	1.013	−34.6
Mississippi	2,573,216	7	1.150	−25.7
Iowa	2,776,755	7	1.107	−28.5
Oregon	2,842,321	7	1.094	−29.3
Oklahoma	3,145,585	8	1.164	−24.8
Connecticut	3,287,116	8	1.139	−26.4
Colorado	3,294,394	8	1.138	−26.5
South Carolina	3,486,703	8	1.106	−28.6
Arizona	3,665,228	8	1.079	−30.3
Kentucky	3,685,296	8	1.076	−30.5

(continued)

Table 20 (continued)

State	Population (1990 Census)	Electoral Votes	Relative Voting Power†	Percent Deviation from Average Voting Power‡
Alabama	4,040,587	9	1.143	−26.2
Louisiana	4,219,973	9	1.119	−27.7
Minnesota	4,375,099	10	1.213	−21.6
Maryland	4,781,468	10	1.161	−25.0
Washington	4,866,692	11	1.243	−19.7
Tennessee	4,877,785	11	1.241	−19.8
Wisconsin	4,891,769	11	1.240	−19.9
Missouri	5,117,073	11	1.212	−21.7
Indiana	5,544,159	12	1.257	−18.8
Massachusetts	6,016,425	12	1.207	−22.0
Virginia	6,187,358	13	1.287	−16.8
Georgia	6,478,216	13	1.258	−18.7
North Carolina	6,628,637	14	1.337	−13.7
New Jersey	7,730,188	15	1.315	−15.1
Michigan	9,295,297	18	1.449	−6.6
Ohio	10,847,115	21	1.536	−0.8
Illinois	11,430,602	22	1.581	2.2
Pennsylvania	11,881,643	23	1.609	3.9
Florida	12,937,926	25	1.663	7.4
Texas	16,986,510	32	1.891	22.1
New York	17,990,455	33	1.888	22.0
California	29,760,021	54	2.663	72.0

Sources: Lawrence D. Longley and James D. Dana, Jr., "The Electoral College's Biases in the 1992 Election—and Beyond," paper delivered at the Annual Meeting of the American Political Science Association, Sept. 3–6, 1992; "The Biases of the Electoral College in the 1990s," *Polity* 25, no. 1 (Fall 1992): 123–45; and "The Electoral College's Biases in the 1992 Election—and Beyond," U.S. Senate Judiciary Committee, Subcommittee on the Constitution, *Hearings on the Electoral College and Direct Election of the President,* 102d Congress, 2d sess., July 22, 1992, pp. 38–76.
†Relative voting power is defined as the ratio of the per citizen–voter voting power to the per citizen voting power of the most deprived state.
‡Percent deviation of per citizen–voter voting power from the average voting power. Average voting power per citizen–voter relative to the most deprived state = 1.548.

states have at least 1.5 times the relative voting power of the inhabitants of the least advantaged state, and the residents of California, the largest state, enjoy a voting power advantage over 2.5 times greater. Column 5 of this table reports the percentages by which the relative voting power (column 4) of citizens in each state deviates from the average (mean) relative voting power per citizen. Thus forty-five of the fifty-one "states" have less than the average relative voting power (in this case, 1.548), while the six most populous states have greater than average voting power. The advantage that citizens in the most populous states enjoy solely because of their place of residence is as great as 72 percent.

The most disadvantaged citizens are those of the medium-to-small-sized states, with from 3 to 21 electoral votes. Voters in North Carolina, the nation's tenth most populous state, have a relative voting power approximately equal to that of the residents of Wyoming, the least populous state. Therefore, the citizens of the forty states with a population size between those of Wyoming and North Carolina are at a disadvantage in comparison with the citizens of those two states and the nine most populous states. Voters in the nine largest states have a disproportionately large relative voting power, which increases in a direct relationship with population. In terms of the percent deviation data, it can be observed that forty-five states have less than average voting power, and only six states have more—the six most populous!

In summary, the electoral college is found to contain two major, partially countervailing biases, each favoring residents of quite different states. Voters in the very smallest states have a slight advantage due to the constant two votes given every state regardless of population; voters in the larger states, however, have an even greater advantage due to the winner-take-all system. The net result, however, is an overall large-state advantage under the electoral college, with the most disadvantaged citizens being residents in the medium-to-small states having from 3 to 21 electoral votes.[12] Specifically, the electoral college, as apportioned for the elections of 1992, 1996, and 2000, gives a citizen voting in California 2.663 times the potential for determining the outcome of the presidential election of a citizen voting in the most disadvantaged state, Montana.[13]*

Measuring Regional and Group Biases of the Electoral College

The biases inherent in the present electoral college for inhabitants of different size *states* have thus far been shown. The data as presented up to now have not, however, dealt with the question of whether various *groups* of voters may be similarly favored or disadvantaged because of their residency in different states. In order to examine this important question, the relative voting power data were used to determine the average voting power of various population categories under the electoral college in comparison with the average voting power of the total population.

The groups chosen were placed in two categories: regions and population groups. Regions chosen were the eastern, southern, midwestern, Mountain, and far western groupings of states. Population groups were residents of rural, urban, and central-city areas, as well as black, Jewish, Hispanic-origin, blue-collar, and foreign-born voters.

The average voting power of black voters for the present electoral college, for example, was calculated by multiplying each state's relative voting power index (table 20, column 4) by its number of

*Samuel Merrill III has presented an alternative empirical model of voting power under the present electoral college based on state-by-state presidential election results since 1900. He concludes that the ratio of disparity ranges up to 10 to 1, somewhat higher than suggested by our analysis. Merrill's model is based on a treatment of blocs of voters as individual voting units rather than as individual voters, as we have done. In Merrill's analysis voting power tends to increase with the number of such blocs (Samuel Merrill, personal letter to authors, June 21, 1979, and "Citizen Voting Power Under the Electoral College: A Stochastic Model Based on State Voting Patterns," *SIAM Applied Journal on Applied Mathematics*, March 1978: 376–90).

black residents. The sum of these products divided by the total black population in the nation produces the average voting power per black voter. Finally, the percent deviation of this average from the per voter average is calculated. This percent deviation gives an indication of how this particular group in the electorate fares in comparison with other groups, as well as with the entire electorate.

Table 21 presents regional and group biases for the electoral college for the electoral college apportionments of the 1960s, 1970s, 1980s, and 1990s—a period of close to fifty years. It can be seen that the one region sharply advantaged by the electoral college is the Far West (which means primarily California), with this region's percent deviation from average voting power increasing from 26.7 to 49.0 percent. In contrast, the East has had a sharp reversal of an earlier advantage and has a net disadvantage under the contemporary electoral college. The South, the Midwest, and, most of all, the Mountain states are all disadvantaged, with the Mountain states having a relatively constant percent deviation disadvantage over the decades.

Estimates concerning various demographic groups under the contemporary electoral college are also reported in table 21. Hispanic-origin, foreign-born, Jewish, and urban voters are found to be the most advantaged groups, with these advantages either increasing or remaining largely unchanged over the decades. Rural and black voters are disadvantaged under the present electoral college; the greatest change was a decline in the black disadvantage from –5.2 to –2.4 between the 1960s and the 1970s, with this net black disadvantage remaining largely unchanged over the most recent three decades. Despite conventional wisdom that black voters achieve a special advantage from the electoral college, this is not found to be the case.[14] Rather, the electoral college *disadvantages* black voters in all four decades, although their disadvantage decreases somewhat during the period surveyed.

Earlier it was found that the electoral college contains countervailing biases, which result in a net large-state advantage and a disadvantage to states with 3 to 21 electoral votes. To this we can now

Table 21 Regional and Group Biases Under the Electoral College in the 1960s, 1970s, 1980s and 1990s, Based on State Populations

	Percent Deviation from National Average Voting Power				
	1960s	1970s	1980s	1990s	Net Change, 1960–1990
Regions					
Eastern States	13.8	8.9	4.9	−3.6	−17.4
Southern States	−15.0	−13.4	−10.1	−7.7	7.3
Midwestern States	−5.6	−6.2	−7.0	−11.8	−6.2
Mountain States	−28.8	−29.0	−25.0	−29.1	−0.3
Far Western States	26.7	33.1	35.4	49.0	22.3
Groups					
Rural Citizen-Voters	−8.8	−9.5	−8.8	−10.4*	−1.6
Urban Citizen-Voters	3.8	3.4	3.1	3.6*	−0.2
Central-City Citizen-Voters	6.3	5.7	5.2		−1.1
Black Citizen-Voters	−5.2	−2.4	−1.7	−2.6	2.6
Jewish Citizen-Voters	26.7		16.7	12.5	−14.2
Hispanic-Origin Citizen-Voters		19.0	20.3	26.3	7.3
Blue-Collar Citizen-Voters		−0.8	−1.0	−0.9*	−0.1
Foreign-Born Citizen-Voters	14.1	14.8	16.4	19.1*	5.0

Data Sources: The 1980 data for occupation, foreign-born, urban, and rural populations are from U.S. Bureau of the Census, U.S. Department of Commerce, 1983, *1980 Census of Population,* Characteristics of the Population, Chapter B, General Population Characteristics: United States Summary, PC80-1-B1.

The 1980 data for black and Hispanic-origin populations, revised from earlier data reported in Longley and Dana (1984), are from U.S. Bureau of the Census, U.S. Department of Commerce, 1983, *1980 Census of Population,* Characteristics of the Population, Chapter A, Number of Inhabitants: United States Summary, PC80-1-A1.

The 1990 data for black and Hispanic-origin populations are from U.S. Bureau of the Census, U.S. Department of Commerce, 1991, *1990 Census of Population and Housing,* Summary Population and Housing Characteristics, State Volumes, 1990, CPH-1-2 through 1990, CPH-1-52.

Table adapted from sources cited in table 20.

*The state population of these groups was estimated to be the 1990 total state population times the percentage of the state population in this group in the 1980 census.

add that the electoral college also advantages Hispanic-origin, for-eign-born, Jewish, and urban voters, as well as inhabitants of the Far West. On the other hand, the present presidential electoral system discriminates against rural and black voters, as well as inhabitants of the Mountain, midwestern, southern, and eastern states.

These data seem in most respects to confirm the often stated hypothesis that the electoral college favors urban and ethnic inter-ests.[15] Urban citizen-voters have above average voting power in the electoral college, while rural voters are relatively disadvantaged by the present electoral college.

The Voting Power of Blacks in the Electoral College

The findings for one group, however, somewhat contradict conven-tional wisdom concerning the biases of the electoral college.[16] Table 21 reports that blacks are disadvantaged by the electoral college in all four decades, including the 1990s. Other findings—that urban and central-city voters are advantaged and rural voters are disad-vantaged under the present system—seem to confirm widely held assumptions about the biases of the electoral college. However, the findings concerning black voters differ from those reached by many analysts.

Actually, one cannot say that *all* blacks are advantaged or that *all* blacks are disadvantaged by the electoral college. A black voter in California has approximately 2.5 times the chance of affecting the election outcome that a black voter in Montana has (see table 20). The differences in voting power arise because people live in different states, not because they are of different races.

The measurement of the bias affecting black voters as a group involves *averaging* the voting power of all blacks in all fifty states and the District of Columbia. If blacks gain from the electoral college—that is, have above-average voting power—then they must be con-centrated more heavily in the six most populous states than is the general population. However, that is indeed not the case. Table 22

Table 22 Black Populations of States Ranked by Voting Power Under the Electoral College in the 1970s

State	Percent Deviation from Average Voting Power	Percentage of U.S. Population	Percentage of U.S. Black Population
California	+53.6	9.8	6.2
New York	+42.4	9.0	9.6
Pennsylvania	+15.4	5.8	4.5
Illinois	+13.9	5.5	6.3
Texas	+13.5	5.5	6.2
Ohio	+9.5	5.2	4.3
Michigan	−0.6	4.4	4.4
Florida	−2.8	3.3	4.6
Alaska	−4.3	0.1	0.0
New Jersey	−5.4	3.5	3.4
Wyoming	−9.0	0.2	0.0
North Carolina	−11.8	2.5	5.0
Massachusetts	−12.0	2.8	0.8
Indiana	−12.8	2.6	1.6
South Dakota	−17.6	0.3	0.0
Montana	−19.3	0.3	0.0
Georgia	−20.1	2.3	5.3
Idaho	−20.4	0.4	0.0
Virginia	−20.6	2.3	3.8
Missouri	−20.8	2.3	2.1
Vermont	−21.3	0.2	0.0
New Hampshire	−21.7	0.4	0.0
Wisconsin	−22.2	2.2	0.6
Louisiana	−22.7	1.8	4.8
Hawaii	−23.3	0.4	0.0
Minnesota	−24.4	1.9	0.2
Nevada	−25.0	0.2	0.1

(continued)

State	Percent Deviation from Average Voting Power	Percentage of U.S. Population	Percentage of U.S. Black Population
Kentucky	−25.0	1.6	1.0
Maryland	−25.6	1.9	3.1
Tennessee	−25.6	1.9	2.8
Oklahoma	−26.5	1.3	0.8
South Carolina	−26.9	1.3	3.5
Washington	−27.1	1.7	0.3
Alabama	−27.5	1.7	4.0
Delaware	−29.1	0.3	0.3
Iowa	−30.0	1.4	0.1
Rhode Island	−30.9	0.5	0.1
Colorado	−31.4	1.1	0.3
Mississippi	−31.6	1.1	3.6
West Virginia	−31.8	0.9	0.3
Kansas	−32.0	1.1	0.5
Arizona	−32.3	0.9	0.2
Connecticut	−32.4	1.5	0.8
Maine	−32.5	0.5	0.0
North Dakota	−33.3	0.3	0.0
New Mexico	−33.3	0.5	0.1
Utah	−34.7	0.5	0.0
Arkansas	−35.0	0.9	1.6
Nebraska	−37.6	0.7	0.2
Oregon	−37.7	1.0	0.1
Dist. of Columbia	−39.7	0.4	2.4

Sources: Lawrence D. Longley, "Minorities and the 1980 Electoral College," paper delivered at the Annual Meeting of the American Political Science Association, August 1980, Washington, D.C., p. 18; Peirce and Longley, *People's President,* pp. 128–29; and Longley, "The Electoral College and the Representation of Minorities: Myths and Realities," in Doris A. Graber, ed., *The President and the Public* (Philadelphia, 1992).

documents that, as of at least the 1970s, blacks are *less* concentrated in these states than the population as a whole.

This table lists the highest-voting-power state, California, at the top of the list, with voting power (as of the 1970s) decreasing as one goes down the list. The percent deviation from average voting power under the electoral college for each state is listed in column 1. Columns 2 and 3 display the percentage of the U.S. population and the percentage of the black population that lives in each state.

In which states is the black population significantly more concentrated than the general population? If we examine states in which the percentage of blacks is 1 percent or more above the percentage of the U.S. population located in that state, we find that they are generally southern states which are *disadvantaged* by the electoral college. Florida, North Carolina, Georgia, Virginia, Louisiana, Maryland, South Carolina, Alabama, Mississippi, and the District of Columbia are in this category, and all have *below*-average voting power. Floridians' voting power is 2.8 percent below average; North Carolina residents are 11.8 percent below average; and the rest have voting power ranging from 20.1 percent to 39.7 percent below average.

Likewise, we should examine those states in which blacks are significantly less concentrated than the general population. The states for which the percentage of the U.S. population is 1 percent or more above the percentage of blacks (as of the 1970s) are California, Pennsylvania, Massachusetts, Indiana, Wisconsin, Minnesota, Washington, and Iowa. This group includes two of the largest states that benefit from the electoral college, California and Pennsylvania. In fact, California has 9.8 percent of the total U.S. population but only 6.2 percent of the blacks in the United States. Furthermore, California is also the state most advantaged by the electoral college, with a voting power 53.6 percent above average. In conclusion, blacks are not any more heavily concentrated in the large states than is the general population. And this unfavorable distribution of blacks among the various states accounts for the net voting disadvantage that blacks have due to the electoral college.

Earlier we cited a number of ways in which the electoral college distorts popular votes as they are transformed into electoral votes. Among these are the constant two electoral votes given every state regardless of population, the winner-take-all procedure by which all of a state's electoral votes are determined by a plurality of the state's voters, the constitutional basing of electoral votes on population figures independent from actual voter turnout, and the fact that these population figures are themselves based on census figures that freeze the electoral vote apportionments among the states for ten to fourteen years.

The result of these various structural features of the electoral college is to ensure that the electoral college can never be a neutral counting device but inherently contains varieties of biases dependent solely upon the state in which voters cast their votes for president. The contemporary electoral college is not just an archaic mechanism for counting the votes; it is an institution that aggregates popular votes in an inherently imperfect manner.

chapter six

The Electoral College in the 1996
Election—and Beyond

In this, the final chapter of the book, we shall bring together some of the key strands of our analysis of the electoral college and apply them to the 1996 election—and those to follow. Our argument is simple: the 1996 election, like any election, vividly illustrates the distortions and imperfections of this fatally flawed means of determining the American president. Further, in 1996 or a future election the electoral college has the potential for creating serious electoral crisis, deeply eroding the security of our democratic processes.

The Electoral College at Its Best

The electoral college is not a neutral and fair counting device for tallying popular votes cast for president in the form of electoral votes. Instead, it invests some votes with more significance than others, according to the state in which they are cast. As a result, these distortions of popular preferences greatly influence candidate strategy: certain key states, their voters, parochial interests, political leaders, and unique local factors are favored.

The electoral college election of the president also discriminates among types of candidates. Independent or third-party contenders with a regional following have great opportunities for electoral college significance, while independent or third-party candidates with broad-based but nationally distributed support may find themselves excluded from winning any electoral college votes. Even without receiving electoral votes, however, such candidates can prove decisive in terms of swinging large blocs of electoral votes from one major-party candidate to the other. Finally, the electoral college can reflect the popular will inaccurately because of the actions of faithless electors—individual electors who vote differently in the electoral college than those who chose them expect.

In short, the electoral college at best is neither neutral nor fair in its counting of the popular votes cast for the president of the United States.

The problems of the electoral college at its best can be summarized as follows:

1. *The electoral college is a distorted counting device.* There are many reasons why the division of electoral votes will always differ from the division of popular votes. Among these are the apportionment of electoral votes among the states on the basis of census population figures that do not reflect population shifts except every ten years or more, the assignment of electoral votes to states on a basis of population figures rather than on a voter-turnout basis, the allocation of a "constant two" electoral votes equally to each state regardless of its size, and the winner-take-all system for determining each state's entire bloc of electoral votes on the basis of a plurality (not even a majority) of popular votes.

The census-based determination of electoral votes allotted each state ensures that states that have grown quickly during a decade (as Sun-Belt states like Arizona or Florida did during the 1990s) will not have their new population growth reflected in their electoral vote total until the presidential election two to four years after the next decade's census—up to fourteen years later. The electoral college vote's neglect of voter turnout, either over time or among states, maintains the same electoral votes for each state despite possible increases in voter turnout in a state or, alternatively, continued low levels of voter participation. It is a curious feature of the electoral college that high turnout in a state is ignored while low levels of voter participation are rewarded.

It is the "constant two" and "winner-take-all" characteristics of the electoral college, however, that are the sources of its most significant distortions. The extra two electoral votes, regardless of population, which correspond to each state's two senators, provide an advantage to the very smallest states by giving them at least three electoral votes, whereas their population might otherwise entitle them to barely one. However, the importance of the winner-take-all feature overshadows all the other distortions: by carrying New York or California—even by the smallest margin of popular votes—a candidate will win *all* of that state's 33 or 54 electoral votes. As a consequence, the electoral college greatly magnifies the political significance of the large-electoral-vote states—even out of proportion to the millions of voters living there. This is even more the case should a large state also be a swing state—one thought likely to go either way in the presidential election, along with all of its electoral votes.

2. Candidate strategy is shaped and determined by these distortions. Strategists for presidential candidates know well the importance of these distortions of the electoral college: any serious presidential candidate will spend inordinate time in the largest states of the country. An additional candidate's day, an extra expenditure of money, a special appeal—any of these might be pivotal in terms of winning an entire large bloc of electoral votes—in the case of California, fully 20 percent of the 270 electoral votes needed to win. Candidates and their strategists do not look at the election in terms of the national popular vote, but rather in terms of popular votes which might tilt a state's winner-take-all bloc of electoral votes.

In the case of a race involving three significant candidates—as was the case in 1992 and might be the case in 1996—the plurality-win and winner-take-all features take on special importance. A candidate in a three-way division of vote does not need 50 percent of California's vote to win its bloc of 54 electoral votes. Forty percent, or even 35 percent, might well do it. A close three-way division of popular votes in a large state increases even further the pivotal value of that state.

3. *The importance of a particular state's parochial interests, political leaders, and unique local factors are magnified by the electoral college.* The distortions of the electoral college lead candidates to focus on large, swingable states in order to win their large blocs of electoral votes, and the best way of appealing to these states is, of course, to concern oneself with the issues and interests special to that state. As a consequence, candidates always will be exceedingly articulate about the problems of Pennsylvania's coal fields or California's defense industry or New York City's crime rates. A special premium is also placed on the role of key large-state political leaders whose enthusiastic efforts might be significant in determining that state's outcome. Mayors Rudolph Giuliani of New York, Richard Daley of Chicago, and Richard Riordan of Los Angeles, as well as Governors George Pataki of New York, Jim Edgar of Illinois, and Pete Wilson of California will be consulted—and courted—by the candidates, as will be leaders of the California Hispanic and New York Jewish communities. Political leaders, local factional feuds, and diverse issues in the large pivotal states play an unusually central role in presidential campaign politics.

In contrast, other states and their distinctive interests are neglected. Smaller states, where candidate effort resulting in a narrow plurality win could at most tilt only 3 or 4 electoral votes, generally are ignored. There is also a lack of candidate attention to states of any size that are viewed as "already decided." Candidates have no incentive, under the electoral college, to waste campaign time or resources on a state or region already likely to go for—or against—them. In short, Delaware, a very small state, is unlikely to be contested vigorously by any candidate because of its size; likewise, many of the southern and Rocky Mountain states may well be conceded to the Republican candidate, and many of the northeastern and Pacific coast states to the Democratic contender, as a consequence being "written off" by all the candidates.

In short, the electoral college focuses candidates' attention and resources on those large states seen as pivotal and away from voters in other states that are too small or that are seen as too predictable in outcome. The political interests of the large, swingable states are more than amply looked after; those of the other states are relatively neglected.

4. *The electoral college differs in impact on different types of candidates.* Besides the distorting effect of the electoral college in terms of voters, the electoral college also discriminates among candidates. The two major-party nominees start off on a relatively equal footing as far as the electoral college goes; each enjoys roughly comparable potential in the large, swingable states (the much-heralded Republican "electoral college lock" having been picked and thus effectively laid to rest by Bill Clinton's decisive electoral college success in the 1992 presidential election). Independent or third-party candidates, however, differ greatly in their potential in the electoral college.

Regionally based independent or third-party candidates—such as George Wallace in 1968 or Strom Thurmond in 1948—can enjoy real benefits from the electoral college. Because of their regional strength, they can hope to carry some states and, with these popular vote pluralities, those states' entire blocs of electoral votes. Their popular vote need not even constitute an absolute majority in a state: a simple plurality of votes will suffice. Independent or third-party candidates with broad-based but *nationally* distributed support, on the other hand, are sharply *disadvantaged* by the electoral college. Without plurality support somewhere, such a candidate may be completely shut out from any electoral votes. Such was precisely the case of independent candidates John B. Anderson in 1980 and Ross Perot in 1992. Unless their support was sufficiently *unevenly* distributed among the states to allow Anderson or Perot to win in some states, their voter support—even when it was as high as 20 to 30 percent—was destined to result in total eradication in the electoral college.

The problem here is more than just a profound unfairness to nationally based independent or third-party candidates when their millions of popular votes result in no electoral votes. A major factor limiting the support of these very same contenders is the view that a popular vote for them is wasted. This can be an enormously difficult problem for any additional candidate attempting to be taken seriously in the 1996 or future election. As the campaign comes to its conclusion, millions of voters who might be inclined to vote for him or her may well decide not to do so because of the electoral college. Voters may reason: "My preferred candidate isn't likely to carry my state. Instead, one of the other, major-party candidates certainly will. I had better vote for one of them (or against one of them by voting for the other). I want to have my vote mean something in the election."

There is, however, a way in which a "third-place" contender with widely distributed national appeal might be truly significant in the 1996 or future election, even should he or she not be in a position to win electoral votes. This is by his or her candidacy and votes being decisive in tilting some of the large, closely competitive states and thereby tilting the outcome of the national election between the major-party candidates.

In short, the electoral college at best treats candidates unequally and creates enormous potential difficulties for many independent or third-party candidates, difficulties that a possible additional candidate may or may not be able to overcome in 1996 or subsequent elections. Whatever their level of success, however, independent or third-party candidates may have great significance in electoral outcomes because of the powerful impact of relatively few popular votes in tightly contested large, marginal states, where the determination of blocs of electoral votes may ride on small and shifting state pluralities.

5. Faithless electors may further distort the popular will. A final problem of the electoral college "at its best"—in other words, while still producing a clear decision—lies in the potential occurrence of faithless electors. In seven of the twelve most recent elections, we have seen electors deciding, after the November election, to vote for someone other than expected. In each of these instances, however, the defections were both singular in occurrence and insignificant in outcome. Nevertheless, they do constitute a disturbing distortion of the popular will. When one of Washington State's nine Republican electors decides, as in 1976, not to vote for the state's popular vote winner, Gerald R. Ford, the voters of Washington have lost a portion of their franchise.

Individual elector defections for whatever reason—strongly held positions or personal whim—have been of minor significance in the past. Faithless electors, however, would be likely to proliferate in an election producing a very close electoral vote tally in which a few shifting electoral votes could change the outcome. In any case, the occurrence of faithless electors is one more way in which the electoral college fails—even when definitive in its choice—to reflect the popular vote faithfully and accurately. The electoral college is not a neutral and fair means of electing the president. Neither, as we shall now see, is it a *sure* way of determining who shall be president.

The Electoral College at Its Worst

The electoral college does not result inevitably in a clear determination of the election outcome. Rather, the result of the popular vote, when transformed into the electoral votes which actually determine the president, may be uncertain and unresolved through December and even into January.

1. In a very close electoral vote count, ambitious electors could determine the outcome. Individual electors have defected from voter expectations in the past for highly individual reasons. In the case of an electoral college majority resting on a thin margin of a few votes, electors seeking personal publicity or attention to a pet cause could withhold—or just threaten to withhold—their electoral votes from the narrow electoral vote leader. Uncertainty and suspense over whether there would be an actual electoral vote majority when the electors voted in mid-December could make the period of forty or so days following the November election a period of political disquiet.

2. *An election can produce a divided verdict, with one candidate receiving the most popular votes and the other candidate winning the election in electoral votes.* An electoral outcome with a divided verdict might be conclusive in the sense that the candidate with the majority of electoral votes would become president, with little question of outright popular upheaval. The electoral college would be seen at its worst, however, in the effect of such a "divided-verdict" election on the legitimacy of a president. Should a person be elected—or reelected—as president despite clearly having run second in popular preference and votes, the president's ability to govern and lead the American people would be weakened. A divided-verdict election is, of course, entirely possible in 1996 or a following election, with *either* two or three major candidates running, if at least two of the candidates run close to each other in popular votes.

3. *An election may be undecided on election night, with deals and actions by the electors at the mid-December electoral college meetings deciding the outcome.* The most frequently expressed fear about the electoral college concerns the possibility of a deadlock, with no candidate winning an electoral vote majority on the basis of the election night popular vote results. Most analysts assume that, in this case, an undecided election would go directly to the House of Representatives in January. In fact, it is entirely possible that an apparent electoral college deadlock, based on the November returns, would set off a sequence of unsavory deals and actions involving the electors themselves.

Should the 1996 election produce an apparent election night electoral college deadlock, a dramatic chain of events, dictated in large part by the Constitution, would be set into action. The forty-one days between election day, November 5, and the day on which the electors will meet in their respective capitals, December 16, would be a period of speculation, conjecture, and crisis. Most electors would certainly follow party lines, but some might deviate from party expectations in order to vote for a clear popular vote winner, or to help a candidate (even of the opposing party) who had *almost* achieved an electoral vote majority, in order to resolve an otherwise deadlocked election. Certainly, these nearly six weeks would be a period of intense uncertainty and unease as unknown and obscure presidential electors decided the outcome of the 1996 presidential election.

Such an occurrence is entirely possible in any close election, especially should a third-party or independent candidate be able to carry one or more states (even by thin pluralities) and thus remove that state's electoral votes from those available to the major-party candidates. The presidency then would be decided *not* on election night but through deals or switches at the electoral college meetings in mid-December, or later in the House of Representatives.

4. If the electoral college fails to produce a majority in December, the extraordinary procedure would be followed of election of the president in January by the House of Representatives. Election of the president by the House of Representatives would be an exceedingly awkward undertaking. According to the Constitution, voting in the House would be by equally weighted states, with an absolute majority of twenty-six needed for a decision. The House would choose from among the top *three* candidates in electoral votes—no other "compromise" candidate could emerge or be considered.

Representatives could be in a great quandary as the House started to vote on January 6. Many would vote strictly along party lines, totally ignoring any strength that might have been shown by an independent or third-party candidate. Other House members might feel it appropriate or even politically necessary to vote for the candidate (the opposing major-party contender, or even an independent candidate) who had carried their district. Some members might even feel influenced by the national popular vote result, or by who had received the most popular votes in their states. In other words, should an election be thrown into the House, representatives would vote in different ways for a number of different reasons. A final outcome would be difficult to predict, despite whatever partisan divisions existed.

As of mid-1996 the House is controlled by the Republican party, not only in terms of the total number of seats (236 of 435) but also very narrowly in terms of state delegations. Twenty-six state delegations (the absolute constitutional minimum for presidential election) presently have a Republican majority, seventeen are Democratic, six are evenly divided between the two parties, and one state delegation (Vermont) consists solely of Socialist Rep. Bernard Sanders. Despite the thin but apparent majority of state delegations controlled by Republicans, House voting for president would be at best confused and unpredictable as members sorted out conflicting pressures of party, constituency, political self-interest, and personal preference.

Another imponderable would result from the fact that the House that would be faced with electing a president in January 1997 would be the new House elected in November 1996, and probably would have partisan balances different from the current House. The favorable Republican position in state delegations as of the midpoint of the 1996 presidential campaign may be eroded by the results of the November 1996 House elections: six of the Republican state delegations presently have Republican majorities by only one seat; a loss of just one Republican representative in any of these six states would make it a Democratic majority state. If the Democratic party should gain even five or ten House seats in the 1996 congressional elections—certainly a realistic possibility given the substantial number of marginal Republican House victories of 1994—the newly elected House, which takes office on January 3, 1997 (just three days prior to being possibly confronted with unique constitutional duties), could easily have fewer than twenty-six state delegations with clear Republican majorities. Even modest partisan shifts would increase significantly the possibility of deadlock in the House of Representatives over the election of the president.

Beyond such calculations, however, lurks the fact that such partisan projections do not take into account the previously mentioned factors of congressional voting influenced by district results, state vote outcome, national popular vote results, or even personal whim. Personal preference would be especially significant in the case of representatives from the smallest states. Seven states (Alaska, Delaware, Montana, North Dakota, South Dakota, Vermont, and Wyoming) have but one representative; each would be able to cast one of the twenty-six House state votes that could elect the president. These 7 individuals, representing slightly more than 4 million citizens, could outvote the 177 House members from the six largest states—California, Florida, Illinois, New York, Pennsylvania, and Texas—who represent a total of more than 100 million citizens. The inequities are even starker for the 600,000 residents of the District of Columbia. Lacking any voting representation in the House of Representatives, they would have no votes at all in the House election of the president of the American people.

5. *A final and definitive decision by the House in January is by no means certain.* If called upon to choose a president in 1997, the House would commence its deliberations and voting on January 6, only fourteen days prior to the constitutionally mandated inauguration day. Such a House vote would be between Republican Bob Dole, incumbent President Bill Clinton, and whatever additional candidate had received the greatest number of electoral votes. No matter how the House vote split, no matter how many state delegations were evenly divided and consequently unable to cast a vote, the constitutional requirement of twenty-six state votes would remain. The House of Representatives might well find it difficult—or even impossible—to decide on a president as inauguration day inexorably

approached. It is entirely possible that the result of the 1996 presidential election would be continued deadlock in the House of Representatives past the immovable date of January 20.

If no president has been elected by the House of Representatives by noon on January 20, the Twentieth Amendment provides that the vice president–elect shall "act as President." This assumes, of course, that a vice president–elect in fact has been chosen by the U.S. Senate by receiving a majority of votes there. This would be a likely outcome, of course, since the voting there is one vote per senator and, most important, is limited to the top *two* contenders. It should be noted, however, that an *exact tie* in the Senate vote is also a possibility should the Senate divide along precisely balanced party lines (the outgoing vice president would be unable to break such a tie since Senate voting is limited to the one hundred members of the Senate). If *both* the House and Senate should deadlock and be unable to resolve their stalemates by January 20, then the Automatic Succession Act of 1947 would apply. In case of a vacancy in both the presidential and vice presidential offices, the act places the Speaker of the House, the president pro tempore of the Senate, and the various Cabinet officers in the line of succession to the presidency.

Another astonishing situation might arise uniquely in the Senate in the admittedly unlikely case that either the Republican or Democratic presidential/vice presidential ticket should run *third* in electoral votes (such was, in fact, the fate of the regular Republican ticket headed by incumbent President William H. Taft in 1912). If, for example, the Republican ticket were in third place and no ticket won an outright electoral vote majority, the presumably Republican-controlled Senate would be faced with a most curious choice— between Democratic Vice President Al Gore and the independent candidate's running mate for vice president—for the post of vice president, who might also be called upon to serve (should the House deadlock) as acting president.

The result of a presidential election giving rise to the necessity of House and Senate decision, then, might be not a decisive, even if delayed, determination of a president but rather the designation of a vice president (or other official) who would only act as president. This person would fill that office for an uncertain tenure, subject to removal at any time by renewed House voting later in his or her term—especially following the midterm congressional elections, when the partisan balance in the House might well shift to the disadvantage of the troubled acting president. Such a presidency would be at best unhappy and weakened, subordinate to Congress because of the administration's congressional creation and possible termination, limited by a nonexistent electoral mandate, and crippled by uncertainty as to how long the temporary presidency could continue.

The electoral college in the 1996 or subsequent election may, happily, exhibit few if any of these extremely serious shortcomings. On the other hand, the American people may be unlucky in this election year or one to follow and be faced by crisis in the electoral college. In any case, the electoral college will be a crucial determining factor shaping and distorting the popular will in the 1996 election— and, if not reformed, even in subsequent elections.

At its best, the electoral college operates in an inherently distorted manner in transforming popular votes into electoral votes. In addition, it has enormous potential as a dangerous institution threatening the certainty of our elections and the legitimacy of our presidents. These defects of the contemporary electoral college cannot be dealt with by patchwork reforms such as abolishing the office of presidential elector. This distorted and unwieldy counting device must be abolished entirely, and the votes of the American people— wherever cast—must be counted directly and equally in determining who shall be president of the United States. It is all too likely that the 1996 presidential election, or one in the future, finally will provide the American public with indisputable evidence of the failings of the electoral college as a means of electing the people's president.

appendix a

The National Vote for President, 1789–1992

The United States has entrusted no single national agency with the official tabulation of the popular votes cast for presidential electors, although the electoral vote itself is certified every four years before a joint session of Congress. The table below records the official electoral vote and indicates the best available tallies of the national popular vote.

Sources for the popular vote: for the elections of 1824 (the year for which the first national count could be compiled) through 1916, Svend Petersen, *A Statistical History of American Presidential Elections* (New York, 1963); for the elections of 1920 through 1964, Richard M. Scammon, *America at the Polls* (Pittsburgh, 1965); for the refinements of the 1960 vote, where a split Democratic elector slate in Alabama raised difficult problems in evaluation, Congressional Quarterly Service; for the elections of 1968 through 1984, Congressional Quarterly, *Guide to U.S. Elections,* 2d ed. (Washington, D.C., 1985); for the election of 1988, Congressional Quarterly, *The People Speak: American Elections in Focus* (Washington, D.C., 1990); for the election of 1992, Congressional Quarterly, *Guide to U.S. Elections,* 3d ed. (Washington, D.C., 1994).

In the elections of 1789 through 1800, each presidential elector cast two equal votes, without distinguishing the person he favored for president from his choice for vice president. The candidate with the most electoral votes was elected president if his total constituted a majority of the number of electors. The runner-up, without a majority requirement, was elected vice president. The Twelfth Amendment, adopted in 1804 and applicable to the election of that year and all subsequent elections, required the electors to cast separate votes for president and vice president.

The elections of 1800 and 1824 were decided by the House of Representatives because no candidate for president received a majority of electoral votes.

The name of the winning candidate is given first for each election year. Key to party designations:

F	Federalist	AM	Anti-Masonic
D	Democratic	W	Whig
NR	National Republican	L	Liberty

FS	Free Soil	U	Union
R	Republican	SR	States' Rights
LR	Land Reform	AIP	American Independent party
CU	Constitutional Union	Amer.	American party
G	Greenback	Peop.	People's party
P	Prohibition	NUC	National Unity Campaign
PO	Populist	Libert.	Libertarian
S	Socialist	New All.	New Alliance party
PR	Progressive	Ind.	Independent

Party designations pose special problems in the early years, when national political parties in the modern sense were still emerging. The designation (D) for Democrat is used in this table for the factions called Anti-Federalist, later Republican, and eventually known as Democratic by the 1820s.

Year	Candidate	Popular Votes Total	Popular Votes Percentage	Electoral Votes Received
1789	George Washington (F)	—	—	69
	John Adams (F)	—	—	34
	John Jay (F)	—	—	9
	Others	—	—	26
1792	George Washington (F)	—	—	132
	John Adams (F)	—	—	77
	George Clinton (D)	—	—	50
	Others	—	—	5
1796	John Adams (F)	—	—	71
	Thomas Jefferson (D)	—	—	68
	Thomas Pinckney (F)	—	—	59
	Aaron Burr (D)	—	—	30
	Samuel Adams (F)	—	—	15
	Oliver Ellsworth (F)	—	—	11
	Others	—	—	22

(continued)

Year	Candidate	Popular Votes Total	Popular Votes Percentage	Electoral Votes Received
1800	Thomas Jefferson (D)	—	—	73
	Aaron Burr (D)	—	—	73
	John Adams (F)	—	—	65
	Charles C. Pinckney (F)	—	—	64
	John Jay	—	—	1
1804	Thomas Jefferson (D)	—	—	162
	Charles C. Pinckney (F)	—	—	14
1808	James Madison (D)	—	—	122
	Charles C. Pinckney (F)	—	—	47
	George Clinton (F)	—	—	6
1812	James Madison (D)	—	—	128
	DeWitt Clinton (F)	—	—	89
1816	James Monroe (D)	—	—	183
	Rufus King (F)	—	—	34
1820	James Monroe (D)	—	—	231
	John Quincy Adams (D)	—	—	1
1824	John Quincy Adams (D)	115,696	31.9	84
	Andrew Jackson (D)	152,933	42.2	99
	William H. Crawford (D)	46,979	13.0	41
	Henry Clay (D)	47,136	13.0	37
1828	Andrew Jackson (D)	647,292	56.0	178
	John Quincy Adams (NR)	507,730	44.0	83
1832	Andrew Jackson (D)	688,242	54.5	219
	Henry Clay (NR)	473,462	37.5	49
	William Wirt (AM)	101,051	8.0	7
	John Floyd (D)	—	—	11

(continued)

Year	Candidate	Popular Votes Total	Popular Votes Percentage	Electoral Votes Received
1836	Martin Van Buren (D)	764,198	50.9	170
	William H. Harrison (W)	549,508	36.6	73
	Hugh L. White (W)	145,352	9.7	26
	Daniel Webster (W)	41,287	2.8	14
	Willie P. Mangum (D)	—	—	11
1840	†William H. Harrison (W)	1,275,612	52.9	234
	Martin Van Buren (D)	1,130,033	46.8	60
	James G. Birney (L)	7,053	0.3	0
1844	James K. Polk (D)	1,339,368	49.6	170
	Henry Clay (W)	1,300,687	48.1	105
	James G. Birney (L)	62,197	2.3	0
1848	†Zachary Taylor (W)	1,362,101	47.3	163
	Lewis Cass (D)	1,222,674	42.5	127
	Martin Van Buren (FS)	291,616	10.1	0
	Gerrit Smith (L)	2,733	0.1	0
1852	Franklin Pierce (D)	1,609,038	50.9	254
	Winfield Scott (W)	1,386,629	43.8	42
	John P. Hale (FS)	156,297	4.9	0
	Others	12,445	0.4	0
1856	James Buchanan (D)	1,839,237	45.6	174
	John C. Frémont (R)	1,341,028	33.3	114
	Millard Fillmore (W)	849,872	21.1	8
	Gerrit Smith (LR)	484	0	0
1860	Abraham Lincoln (R)	1,867,198	39.8	180
	Steven A. Douglas (D)	1,379,434	29.4	12
	John C. Breckinridge (D)	854,248	18.2	72
	John Bell (CU)	591,658	12.6	39
	Gerrit Smith	172	0	0

(continued)

Year	Candidate	Popular Votes Total	Popular Votes Percentage	Electoral Votes Received
1864	†Abraham Lincoln (R)	2,219,362	55.2	212
	George B. McClellan (D)	1,805,063	44.9	21
1868	Ulysses S. Grant (R)	3,013,313	52.7	214
	Horatio Seymour (D)	2,703,933	47.3	80
1872	Ulysses S. Grant (R)	3,597,375	55.6	286
	†Horace Greeley (D)	2,833,711	43.8	0
	Others	35,052	0.6	63
1876	Rutherford B. Hayes (R)	4,035,924	47.9	185
	Samuel J. Tilden (D)	4,287,670	50.9	184
	Others	94,935	1.1	0
1880	†James A. Garfield (R)	4,454,433	48.3	214
	Winfield S. Hancock (D)	4,444,976	48.2	155
	James B. Weaver (G)	308,649	3.4	0
	Others	11,409	0.1	0
1884	Grover Cleveland (D)	4,875,971	48.5	219
	James G. Blaine (R)	4,852,234	48.3	182
	Benjamin F. Butler (G)	175,066	1.7	0
	John P. St. John (P)	150,957	1.5	0
1888	Benjamin Harrison (R)	5,445,269	47.8	233
	Grover Cleveland (D)	5,540,365	48.6	168
	Clinton B. Fisk (P)	250,122	2.2	0
	Others	154,083	1.4	0
1892	Grover Cleveland (D)	5,556,982	46.0	277
	Benjamin Harrison (R)	5,191,466	43.0	145
	James B. Weaver (PO)	1,029,960	8.5	22
	Others	292,672	2.4	0

(continued)

Year	Candidate	Popular Votes Total	Popular Votes Percentage	Electoral Votes Received
1896	William McKinley (R)	7,113,734	51.0	271
	William J. Bryan (D)	6,516,722	46.7	176
	Others	317,219	2.3	0
1900	†William McKinley (R)	7,219,828	51.7	292
	William J. Bryan (D)	6,358,160	45.5	155
	Others	396,200	2.8	0
1904	Theodore Roosevelt (R)	7,628,831	56.4	336
	Alton B. Parker (D)	5,084,533	37.6	140
	Eugene V. Debs (S)	402,714	3.0	0
	Silas C. Swallow (P)	259,163	1.9	0
	Others	149,357	1.1	0
1908	William H. Taft (R)	7,679,114	51.6	321
	William J. Bryan (D)	6,410,665	43.1	162
	Eugene V. Debs (S)	420,858	2.8	0
	Eugene W. Chafin (P)	252,704	1.7	0
	Others	127,379	0.9	0
1912	Woodrow Wilson (D)	6,301,254	41.9	435
	Theodore Roosevelt (PR)	4,127,788	27.4	88
	William H. Taft (R)	3,485,831	23.3	8
	Eugene V. Debs (S)	901,255	6.0	0
	Others	238,934	1.6	0
1916	Woodrow Wilson (D)	9,131,511	49.3	277
	Charles E. Hughes (R)	8,548,935	46.1	254
	Allan L. Benson (S)	585,974	3.2	0
	Others	269,812	1.5	0
1920	†Warren G. Harding (R)	16,153,115	60.3	404
	James M. Cox (D)	9,133,082	34.1	127
	Eugene V. Debs (S)	915,490	3.4	0
	Others	566,916	2.1	0

(continued)

Year	Candidate	Popular Votes Total	Popular Votes Percentage	Electoral Votes Received
1924	Calvin Coolidge (R)	15,719,921	54.0	382
	John W. Davis (D)	8,386,704	28.8	136
	Robert M. LaFollette (PR)	4,832,532	16.6	13
	Others	155,866	0.5	0
1928	Herbert C. Hoover (R)	21,437,277	58.2	444
	Alfred E. Smith (D)	15,007,698	40.8	87
	Others	360,976	1.0	0
1932	Franklin D. Roosevelt (D)	22,829,501	57.4	472
	Herbert C. Hoover (R)	15,760,684	39.6	59
	Norman M. Thomas (S)	884,649	2.2	0
	Others	283,925	0.8	0
1936	Franklin D. Roosevelt (D)	27,757,333	60.8	523
	Alfred M. Landon (R)	16,684,231	36.5	8
	William Lemke (U)	892,267	2.0	0
	Others	320,932	0.7	0
1940	Franklin D. Roosevelt (D)	27,313,041	54.7	449
	Wendell Willkie (R)	22,348,480	44.8	82
	Others	238,897	0.5	0
1944	†Franklin D. Roosevelt (D)	25,612,610	53.4	432
	Thomas E. Dewey (R)	22,017,617	45.9	99
	Others	346,443	0.7	0
1948	Harry S Truman (D)	24,179,345	49.6	303
	Thomas E. Dewey (R)	21,991,291	45.1	189
	J. Strom Thurmond (SR)	1,176,125	2.4	39
	Henry A. Wallace (PR)	1,157,326	2.4	0
	Others	289,739	0.6	0
1952	Dwight D. Eisenhower (R)	33,936,234	55.1	442
	Adlai E. Stevenson (D)	27,314,992	44.4	89
	Others	299,692	0.5	0

(continued)

Year	Candidate	Popular Votes Total	Percentage	Electoral Votes Received
1956	Dwight D. Eisenhower (R)	35,590,472	57.4	457
	Adlai E. Stevenson (D)	26,022,752	42.0	73
	Unpledged Elector Slates	196,318	0.3	0
	Others	217,366	0.3	1
1960	†John F. Kennedy (D)	34,220,984	49.5	303
	Richard M. Nixon (R)	34,108,157	49.3	219
	Unpledged Elector Slates	638,822	0.9	15
	Others	188,559	0.3	0

Alternate Computation: This method avoids a major defect of the method used above, which counts Alabama Democratic votes twice, once for Kennedy and once for unpledged slates. The alternate computation credits five-elevenths of Alabama's Democratic votes to Kennedy and six-elevenths to the unpledged electoral slate totals. (See discussion in Chapter 3.)

Year	Candidate	Popular Votes Total	Percentage	Electoral Votes Received
	†John F. Kennedy (D)	34,049,976	49.2	303
	Richard M. Nixon (R)	34,108,157	49.3	219
	Unpledged Elector Slates	491,527	0.7	15
	Others	188,559	0.3	0
1964	Lyndon B. Johnson (D)	43,129,484	61.1	486
	Barry M. Goldwater (R)	27,178,188	38.5	52
	Others	336,838	0.4	0
1968	Richard M. Nixon (R)	31,785,148	43.4	301
	Hubert H. Humphrey (D)	31,274,503	42.7	191
	George C. Wallace (AIP)	9,901,151	13.5	46
	Others	242,568	0.3	0

(continued)

Year	Candidate	Popular Votes Total	Popular Votes Percentage	Electoral Votes Received
1972	†Richard M. Nixon (R)	47,170,179	60.7	520
	George S. McGovern (D)	29,171,791	37.5	17
	John G. Schmitz (Amer.)	1,090,673	1.4	0
	Benjamin Spock (Peop.)	78,751	0.1	0
	Others	216,198	0.3	1
1976	Jimmy Carter (D)	48,830,763	50.1	297
	Gerald R. Ford (R)	39,147,793	48.0	240
	Eugene J. McCarthy (Ind.)	756,691	0.9	0
	Roger MacBride (Libert.)	173,011	0.2	0
	Others	647,631	0.8	1
1980	Ronald Reagan (R)	43,904,153	50.7	489
	Jimmy Carter (D)	35,483,883	41.0	49
	John B. Anderson (NUC)	5,720,060	6.6	0
	Ed Clark (Libert.)	921,299	1.1	0
	Others	485,826	0.6	0
1984	Ronald Reagan (R)	54,455,074	58.8	525
	Walter F. Mondale (D)	37,577,137	40.6	13
	David Bergland (Libert.)	228,314	0.3	0
	Lyndon H. LaRouche, Jr. (Ind.)	78,807	0.1	0
	Others	241,261	0.3	0
1988	George Bush (R)	48,886,097	53.4	426
	Michael S. Dukakis (D)	41,809,074	45.6	111
	Ron Paul (Libert.)	432,179	0.5	0
	Lenora B. Fulani (New All.)	217,219	0.2	0
	Others	250,240	0.3	1

(continued)

Year	Candidate	Popular Votes Total	Percentage	Electoral Votes Received
1992	Bill Clinton (D)	44,909,326	43.0	370
	George Bush (R)	39,103,882	37.4	168
	Ross Perot (Ind.)	19,741,657	18.9	0
	Andre V. Marrou (Libert.)	291,627	0.3	0
	Others	378,522	0.4	0

†*Notes on Candidates:*

William Henry Harrison died in office April 4, 1841, and was succeeded by Vice President John Tyler.

Zachary Taylor died in office July 9, 1850, and was succeeded by Vice President Millard Fillmore.

Abraham Lincoln was shot April 14, 1965, and died the following day. He was succeeded by Vice President Andrew Johnson.

Horace Greeley died Nov. 29, 1872, before the counting of the electoral votes, which the Democratic electors divided among a scattering of candidates.

James A. Garfield was shot July 2, 1881, and died Sept. 19, 1881. He was succeeded by Vice President Chester A. Arthur.

William McKinley was shot Sept. 6, 1901, and died Sept. 14, 1901. He was succeeded by Vice President Theodore Roosevelt.

Warren G. Harding died in office Aug. 2, 1923, and was succeeded by Vice President Calvin Coolidge.

Franklin D. Roosevelt died in office April 12, 1945, and was succeeded by Vice President Harry S Truman.

John F. Kennedy was assassinated Nov. 22, 1963, and was succeeded by Vice President Lyndon B. Johnson.

Richard M. Nixon resigned Aug. 9, 1974, and was succeeded by Vice President Gerald R. Ford, who had become vice president following the resignation, on Oct. 10, 1973, of Vice President Spiro T. Agnew.

appendix b

Electoral College Membership, 1789–2000

Total Membership of the Electoral College since 1789 (with totals for selected states)

Election Years*	Number of States†	Total Electoral Vote†	Calif.	Ill.	N.Y.	Va.
1789	13	91			8	12
1792–1800	16	138			12	21
1804–1808	17	176			19	24
1812–1820	23	232		3	29	25
1824–1828	24	261		3	36	24
1832–1840	26	294		5	42	23
1844–1848	31	294		9	36	17
1852–1860	33	303	4	11	35	15
1864–1868	36	315	5	16	33	13
1872–1880	38	369	6	21	35	11
1884–1888	44	420	8	22	36	12
1892–1900	45	447	9	24	36	12
1904–1908	46	483	10	27	39	12
1912–1928‡	48	531	13	29	45	12
1932–1940	48	531	22	29	47	11
1944–1948	48	531	25	28	47	11
1952–1960	50	537§	32	27	45	12
1964–1968	50	538‖	40	26	43	12
1972–1980	50	538‖	45	26	41	12
1984–1988	50	538‖	47	24	36	12
1992–2000	50	538‖	54	22	33	13

Sources: Biographical Directory of the American Congress (Washington, D.C., 1961), p. 45; *Representation and Apportionment* (Washington, D.C., 1966), pp. 53, 61; *Congressional Quarterly Weekly Report,* Jan. 10, 1981: 71; and Rhodes Cook, *Race for the Presidency* (Washington, D.C., 1991), p. 5.

Electoral College Membership State by State, 1904–2000*

State	1904–1908	1912–1928‡	1932–1940	1944–1948	1952–1960	1964–1968	1972–1980	1984–1988	1992–2000
Alabama	11	12	11	11	11	10	9	9	9
Alaska					3	3	3	3	3
Arizona		3	3	4	4	5	6	7	8
Arkansas	9	9	9	9	8	6	6	6	6
California	10	13	22	25	32	40	45	47	54
Colorado	5	6	6	6	6	6	7	8	8
Connecticut	7	7	8	8	8	8	8	8	8
Delaware	3	3	3	3	3	3	3	3	3
Dist. of Columbia						3	3	3	3
Florida	5	6	7	8	10	14	17	21	25
Georgia	13	14	12	12	12	12	12	12	13
Hawaii					3	4	4	4	4
Idaho	3	4	4	4	4	4	4	4	4
Illinois	27	29	29	28	27	26	26	24	22
Indiana	15	15	14	13	13	13	13	12	12
Iowa	13	13	11	10	10	9	8	8	7

Kansas	10	10	9	8	8	7	7	7	6
Kentucky	13	13	11	11	10	9	9	9	8
Louisiana	9	10	10	10	10	10	10	10	9
Maine	6	6	5	5	5	4	4	4	4
Maryland	8	8	8	8	9	10	10	10	10
Massachusetts	16	18	17	16	16	14	14	13	12
Michigan	14	15	19	19	20	21	21	20	18
Minnesota	11	12	11	11	11	10	10	10	10
Mississippi	10	10	9	9	8	7	7	7	7
Missouri	18	18	15	15	13	12	12	11	11
Montana	3	4	4	4	4	4	4	4	3
Nebraska	8	8	7	6	6	5	5	5	5
Nevada	3	3	3	3	3	3	3	4	4
New Hampshire	4	4	4	4	4	4	4	4	4
New Jersey	12	14	16	16	16	17	17	16	15
New Mexico		3	3	4	4	4	4	5	5
New York	39	45	47	47	45	43	41	36	33
North Carolina	12	12	13	14	14	13	13	13	14
North Dakota	4	5	4	4	4	4	3	3	3

(continued)

Electoral College Membership State by State, 1904–2000* (continued)

State	1904–1908	1912–1928‡	1932–1940	1944–1948	1952–1960	1964–1968	1972–1980	1984–1988	1992–2000
Ohio	23	24	26	25	25	26	25	23	21
Oklahoma	7	10	11	10	8	8	8	8	8
Oregon	4	5	5	6	6	6	6	7	7
Pennsylvania	34	38	36	35	32	29	27	25	23
Rhode Island	4	5	4	4	4	4	4	4	4
South Carolina	9	9	8	8	8	8	8	8	8
South Dakota	4	5	4	4	4	4	4	3	3
Tennessee	12	12	11	12	11	11	10	11	11
Texas	18	20	23	23	24	25	26	29	32
Utah	3	4	4	4	4	4	4	5	5
Vermont	4	4	3	3	3	3	3	3	3
Virginia	12	12	11	11	12	12	12	12	13
Washington	5	7	8	8	9	9	9	10	11
West Virginia	7	8	8	8	8	7	6	6	5
Wisconsin	13	13	12	12	12	12	11	11	11
Wyoming	3	3	3	3	3	3	3	3	3
Totals†	483	531	531	531	537§	538‖	538‖	538‖	538‖

*Apportionments are based on the last decennial census preceding the actual year of the election. Thus the electoral college membership for the presidential elections of 1792 through 1800 was based on the 1790 census, that of 1804 and 1808 on the 1800 census, etc. The electoral college membership for the first presidential election, in 1789, was based on the temporary apportionment specified in the Constitution.

†Figures given are those at the end of the decade, including temporary apportionment for states that may have joined the Union since the preceding census.

‡Congress made no reapportionment following the 1920 census.

§Total rose temporarily to 537 for the 1960 election to allow the newly admitted states of Alaska and Hawaii to cast electoral votes.

‖Increase to 538 from 535, which would be the 50-state base, accounted for by the Twenty-third Amendment, giving the District of Columbia a minimum of 3 electoral votes.

appendix c

Comparison of Popular and Electoral Vote Percentages, 1824–1992

Year	Winning Candidate	Percentage of Popular Vote	Percentage of Electoral Vote	Disparity (in percentage points)
1824	John Quincy Adams (D)	32	32	0
1828	Andrew Jackson (D)	56	68	12
1832	Andrew Jackson (D)	55	77	22
1836	Martin Van Buren (D)	51	58	7
1840	William H. Harrison (W)	53	80	27
1844	James K. Polk (D)	50	62	12
1848	Zachary Taylor (W)	47	56	9
1852	Franklin Pierce (D)	51	86	35
1856	James Buchanan (D)	46	59	13
1860	Abraham Lincoln (R)	40	59	19
1864	Abraham Lincoln (R)	55	91	36
1868	Ulysses S. Grant (R)	53	73	20
1872	Ulysses S. Grant (R)	56	82	26
1876	Rutherford B. Hayes (R)	48	50	2
1880	James A. Garfield (R)	48	58	10
1884	Grover Cleveland (D)	49	55	6
1888	Benjamin Harrison (R)	48	58	10
1892	Grover Cleveland (D)	46	62	16
1896	William McKinley (R)	51	61	10
1900	William McKinley (R)	52	65	13

(continued)

Year	Winning Candidate	Percentage of Popular Vote	Percentage of Electoral Vote	Disparity (in percentage points)
1904	Theodore Roosevelt (R)	56	71	15
1908	William H. Taft (R)	52	66	14
1912	Woodrow Wilson (D)	42	82	40
1916	Woodrow Wilson (D)	49	52	3
1920	Warren G. Harding (R)	60	76	16
1924	Calvin Coolidge (R)	54	71	17
1928	Herbert C. Hoover (R)	58	84	26
1932	Franklin D. Roosevelt (D)	57	89	32
1936	Franklin D. Roosevelt (D)	61	98	37
1940	Franklin D. Roosevelt (D)	55	85	30
1944	Franklin D. Roosevelt (D)	53	81	28
1948	Harry S Truman (D)	50	57	7
1952	Dwight D. Eisenhower (R)	55	83	28
1956	Dwight D. Eisenhower (R)	57	86	29
1960	John F. Kennedy (D)	50	62	12
1964	Lyndon B. Johnson (D)	61	90	29
1968	Richard M. Nixon (R)	43	56	13
1972	Richard M. Nixon (R)	61	97	36
1976	Jimmy Carter (D)	50	55	5
1980	Ronald Reagan (R)	51	91	40
1984	Ronald Reagan (R)	59	98	39
1988	George Bush (R)	53	79	26
1992	Bill Clinton (D)	43	69	26

appendix d

U.S. Constitutional Provisions Relating to Presidential Elections

Article II

Section 1. The executive Power shall be vested in a President of the United States of America. He shall hold his Office during the Term of four Years, and, together with the Vice President, chosen for the same Term, be elected, as follows.

Each State shall appoint, in such Manner as the Legislature thereof may direct, a Number of Electors, equal to the whole Number of Senators and Representatives to which the State may be entitled in the Congress; but no Senator or Representative, or Person holding an Office of Trust or Profit under the United States, shall be appointed an Elector.

[The Electors shall meet in their respective States, and vote by Ballot for two Persons, of whom one at least shall not be an Inhabitant of the same State with themselves. And they shall make a List of all the Persons voted for, and of the Number of Votes for each; which List they shall sign and certify, and transmit sealed to the Seat of the Government of the United States, directed to the President of the Senate. The President of the Senate shall, in the Presence of the Senate and House of Representatives, open all the Certificates, and the Votes shall then be counted. The Person having the greatest Number of Votes shall be the President, if such Number be a Majority of the whole Number of Electors appointed; and if there be more than one who have such Majority, and have an equal Number of Votes, then the House of Representatives shall immediately chuse by Ballot one of them for President; and if no Person have a majority, then from the five highest on the List the said House shall in like Manner chuse the President. But in chusing the President, the Votes shall be taken by States, the Representation from each State having one Vote; a quorum for this Purpose shall consist of a Member or Members from two-thirds of the States, and a Majority of all the States shall be necessary to a Choice. In every Case, after the Choice of the President, the Person having the greatest Number of Votes of the Electors shall be the Vice President. But if there should remain two or more who have equal Votes, the Senate shall chuse from them by Ballot the Vice President.]*

*Paragraph in brackets superseded by Twelfth Amendment.

The Congress may determine the Time of chusing the Electors, and the Day on which they shall give their Votes; which Day shall be the same throughout the United States.

No Person except a natural born Citizen, or a Citizen of the United States, at the time of the Adoption of this Constitution, shall be eligible to the Office of President; neither shall any person be eligible to that Office who shall not have attained to the Age of thirty five Years, and been fourteen Years a Resident within the United States.

In Case of the Removal of the President from Office, or of his Death, Resignation, or Inability to discharge the Powers and Duties of the said Office, the Same shall devolve on the Vice President, and the Congress may by Law provide for the Case of Removal, Death, Resignation or Inability, both of the President and Vice President, declaring what Officer shall then act as President, and such Officer shall act accordingly, until the Disability be removed, or a President shall be elected.

The President shall, at stated Times, receive for his Services, a Compensation, which shall neither be increased nor diminished during the Period for which he shall have been elected, and he shall not receive within that Period any other Emolument from the United States, or any of them.

Before he enter on the Execution of his Office, he shall take the following Oath or Affirmation—"I do solemnly swear (or affirm) that I will faithfully execute the Office of President of the United States, and will to the best of my Ability, preserve, protect and defend the Constitution of the United States."

Section 2. The President shall be Commander in Chief of the Army and Navy of the United States, and of the Militia of the several States, when called into the actual Service of the United States; he may require the Opinion, in writing, of the principal Officer in each of the executive Departments, upon any Subject relating to the Duties of their respective Offices, and he shall have Power to grant Reprieves and Pardons for Offenses against the United States, except in Cases of Impeachment.

He shall have Power, by and with the Advice and Consent of the Senate, to make Treaties, provided two thirds of the Senators present concur; and he shall nominate, and by and with the Advice and Consent of the Senate, shall appoint Ambassadors, other public Ministers and Consuls, Judges of the supreme Court, and all other Officers of the United States, whose Appointments are not herein otherwise provided for, and which shall be established by Law: but the Congress may by Law vest the Appointment of such inferior Officers, as they think proper, in the President alone, in the Courts of Law, or in the Heads of Departments.

The President shall have Power to fill up all Vacancies that may happen during the Recess of the Senate, by granting Commissions which shall expire at the End of their next Session.

Section 3. He shall from time to time give to the Congress Information of the State of the Union, and recommend to their Consideration such Measures as he shall judge necessary and expedient; he may, on extraordinary Occasions, convene both Houses, or either of them, and in Case of Disagreement between them, with Respect to the Time of Adjournment, he may adjourn them to such Time as he shall think proper; he shall receive Ambassadors and other public Ministers; he shall take Care that the Laws be faithfully executed, and shall Commission all the Officers of the United States.

Section 4. The President, Vice President and all Civil Officers of the United States, shall be removed from Office on Impeachment for, and Conviction of, Treason, Bribery, or other high Crimes and Misdemeanors.

Amendment XII (declared ratified Sept. 25, 1804)

The Electors shall meet in their respective states and vote by ballot for President and Vice-President, one of whom, at least, shall not be an inhabitant of the same state with themselves; they shall name in their ballots the person voted for as President, and in distinct ballots the person voted for as Vice-President, and they shall make distinct lists of all persons voted for as President, and of all persons voted for as Vice-President, and of the number of votes for each, which lists they shall sign and certify, and transmit sealed to the seat of the government of the United States, directed to the President of the Senate;—The President of the Senate shall, in the presence of the Senate and House of Representatives, open all the certificates and the votes shall then be counted;—The person having the greatest number of votes for President, shall be the President, if such number be a majority of the whole number of Electors appointed; and if no person have such majority, then from the persons having the highest numbers not exceeding three on the list of those voted for as President, the House of Representatives shall choose immediately, by ballot, the President. But in choosing the President, the votes shall be taken by states, the representation from each state having one vote; a quorum for this purpose shall consist of a member or members from two-thirds of the states, and a majority of all the states shall be necessary to a choice. [And if the House of Representatives shall not choose a President whenever the right of choice shall devolve upon them, before the fourth day of March next following, then the Vice-President shall act as President, as in the case of the death or other constitutional disability of the President]*—The person having the greatest number of votes as Vice-President, shall be the Vice-President, if such number be a majority of the

*Sentence in brackets superseded by Twentieth Amendment.

whole number of Electors appointed, and if no person have a majority, then from the two highest numbers on the list, the Senate shall choose the Vice-President; a quorum for the purpose shall consist of two-thirds of the whole number of senators, and a majority of the whole number shall be necessary to a choice. But no person constitutionally ineligible to the office of President shall be eligible to that of Vice-President of the United States.

Amendment XIV (declared ratified July 28, 1868)

Section 1. All persons born or naturalized in the United States and subject to the jurisdiction thereof, are citizens of the United States and of the State wherein they reside. No State shall make or enforce any law which shall abridge the privileges or immunities of citizens of the United States; or shall any State deprive any person of life, liberty, or property, without due process of law; nor deny to any person within its jurisdiction the equal protection of the laws.

Section 2. Representatives shall be apportioned among the several States according to their respective numbers, counting the whole number of persons in each State, excluding Indians not taxed. But when the right to vote at any election for the choice of electors for President and Vice President of the United States, Representatives in Congress, the Executive and Judicial officers of a State, or the members of the Legislature thereof, is denied to any of the male inhabitants of such State, being twenty-one years of age, and citizens of the United States, or in any way abridged, except for participation in rebellion, or other crime, the basis of representation therein shall be reduced in the proportion which the number of such male citizens shall bear to the whole number of male citizens twenty-one years of age in such State.*

Section 3. No person shall be a Senator or Representative in Congress, or elector of President and Vice President, or hold any office, civil or military, under the United States, or under any State, who, having previously taken an oath, as a member of Congress, or as an officer of the United States, or as a member of any State legislature, or as an executive or judicial officer of any State, to support the Constitution of the United States, shall have engaged in insurrection or rebellion against the same, or given aid or comfort to the enemies thereof. But Congress may by a vote of two-thirds of each House, remove such disability. . . .

Section 5. The Congress shall have power to enforce, by appropriate legislation, the provisions of this article.

*The sections of this amendment which would reduce a state's congressional representation (and thus its votes in the electoral college) have never been enforced.

Amendment XV (declared ratified March 30, 1870)

Section 1. The right of citizens of the United States to vote shall not be denied or abridged by the United States or by any State on account of race, color, or previous condition of servitude.

Section 2. The Congress shall have power to enforce this article by appropriate legislation.

Amendment XVII (declared ratified May 31, 1913)

The Senate of the United States shall be composed of two Senators from each State, elected by the people thereof, for six years, and each Senator shall have one vote. The electors in each State shall have the qualifications requisite for electors of the most numerous branch of the State legislatures . . . .

Amendment XIX (declared ratified Aug. 26, 1920)

The right of citizens of the United States to vote shall not be denied or abridged by the United States or by any State on account of sex.

Congress shall have power to enforce this article by appropriate legislation.

Amendment XX (declared ratified Feb. 6, 1933)

Section 1. The terms of the President and Vice President shall end at noon on the 20th day of January, and the terms of Senators and Representatives at noon on the 3rd day of January, of the years in which such terms would have ended if this article had not been ratified; and the terms of their successors shall then begin.

Section 2. The Congress shall assemble at least once in every year, and such meeting shall begin at noon on the 3rd day of January, unless they shall by law appoint a different day.

Section 3. If, at the time fixed for the beginning of the term of the President, the President elect shall have died, the Vice President elect shall become President. If a President shall not have been chosen before the time fixed for the beginning of his term, or if the President elect shall have failed to qualify, then the Vice President elect shall act as President until a President shall have qualified; and the Congress may by law provide for the case wherein neither a President elect nor a Vice President elect shall have qualified, declaring who shall then act as President, or the manner in which one who is to act shall be selected, and such person shall act accordingly until a President or Vice President shall have qualified.

Section 4. The Congress may by law provide for the case of the death of any of the persons from whom the House of Representatives may choose a President whenever the right of choice shall have devolved upon them, and for the case of the death of any of the persons from whom the Senate may choose a Vice President whenever the right of choice shall have devolved upon them . . . .

Amendment XXII (declared ratified Feb. 26, 1951)

Section 1. No person shall be elected to the office of the President more than twice, and no person who has held the office of President, or acted as President, for more than two years of a term to which some other person was elected President shall be elected to the office of the President more than once. But this Article shall not apply to any person holding the office of President when this Article was proposed by the Congress, and shall not prevent any person who may be holding the office of President, or acting as President, during the term within which this Article becomes operative from holding the office of President or acting as President during the remainder of such term . . . .

Amendment XXIII (declared ratified March 29, 1961)

Section 1. The District constituting the seat of Government of the United States shall appoint in such manner as the Congress may direct:

A number of electors of President and Vice President equal to the whole number of Senators and Representatives in Congress to which the District would be entitled if it were a State, but in no event more than the least populous State; they shall be considered, for the purposes of the election of President and Vice President, to be electors appointed by a State; and they shall meet in the District and perform such duties as provided by the twelfth article of amendment.

Section 2. The Congress shall have power to enforce this article by appropriate legislation.

Amendment XXIV (declared ratified Jan. 23, 1964)

Section 1. The right of citizens of the United States to vote in any primary or other election for President or Vice President, for electors for President or Vice President, or for Senator or Representative in Congress, shall not be denied or abridged by the United States or any State by reason of failure to pay any poll tax or other tax.

Section 2. The Congress shall have the power to enforce this article by appropriate legislation.

Amendment XXV (declared ratified Feb. 10, 1967)

Section 1. In case of the removal of the President from office or of his death or resignation, the Vice President shall become President.

Section 2. Whenever there is a vacancy in the office of the Vice President, the President shall nominate a Vice President who shall take office upon confirmation by a majority vote of both houses of Congress.

Section 3. Whenever the President transmits to the President pro tempore of the Senate and the Speaker of the House of Representatives his written declaration that he is unable to discharge the powers and duties of his office, and until he transmits to them a written declaration to the contrary, such powers and duties shall be discharged by the Vice President as Acting President.

Section 4. Whenever the Vice President and a majority of either the principal officers of the Executive departments or of such other body as Congress may by law provide transmit to the President pro tempore of the Senate and the Speaker of the House of Representatives their written declaration that the President is unable to discharge the powers and duties of his office, the Vice President shall immediately assume the powers and duties of the office as Acting President.

Thereafter, when the President transmits to the President pro tempore of the Senate and the Speaker of the House of Representatives his written declaration that no inability exists, he shall resume the powers and duties of his office unless the Vice President and a majority of either the principal officers of the executive departments or of such other body as Congress may by law provide transmits within four days to the President pro tempore of the Senate and the Speaker of the House of Representatives their written declaration that the President is unable to discharge the powers and duties of his office. Thereupon Congress shall decide the issue, assembling within forty-eight hours for that purpose if not in session. If the Congress, within twenty-one days after receipt of the latter written declaration, or, if Congress is not in session, within twenty-one days after Congress is required to assemble, determines by two-thirds vote of both houses that the President is unable to discharge the powers and duties of his office, the Vice President shall continue to discharge the same as Acting President; otherwise, the President shall resume the powers and duties of his office.

appendix e

Federal Law Relating to Presidential Elections

United States Code

Title 3: The President

Chapter 1: Presidential Elections and Vacancies (excerpts)

§1. Time of appointing electors.

The electors of President and Vice President shall be appointed, in each State, on the Tuesday next after the first Monday in November, in every fourth year succeeding every election of a President and Vice President.

§4. Vacancies in electoral college.

Each State may, by law, provide for the filling of any vacancies which may occur in its college of electors when such college meets to give its electoral vote.

§7. Meeting and vote of electors.

The electors of President and Vice President of each State shall meet and give their votes on the first Monday after the second Wednesday in December next following their appointment at such place in each State as the legislature of such State shall direct.

§9. Certificates of votes for President and Vice President.

The electors shall make and sign six certificates of all the votes given by them, each of which certificates shall contain two distinct lists, one of the votes for President and the other of the votes for Vice President, and shall annex to each of the certificates one of the lists of the electors which shall have been furnished to them by direction of the executive of the State.

§11. Disposition of certificates.

The electors shall dispose of the certificates so made by them and the lists attached thereto in the following manner:

First. They shall forthwith forward by registered mail one of the same to the President of the Senate at the seat of government.

Second. Two of the same shall be delivered to the secretary of state of the State, one of which shall be held subject to the order of the President of the Senate, the other to be preserved by him for one year and shall be a part of the public records of his office and shall be open to public inspection.

Third. On the day thereafter they shall forward by registered mail two of such certificates and lists to the Administrator of General Services at the seat of government, one of which shall be held subject to the order of the President of the Senate. The other shall be preserved by the Administrator of General Services for one year and shall be a part of the public records of his office and shall be open to public inspection.

Fourth. They shall forthwith cause the other of the certificates and lists to be delivered to the judge of the district in which the electors shall have assembled.

§15. Counting electoral votes in Congress.

Congress shall be in session on the sixth day of January succeeding every meeting of the electors. The Senate and House of Representatives shall meet in the Hall of the House of Representatives at the hour of 1 o'clock in the afternoon on that day, and the President of the Senate shall be their presiding officer. Two tellers shall be previously appointed on the part of the Senate and two on the part of the House of Representatives, to whom shall be handed, as they are opened by the President of the Senate, all the certificates and papers purporting to be certificates of the electoral votes, which certificates and papers shall be opened, presented, and acted upon in the alphabetical order of the States, beginning with the letter A; and said tellers, having then read the same in the presence and hearing of the two Houses, shall make a list of the votes as they shall appear from the said certificates; and the votes having been ascertained and counted according to the rules in this subchapter provided, the result of the same shall be delivered to the President of the Senate, who shall thereupon announce the state of the vote, which announcement shall be deemed a sufficient declaration of the persons, if any, elected President and Vice President of the United States, and, together with a list of the votes, be entered on the Journals of the two Houses. Upon such reading of any such certificate or paper, the President of the Senate shall call for objections, if any. Every objection shall be made in writing, and shall state clearly and concisely, and without argument, the ground thereof, and shall be signed by at least one Senator and one Member of the House of Representatives before the same shall be received. When all objections so made to any vote or paper from a State shall have been received and read, the Senate shall thereupon withdraw, and such objections shall be submitted to the Senate for its decision; and the Speaker of the House of Representatives shall, in like manner, submit such objections to the House of Representatives for its decision; and no electoral vote or votes from any State which shall have been regularly given by electors whose appointment has been lawfully certified to according to section 6* of this title from which but one return has been

---

*Section 6 provides for certification of votes by electors by state governors.

received shall be rejected, but the two Houses concurrently may reject the vote or votes when they agree that such vote or votes have not been so regularly given by electors whose appointment has been so certified. If more than one return or paper purporting to be a return from a State shall have been received by the President of the Senate, those votes, and those only, shall be counted which shall have been regularly given by the electors who are shown by the determination mentioned in section 5* of this title to have been appointed, if the determination in said section provided for shall have been made, or by such successors or substitutes, in case of a vacancy in the board of electors so ascertained, as have been appointed to fill such vacancy in the mode provided by the laws of the State; but in case there shall arise the question which of two or more of such State authorities determining what electors have been appointed, as mentioned in section 5 of this title, is the lawful tribunal of such State, the votes regularly given of those electors, and those only, of such State shall be counted whose title as electors the two Houses, acting separately, shall concurrently decide is supported by the decision of such State so authorized by its law; and in such case of more than one return or paper purporting to be a return from a State, if there shall have been no such determination of the question in the State aforesaid, then those votes, and those only, shall be counted which the two Houses shall concurrently decide were cast by lawful electors appointed in accordance with the laws of the State, unless the two Houses, acting separately, shall concurrently decide such votes not to be the lawful votes of the legally appointed electors of such State. But if the two Houses shall disagree in respect of the counting of such votes, then, and in that case, the votes of the electors whose appointment shall have been certified by the executive of the State, under the seal thereof, shall be counted. When the two Houses have voted, they shall immediately again meet, and the presiding officer shall then announce the decision of the questions submitted. No votes or papers from any other State shall be acted upon until the objections previously made to the votes or papers from any State shall have been finally disposed of.

§16. Same; seats for officers and Members of two Houses in joint meeting.

At such joint meeting of the two Houses seats shall be provided as follows: For the President of the Senate, the Speaker's chair; for the Speaker, immediately upon his left; for the Senators, in the body of the Hall upon the right of the presiding officer; for the Representatives, in the body of the Hall not provided for the Senators; for the tellers, Secretary of the Senate, and Clerk of the House of Representatives, at the Clerk's desk; for the other officers of the two Houses in front of the Clerk's desk and upon each side of the Speaker's platform. Such joint meeting shall not be dissolved

*Section 5 provides that if state law specifies a method for resolving disputes concerning the vote for presidential electors, Congress must respect any determination so made by a state.

until the count of electoral votes shall be completed and the result declared; and no recess shall be taken unless a question shall have arisen in regard to counting any such votes, or otherwise under this subchapter, in which case it shall be competent for either House, acting separately, in the manner hereinbefore provided, to direct a recess of such House not beyond the next calendar day, Sunday excepted, at the hour of 10 o'clock in the forenoon. But if the counting of the electoral votes and the declaration of the result shall not have been completed before the fifth calendar day next after such first meeting of the two Houses, no further or other recess shall be taken by either House.

§17. Same; limit of debate in each House.

When the two Houses separate to decide upon an objection that may have been made to the counting of any electoral vote or votes from any State, or other question arising in the matter, each Senator and Representative may speak to such objection or question five minutes, and not more than once; but after such debate shall have lasted two hours it shall be the duty of the presiding officer of each House to put the main question without further debate.

§18. Same; parliamentary procedure at joint meeting.

While the two Houses shall be in meeting as provided in this chapter, the President of the Senate shall have power to preserve order; and no debate shall be allowed and no question shall be put by the presiding officer except to either House on a motion to withdraw.

appendix f

Rules of 1825 for Election of a President in the House of Representatives

The following rules* were adopted by the House of Representatives on February 7, 1825, for the election of a president after the failure of the electoral college to produce a majority for any candidate following the presidential election of 1824. No subsequent election has ever gone to the House for decision. These rules would be the governing precedent if the House should again be called upon to elect a president, though the House might alter the rules at any time.

1. In the event of its appearing, on opening all the certificates, and counting the votes given by the electors of the several States for President, that no person has a majority of the votes of the whole number of electors appointed, the same shall be entered on the Journals of this House.

2. The roll of the House shall then be called by States; and, on its appearing that a Member or Members from two-thirds of the States are present, the House shall immediately proceed, by ballot, to choose a President from the persons having the highest numbers, not exceeding three, on the list of those voted for as President; and, in case neither of those persons shall receive the votes of a majority of all the States on the first ballot, the House shall continue to ballot for a President, without interruption by other business, until a President be chosen.

3. The doors of the Hall shall be closed during the balloting, except against the Members of the Senate, stenographers, and the officers of the House.

4. From the commencement of the balloting until an election is made no proposition to adjourn shall be received, unless on the motion of one State, seconded by another State, and the question shall be decided by States. The same rule shall be observed in regard to any motion to change the usual hour for the meeting of the House.

5. In balloting the following mode shall be observed, to wit:

The Representatives of each State shall be arranged and seated together, beginning with the seats at the right hand of the Speaker's chair, with the Members from

*Hind's Precedents of the House of Representatives, vol. 3 (Washington, D.C., 1907), pp. 292–93.

the State of Maine; thence, proceeding with the Members from the States, in the order the States are usually named for receiving petitions,* around the Hall of the House, until all are seated.

A ballot box shall be provided for each State.

The Representatives of each State shall, in the first instance, ballot among themselves, in order to ascertain the vote of their State; and they may, if necessary, appoint tellers of their ballots.

After the vote of each State is ascertained, duplicates thereof shall be made out; and in case any one of the persons from whom the choice is to be made shall receive a majority of the votes given, on any one balloting by the Representatives of a State, the name of that person shall be written on each of the duplicates; and in case the votes so given shall be divided so that neither of said persons shall have a majority of the whole number of votes given by such State, on any one balloting, then the word "divided" shall be written on each duplicate.

After the delegation from each State shall have ascertained the vote of their State, the Clerk shall name the States in the order they are usually named for receiving petitions; and as the name of each is called the Sergeant-at-Arms shall present to the delegation of each two ballot boxes, in each of which shall be deposited, by some Representative of the State, one of the duplicates made as aforesaid of the vote of said State, in the presence and subject to the examination of all the Members from said State then present; and where there is more than one Representative from a State, the duplicates shall not both be deposited by the same person.

When the votes of the States are thus all taken in, the Sergeant-at-Arms shall carry one of said ballot boxes to one table and the other to a separate and distinct table.

One person from each State represented in the balloting shall be appointed by the Representatives to tell off said ballots; but, in case the Representatives fail to appoint a teller, the Speaker shall appoint.

The said tellers shall divide themselves into two sets, as nearly equal in number as can be, and one of the said sets of tellers shall proceed to count the votes in one of said boxes, and the other set the votes in the other box.

When the votes are counted by the different sets of tellers, the result shall be reported to the House; and if the reports agree, the same shall be accepted as the true votes of the States; but if the reports disagree, the States shall proceed, in the same manner as before, to a new ballot.

*Petitions are no longer introduced in this way. The old order of calling the states began with Maine and proceeded through the original thirteen states and then through the remaining states in the order of their admission to the Union.

6. All questions arising after the balloting commences, requiring the decision of the House, which shall be decided by the House, voting per capita, to be incidental to the power of choosing a President, shall be decided by States without debate; and in case of an equal division of the votes of States, the question shall be lost.

7. When either of the persons from whom the choice is to be made shall have received a majority of all the States, the Speaker shall declare the same, and that person is elected President of the United States.

8. The result shall be immediately communicated to the Senate by message, and a committee of three persons shall be appointed to inform the President of the United States and the President-elect of said election.

On February 9, 1825, the election of John Quincy Adams took place in accordance with these rules.

notes

Chapter 1

1. This fictionalized account of crisis in the 1996 electoral college is inspired in part by a classic short fantasy written early in the election year of 1968 by *New York Times* columnist Russell Baker, *Our Next President: The Incredible Story of What Happened in the 1968 Elections* (New York, 1968). All the quotations in this chapter are, of course, hypothetical. Two less plausible fictional accounts of events surrounding possible electoral college deadlock in 1968 and subsequent contingent activities in the House are Theodore G. Ventoulis, "1968: The Year No President Was Elected," in *The House Shall Choose* (Margate, N.J., 1968), pp. 154–77; and Sherwin Markman, *The Election* (New York, 1970). The latter novel includes a black insurrection in California complicating House deliberations on the presidency.

   The 1980 election spawned at least two similar fantasies: Daniel Rapoport, "The Scandinavian Connection," *National Journal*, May 10, 1980: 779; and Walter Shapiro, "The Anderson Crisis," *Washington Post Magazine*, June 1, 1980: 16–21. Each of these accounts envisioned the candidacy of John B. Anderson resulting in electoral college deadlock and subsequent electoral stalemate in the House.

   The leading 1992 fictionalized anticipation of electoral college deadlock and stymied efforts to elect a president in the House was Norman J. Ornstein, "Along Came Bill: Or How to Be Named Leader of the Western World in 1993," *New York Times Magazine*, May 24, 1992: 20–21, 36. In this account, Sen. Bill Bradley (D., N.J.), the Democratic vice presidential nominee, becomes president following presidential electoral paralysis in the House.

Chapter 2

1. John Dickinson, quoted in John P. Roche, "The Founding Fathers: A Reform Caucus in Action," *American Political Science Review* 55 (December 1961): 799. Roche describes the convention delegates as "first and foremost superb democratic politicians" who "*made* history and did it within the limits of consensus," and the convention itself as "a *nationalist* reform caucus which had to operate with great delicacy and skill in a political cosmos full of enemies to achieve the one definitive goal—popular approbation."

2. Richard C. Welty, "Who *Really* Elects Our Presidents?" *Midwest Quarterly* 2 (Autumn 1960): 23.

3. This first assessment of the probable consequences of a direct vote for the president seems reasonably accurate for this historical period. What was not anticipated, of course, was the later development of political parties able to popularize national contenders, inform the nation's electorate about them, and actively engage in aggregating support for candidates across state lines.

4. Charles A. O'Neil, *The American Electoral System* (New York, 1887), pp. 3–4, and J. Hampden Dougherty, *The Electoral System of the United States* (New York, 1906), p. 1.

5. Neal R. Peirce and Lawrence D. Longley, *The People's President: The Electoral College in American History and the Direct Vote Alternative,* rev. ed. (New Haven, 1981), p. 22.

6. The practical effect of this provision would be to retain the same state proportions as if the selection had been by a joint session of Congress, as had been proposed in the earlier congressional selection plan.

7. This change in the contingent procedure from the Senate to the House was due to fears that the Senate, which had already been given treaty ratification powers and advice and consent responsibilities, was accumulating too much authority in comparison with the House of Representatives.

8. Peirce and Longley, *People's President,* p. 28.

9. William T. Gossett, "Electing the President: New Hope for an Old Ideal," *American Bar Association Journal* 53 (December 1967): 1103.

10. Roche, "Founding Fathers," p. 811.

11. Felix Morley, "Democracy and the Electoral College," *Modern Age* 5 (Fall 1961): 377.

12. Roche, "Founding Fathers," p. 811.

13. James Madison, quoted in Peirce and Longley, *People's President,* p. 17.

14. John P. Feerick, "Electoral College: Why It Was Created," *American Bar Association Journal* 54 (March 1968): 254; and Peirce and Longley, *People's President.*

15. Feerick, "Electoral College," p. 255.

16. "The Electoral College," *Congressional Quarterly Guide to Current American Government,* Spring 1970: 141.

17. James A. Michener, *Presidential Lottery: The Reckless Gamble in Our Electoral System* (New York, 1969), p. 9.

18. These thirty-two states and the District of Columbia use what is called the *short ballot* for president, where the ballot lists only the presidential contenders, but not the electors. Three other states also use the short ballot in those areas with voting machines. Fourteen states retain the long ballot, listing both presidential candidates and electors. Alabama, uniquely, lists the names of electors, but leaves

it up to the voter to know to whom they are pledged—if at all. In 1960 five
Alabama Democratic electors were pledged to Kennedy, while six were
unpledged. In 1964 all Alabama electors under the Democratic column were
unpledged; no electors were pledged to the incumbent Democratic president,
Lyndon Johnson. League of Women Voters, *Who Should Elect the President?*
(Washington, D.C., 1969), p. 4.

19. Quoted in Peirce and Longley, *People's President*, p. 36. An interesting and more
eloquent echo of these sentiments was expressed by James Russell Lowell, a
Republican elector in Massachusetts in 1876, who was urged to switch his vote
from Hayes to Tilden in order to resolve the political uncertainties of that year.
He declined so to act, stressing that "it is a plain question of trust." Quoted in
ibid., p. 99.

20. Adapted and updated from ibid., p. 99. The faithless elector of 1956 was a particularly interesting case. As quoted in Chapter 4, when asked to explain his vote,
elector W. F. Turner justified his action by citing his duty to white people. Harry
L. Selden, "The Electoral College: Does It Choose the Best Man?" *American Heritage* 13 (October 1962): 142. In 1972 Roger MacBride, a Virginia Nixon elector,
cast an unexpected vote—for Libertarian party candidate John Hospers. Similarly, in 1976, Republican elector Mike Padden of the state of Washington
declined to vote for Republican nominee Gerald Ford, and instead voted for
Ronald Reagan. Finally, a West Virginia Democratic elector in 1988, for unex-
plained reasons, cast her *presidential* electoral vote for *vice presidential* nominee
Lloyd Bentsen and her *vice presidential* electoral vote for *presidential* candidate
Michael Dukakis.

21. See James C. Kirby, Jr., "Limitations on the Power of State Legislatures over Presidential Elections," *Law and Contemporary Problems* 27 (Spring 1962): 495–509.

22. For additional discussion of possible House election of the president, see Chap.
4—as well as the fable recounted in Chap. 1.

23. Peirce and Longley, *People's President*, pp. 44–47. The legislature chose presidential electors also, for a brief period, in the reconstructed state of Florida in
1868 and in the newly admitted state of Colorado in 1876. "The Electoral College," *Congressional Quarterly Guide to Current American Government*, Spring
1970: 141.

24. See Peirce and Longley, *People's President*, pp. 44–47. The district division of electoral votes had been common early in the nineteenth century but completely disappeared by 1836. It momentarily reappeared in Michigan for one election late
in the nineteenth century, for short-term partisan reasons.

As will be discussed in Chapter 4, Maine resurrected the district division of
electoral votes in 1969 through adoption of a plan, effective as of the presidential election of 1972, which determines two of Maine's four electoral votes on the

basis of the popular vote in its two congressional districts. Nebraska adopted a similar arrangement for its five electoral votes starting with the 1992 election. As of the 1996 presidential election, neither Maine nor Nebraska has, in fact, divided its bloc of four or five electoral votes.

Despite Maine's use of the district plan for over twenty years, in each of the presidential elections from 1972 to 1992, its state electoral vote has been unanimous because the candidate who carried the state popular vote also carried each of Maine's two congressional districts. Such was also the case in Nebraska in the presidential election of 1992: George Bush carried each of that state's three congressional districts while also soundly carrying the state.

In 1992, efforts were made in the legislatures of a number of states—most notably in the large state of Florida—to adopt a district division of electoral votes for the state. Ultimately, each such effort failed.

25. See ibid., pp. 41–44. The Twelfth Amendment, however, also provided that if a subsequent election were thrown into the House, the choice would be from the top three candidates rather than from the top five, as previously; that if by inauguration day no president had been selected, the new vice president would become president; that a vice president would need a majority of electoral votes (previously he only needed the second highest number); and that age, citizenship, and residency requirements would be the same for vice president as for president.

26. Ibid., p. 53.

27. Historian Eugene H. Roseboom writes that "fortune seemed to reserve her smiles for the Republicans during these years, but in this case asinine blundering by the Illinois Democrats would seem to be a more logical explanation." *A History of Presidential Elections* (New York, 1959), p. 247.

28. See Michener, *Presidential Lottery,* pp. 78–91, and Paul L. Haworth, *The Hayes-Tilden Disputed Election of 1876* (New York, 1966).

29. What House action might have been in 1825 had its widely revered and very powerful Speaker been among the candidates that could be considered is unknown but interesting speculation. Clay had only 13 percent of the popular vote, but institutional and personal loyalty among House members toward their Speaker might have been very potent.

30. Letter to George Hay, Aug. 17, 1823, in Paul L. Ford, ed., *The Works of Thomas Jefferson* (New York, 1905), vol. 12, p. 303.

Chapter 3

1. The terms *colleges of electors* and *electoral college* appeared first in congressional debates around 1800. They were first incorporated into legislation in 1845. J.

Hampden Dougherty, *The Electoral System of the United States* (New York, 1906), p. 74.

2. For more detailed background on the 1948 campaign, see Congressional Quarterly, *Congress and the Nation* (Washington, D.C., 1965), pp. 5–8; also Jules Abels, *Out of the Jaws of Victory* (New York, 1959).

3. Richard M. Scammon, "How Barkley Became President," *Northern Virginia Sun,* March 7, 1960.

4. For further background on the 1960 campaign, see Theodore H. White, *The Making of the President, 1960* (New York, 1961); also *Congress and the Nation,* pp. 32–39; and Lawrence D. Longley and Alan G. Braun, *The Politics of Electoral College Reform* (New Haven, 1972), chap. 1. The congressional apportionment in effect in 1960—consequently determining the electoral vote apportionment—was based on the 1950 census. As a result, the president chosen in 1960 to serve from 1961 to 1965 was selected by an electoral college apportioned according to population distributions already ten years old.

5. The commonly accepted practice in determining popular votes for president is to credit the candidate with the number of votes received by the highest-polling elector pledged to him in the state. For further discussion, see Chap. 4.

6. *Congressional Quarterly Weekly Report,* Feb. 17, 1961: 285–88. See also U.S. Congress, Senate Committee on the Judiciary, Subcommittee on Constitutional Amendments, *Hearings on Nomination and Election of President and Vice President and Qualifications for Voting,* 87th Cong., 1st sess., 1961, pp. 391–99 (hereafter cited as 1961 Senate *Hearings*).

7. *Chicago Tribune,* Nov. 14, 1960.

8. *New York Herald Tribune,* July 14, 1961.

9. In painstaking research into the 1960 Illinois vote more than two decades later, historian Edmund F. Kallina has found that although there was a widespread pattern of miscounted votes in Cook County in 1960 benefiting all Democratic candidates, the presidential campaign of John F. Kennedy benefited least from these efforts, which were focused more on local races. Further, Kallina concludes that the best estimate of "stolen" Democratic presidential votes, fewer than 8,000, is slightly less than the margin of 8,858 votes by which Kennedy carried the state, and thus there is insufficient evidence "to make a convincing case that Nixon was cheated out of Illinois' electoral votes." Edmund F. Kallina, "Was the 1960 Presidential Election Stolen? The Case of Illinois," *Presidential Studies Quarterly* 15 (1985): 113–18, quote from p. 113; and *Courthouse Over White House: Chicago and the Presidential Election of 1960* (Orlando, 1988).

10. *New York Times,* March 4, 1962.

11. Ibid., Dec. 11, 1960.

12. *Washington Evening Star,* Dec. 12, 1960.

13. Associated Press dispatch, Dec. 12, 1960.

14. 1961 Senate *Hearings*, p. 622.

15. For Irwin's testimony, which includes copies of his correspondence with other Republican electors and southern unpledged elector leaders, see 1961 Senate *Hearings*, pp. 562–655. One result of Henry Irwin's action was that Oklahoma, in 1961, passed the nation's most stringent law binding electors to oaths to support their party's nominees or face penalties up to a fine of $1,000. Such laws, however, are probably unconstitutional on the grounds that the Constitution provides for electors *voting*, which implies a freedom of action. See James C. Kirby, Jr., "Limitations on the Power of State Legislatures Over Presidential Elections," *Law and Contemporary Problems*, Spring 1962: 495–509.

16. The unpledged electors from Alabama and Mississippi had voted for Thurmond for vice president, while the bolting Republican elector from Oklahoma, Henry D. Irwin, had cast his vice presidential vote for Goldwater. See *Congressional Record*, Jan. 6, 1961: 291. For a journalistic account of the joint session, see *New York Times*, Jan. 7, 1961.

17. The following discussion draws upon material originally published in Longley and Braun, *Politics of Electoral College Reform*, pp. 7–17; and Neal R. Peirce, *The Deep South States of America* (New York, 1974), pp. 253–55.

18. This and the following three paragraphs are based on interviews and materials originally published in Peirce, *Deep South States*, pp. 254–55.

19. Sen. Birch Bayh, quoted in "The Electoral College," *Congressional Quarterly Guide to Current American Government*, Spring 1970: 144.

20. "Wallace Candidacy Raises Fears of Electoral Stalemate," *Congressional Quarterly Weekly Report*, July 19, 1968: 1818.

21. League of Women Voters of the United States, *Who Should Elect the President?* (Washington, D.C., 1969).

22. As we note below, Wallace's electoral vote was later increased by one and Nixon's decreased by a like amount by the actions of an individual Nixon elector.

23. An electoral college majority in 1968 was 270 votes out of a total of 538, while in 1960 it was 269 votes out of a total of 537. The reason for this change was that the total electoral college vote rose temporarily for the 1960 election to 537 to accommodate the new states of Alaska and Hawaii, while by 1968 the total electoral college vote had increased permanently to 538 electoral votes when the Twenty-third Amendment gave the District of Columbia 3 electoral votes.

24. The state break-downs were: 30,631 votes in New Jersey, 10,245 in Missouri, and 12,158 in New Hampshire. Based on "Final 1968 Presidential Election Results as Reported to *Congressional Quarterly* by the Governmental Affairs Institution," in Congressional Quarterly, *Politics in America*, 3d ed. (Washington, D.C., 1969), p. 127. This analysis is, of course, based solely on the actual November election

results. If one takes into account the later action of Nixon elector Dr. Lloyd W. Bailey in voting for Wallace, different results would apply, since only 32 rather than 33 electoral votes would have to shift. In this case, a shift of 41,971 votes from Nixon to Humphrey in New Jersey (30,631), Missouri (10,245), and Alaska (1,095) could have deadlocked the election.

25. Bailey's action gave rise to debate by both houses of Congress on Jan. 6, 1969, over a challenge to his vote by Sen. Edmund Muskie (D., Maine) and Rep. James G. O'Hara (D., Mich.), which was finally defeated. For detailed discussion, see Chap. 4; see also Congressional Quarterly, *Guide to Congress*, 2d ed. (Washington, D.C., 1976), pp. 240–41, and Congressional Quarterly, *Guide to U.S. Elections* (Washington, D.C., 1975), pp. 211–12.

26. Judson L. James, *American Political Parties: Potential and Performance* (New York, 1969), p. 52.

27. James A. Michener, *Presidential Lottery: The Reckless Gamble in Our Electoral System* (New York, 1969), pp. 16 and 56. Another plan, widely reported during the months before the election, had been advanced by Gary Orfield, an assistant professor of government at the University of Virginia, in an article in the *Washington Post* of July 7, 1968. The Orfield proposal, quickly adopted by Rep. (later Sen.) Charles E. Goodell (R., N.Y.) and Rep. Morris K. Udall (D., Ariz.), would have the leaders of both parties pledge that if the 1968 election resulted in an electoral college deadlock, they would provide sufficient House votes to elect whomever had been the popular vote winner. This plan, of course, could have been as easily implemented in the electoral college as in the House of Representatives. "Wallace Candidacy Raises Fears of Electoral Stalemate," p. 1820.

28. This potential tension actually appeared in a rather subtle form in the campaign statements of the two candidates about the possibility of electoral college deadlock. Humphrey stressed the need to follow the prescribed constitutional contingent procedure, while Nixon stated his belief that "whoever wins the popular vote should be the next President of the United States." Quoted in "The Electoral College," *Congressional Quarterly Guide to Current American Government*, Spring 1970: 144.

29. Among the nastiest rumors of the 1968 election was that if electoral college deadlock appeared imminent and if the new House appeared likely to elect Nixon, outgoing President Lyndon Johnson might reconvene the old Congress for the purpose of moving the meeting time of the new Congress back beyond January 6 so that the old Democratic Congress could choose the new president. This rumor never had any substance, but it illustrates both the suspicions generated by threatened deadlock and the frightening possibilities under the contingent proceedings.

30. "House Membership in the 91st Congress, 1st Session," *Congressional Quarterly Weekly Report,* Jan. 3, 1969: 38–39.

31. Much of this material is adapted from Longley and Braun, *Politics of Electoral College Reform,* pp. 15–17.

32. "Wallace Candidacy Raises Fears of Electoral Stalemate," pp. 1821–22.

33. "House Candidates Pledges," *Congressional Quarterly Weekly Report,* Oct. 25, 1968: 2956. The pledges were made as a result of widespread speculation that the election might go to the House and that in that case representatives would vote for the nominee of their party. For Democrats in districts that were expected to go to Nixon or Wallace, this was potentially a detrimental campaign issue. In order to protect themselves, candidates pledged to follow the mandate of their districts and to vote in the House for the winner of their districts, regardless of party affiliation.

34. Compiled from National Municipal League, *Apportionment in the Nineteen Sixties* (New York, 1967), n.p.; and Luman H. Long, ed., *World Almanac, 1969* (New York, 1968), pp. 907–8.

35. National Municipal League, *Apportionment,* and Long, *World Almanac, 1969,* pp. 907–8.

36. This incomplete analysis of possible voting alignments in the House following the 1968 presidential election highlights another aspect of the inequality of the contingent election scheme. One man, representing the 285,278 citizens of Nevada, would cast one-fiftieth of the vote for president. At the same time, had the Illinois, Maryland, Montana, and Oregon delegations voted along party lines, they would have been split and would have lost their vote; over 15 million people would, therefore, have been disenfranchised. This is in addition to the total and automatic disenfranchisement of the 700,000 residents of the District of Columbia.

37. For fascinating speculations about the possibilities inherent in the 1968 election as the House moves through successive ballots, see the political fantasies cited in Chap. 1, n. 1. One can carry this type of analysis on and on—for example, to show how a Democratic Senate might have had to choose for vice president between Spiro Agnew and Curtis Le May, if, as some September predictions had suggested, the Wallace–Le May ticket had run ahead, in electoral votes, of the Humphrey-Muskie ticket, thus becoming the second ticket and thereby excluding Senator Muskie from Senate consideration.

38. Some of the following analysis of the 1976 election is adapted from material originally appearing in Lawrence D. Longley, "Electoral College Reform: Problems, Politics, and Prospects," in *Paths to Political Reform,* ed. William J. Crotty (Lexington, Mass., 1980).

39. See "Testimony of Douglas Bailey," media manager of the Ford-Dole campaign, Aug. 2, 1977, in U.S. Congress, Senate Judiciary Committee, Subcommittee on the Constitution, *Hearings on Electoral College and Direct Election,* 95th Cong., 1st sess., July 20, 22, 28, and Aug. 2, 1977 (hereafter cited as July 1977 Senate *Hearings*), pp. 258–73, as well as the testimony at the same hearings by Sen. Robert Dole, who also stressed the campaign distortions created by the electoral college (pp. 26–40). See also "Impact of Direct Election on the Smaller States," in U.S. Congress, Senate Judiciary Committee, *Direct Popular Election of the President and Vice President of the United States,* December 1977 (hereafter cited as December 1977 Senate *Report*), pp. 14–16.

40. For a discussion of campaign resource allocation biases, see Claude S. Colantoni, Terrance J. Levesque, and Peter C. Ordeshook, "Campaign Resource Allocations Under the Electoral College," *American Political Science Review* 69 (March 1975): 141–54, and the discussion concerning this article in the same issue, pp. 155–61; Steven J. Brams and Morton D. Davis, "The 3/2s Rule in Presidential Campaigning," *American Political Science Review* 68 (March 1974): 113–34 (repr. in U.S. Congress, Senate Judiciary Committee, Subcommittee on the Constitution, *Hearings on the Electoral College and Direct Election,* 95th Cong. 1st sess., Jan. 27, Feb. 1, 2, 7, and 10, 1977 [hereafter cited as February 1977 Senate *Hearings*], pp. 515–37); Stephen J. Brams, *The Presidential Election Game* (New Haven, 1978), esp. chap. 3; and "Testimony of the Honorable Hubert H. Humphrey, U.S. Senator from the State of Minnesota," Jan. 27, 1977, in February 1977 Senate *Hearings,* p. 25.

41. The faithless elector of 1972 was Republican Roger Lea MacBride of Virginia, who deserted Republican nominee Richard Nixon to vote for Libertarian party candidate John Hospers, head of the School of Philosophy at the University of Southern California. Roger MacBride was the cocreator of the television series *The Little House on the Prairie* and also the author of an obscure book on the electoral college, *The Electoral College* (Caldwell, Idaho, 1953). His is the first known case of a writer about the electoral college creating a personal footnote in the history of the electoral college by being a faithless elector. MacBride went on to become the 1976 presidential candidate of the Libertarian party, receiving 173,019 votes in that year, including a noteworthy 5.5 percent of all votes cast for president in Alaska.

42. "Testimony of Honorable Robert Dole, U.S. Senator from the State of Kansas," February 1977 Senate *Hearings,* pp. 36–37. A *Washington Post* editorial commenting upon this Dole statement can be found reprinted in these same *Hearings,* pp. 114–15.

43. See ibid., p. 115.

44. This analysis assumes, of course, the nondefection of Republican elector Mike Padden of Washington. If he had nevertheless declined to vote for Ford, the election would have been inconclusive and would have gone to the House in January 1977.

45. The fourteen states were Alabama, Arkansas, Connecticut, Delaware, Kentucky, Maine, Massachusetts, Michigan, Mississippi, New York, North Carolina, Tennessee, Vermont, and Wisconsin.

46. *Newsweek*, Nov. 10, 1980.

47. Congressional Quarterly, *Guide to U.S. Elections*, 3d ed. (Washington, D.C., 1994), p. 336.

48. Michael Duffy, "The 34% Solution," *Time* 139 (June 1, 1992). For other contemporary reflections on the implications of a three-way division of the presidential vote, see Guy Gugliotta, "Three-Way House Race Could Greatly Complicate Electoral Process," *Washington Post*, May 18, 1992: A19; Norman J. Ornstein, "Along Came Bill: Or How to Be Named Leader of the Western World in 1993," *New York Times Magazine*, May 24, 1992: 20–21, 36; Rhodes Cook, "Perot Positioned to Defy a Past Seemingly Carved in Stone," *Congressional Quarterly Weekly Report*, June 13, 1992: 1721; Lloyd Cutler, "Electoral College Drama," *Washington Post*, June 22, 1992: A17; Mark A. Siegel, "Don't Steal the People's Vote," *Washington Post*, June 22, 1992: A17; R. W. Apple, "Close Three-Way Race Holds Opportunities for Clinton," *New York Times*, June 23, 1992: A18; Maggie Mahar, "Suppose It's None of the Above: What Happens If No Candidate Is Elected?" *Barron's*, July 6, 1992: 18; and Guy Gugliotta, "Losers Could Become Kingmakers After a Three-Way Race for President," *Washington Post*, July 15, 1992: A17.

49. Later in the campaign, these concerns about elector loyalty were a special concern of the Perot campaign because of its off-and-on-again character. See Timothy Noah, "Perot Could Face Hurdle of Reversals in Electoral College: Some Electors No Longer Back Texan, Threaten Attempt to Give His Race Meaning," *Wall Street Journal*, Oct. 28, 1992.

50. Thomas Galvin, "House Warily Dusts off Rules on Choosing a President," *Congressional Quarterly Weekly Report*, May 23, 1992: 1420.

51. Examples of the memoranda and fact sheets being carefully studied around the Capitol during the spring of 1992 were two analyses originally prepared in the context of John Anderson's independent campaign of 1980: Congressional Research Service, American Law Division, "Majority or Plurality Vote Within State Delegations When House of Representatives Votes for the President," June 10, 1980; and Rep. Martin Frost, "Election of the President in the House of Representatives," unpublished memorandum to Richard Bolling, chairman, House Rules Committee, July 1, 1980.

52. Congressional reaction is reported in Tim Curran and Susan B. Glasser, "Members Sigh in Relief as Perot Quits the Race: Excruciating January Vote by Full House Avoided," *Roll Call—The Newspaper of Capitol Hill,* July 20, 1992.

53. Congressional Quarterly, *Guide to U.S. Elections,* p. 338.

54. The lowest national popular vote to produce an outright electoral vote majority was the 1860 electoral college majority of Abraham Lincoln based on only 39.8 percent of the popular vote in a four-way contest. The next lowest was three-way 1912 electoral victory by Woodrow Wilson based on 41.9 percent of the popular vote. Clinton's 1992 magnification of electoral votes over his popular votes was a relatively high 26 percentage points. (See Chap. 5 for further discussion of electoral college magnification.)

55. For additional discussion of the problems of the electoral college in the 1992 election, see "Prepared Statement of Lawrence D. Longley," U.S. Senate Judiciary Committee, Subcommittee on the Constitution, *Hearings on the Electoral College and Direct Election of the President,* 102d Cong., 2d sess., July 22, 1992, pp. 29–76; as well as the other statements in this, the most recent general congressional examination of the electoral college.

56. *The Federalist* (Modern Library, 2d ed.), p. 441.

Chapter 4

1. Carl Becker, "The Will of the People," *Yale Review,* March 1945: 389, 399.

2. For comprehensive background on political conventions, see Paul T. David, Ralph M. Goldman, and Richard C. Bain, *The Politics of National Party Conventions* (Washington, D.C., 1960). Excellent overviews of the presidential selection process that include insightful analyses of the national conventions are provided in Nelson W. Polsby and Aaron B. Wildavsky, *Presidential Elections: Strategies and Structures of American Politics,* 9th ed. (Chatham, N.J., 1996); and Stephen J. Wayne, *The Road to the White House, 1996* (New York, 1996).

3. For data on congressional apportionment procedures and patterns, see Congressional Quarterly, *Representation and Apportionment* (Washington, D.C., 1966), pp. 51–61; Congressional Quarterly, *Guide to U.S. Elections,* 3d ed. (Washington, D.C., 1994); and Floyd M. Riddick, *The United States Congress: Organization and Procedure* (Manassas, Va., 1948), pp. 6–10.

4. 481 U.S. 1 (1892).

5. U.S. Congress, *Register of Debates,* vol. 2, p. 1405, cited by Lucius Wilmerding, *The Electoral College* (New Brunswick, N.J., 1958), p. 43.

6. *Ex parte Yarbrough,* 110 U.S. 651 (1884); *Burroughs and Cannon v. United States,* 290 U.S. 534 (1934).

7. See James C. Kirby, Jr., "Limitations on the Power of State Legislatures Over Presidential Elections," *Law and Contemporary Problems,* Spring 1962: 497–504.

8. Senate Report No. 22, 19th Cong., 1st sess., Jan. 19, 1826 (hereafter cited as 1826 Senate *Report*), p. 4.

9. Wilmerding, *Electoral College,* p. 175.

10. U.S. Congress, Senate, Committee on the Judiciary, Subcommittee on Constitutional Amendments, *Hearings, Nomination and Election of President and Vice President and Qualifications for Voting,* 87th Cong., 1st sess., 1961, p. 546 (hereafter cited as 1961 Senate *Hearings*).

11. James A. Michener, *Presidential Lottery: The Reckless Gamble in Our Electoral System* (New York, 1969), p. 9.

12. Robert G. Dixon, Jr., "Electoral College Procedure," *Western Political Quarterly,* June 1950: 216.

13. The Congress apparently refrained from setting a specific date for two reasons: because it would be inconvenient for state legislatures that might choose the electors themselves and would need more than a single day to complete their debates and action, and because states' rights advocates said Congress should not place unnecessary restrictions on the states. See Charles A. O'Neil, *The American Electoral System* (New York, 1887), pp. 41–43.

14. Ibid., pp. 43–44.

15. J. Hampden Dougherty, *The Electoral System of the United States* (New York, 1906), pp. 392–93.

16. Dixon, "Electoral College Procedure," p. 217.

17. "The Electoral College: Operation and Effect of Proposed Amendments," memorandum prepared by the staff of the Senate Judiciary Committee, Subcommittee on Constitutional Amendments, Oct. 10, 1961, p. 16 (hereafter cited as 1961 Senate Committee *Memorandum*).

18. Dixon, "Electoral College Procedure," p. 217. Other instances where close votes resulted in election of split elector slates: North Dakota in 1892 (1 Republican, 2 Democratic electors); Maryland in 1908 (2 Republican, 6 Democratic); Ohio in 1892 (22 Republican, 1 Democratic); West Virginia in 1916 (7 Republican, 1 Democratic); California in 1880 (5 Republican, 1 Democratic); California in 1892 (8 Democratic, 1 Republican). See Wilmerding, *Electoral College,* p. 74.

19. O'Neil, *American Electoral System,* p. 48.

20. Wilmerding, *Electoral College,* p. 174.

21. Cited by O'Neil, *American Electoral System,* p. 56.

22. 1826 Senate *Report,* p. 4.

23. Cited by Dougherty, *Electoral System of the United States,* p. 250.

24. Ibid., p. 251.

25. Justice Jackson's inspiration obviously came from a song by Sir Joseph Porter and the chorus in act 1 of Gilbert and Sullivan's *H.M.S. Pinafore*: "I grew so rich that I was sent / By a pocket borough into Parliament. / I always voted at my party's call, / And I never thought of thinking for myself at all."

26. *Ray v. Blair*, 343 U.S. 214 (1952).

27. *Rotarian Magazine*, July 1949.

28. 1826 Senate *Report*, p. 5.

29. Cited by Edward D. Corwin, *The President: Office and Powers* (New York, 1957), p. 41.

30. Everett S. Brown, *William Plumer's Memorandum of Proceedings in the United States Senate* (New York, 1932), p. vii, cited by Wilmerding, *Electoral College*, p. 176.

31. John Bach McMaster, *A History of the People of the United States From the Revolution to the Civil War*, 8 vols. (New York, 1893–1924), vol. 5, pp. 74–75; A. R. Newsome, *The Presidential Election of 1824 in South Carolina* (Chapel Hill, N.C., 1939), chap. 8, cited in Wilmerding, *Electoral College*, pp. 177–78.

32. Wilmerding, *Electoral College*, pp. 178–79.

33. *New York Times*, Dec. 18, 1956.

34. 1961 Senate *Hearings*, pp. 445–46, 634. The television program, a transcript of which was printed in the *Hearings*, was a *CBS Reports* program of Jan. 5, 1961.

35. Letter from Lowell to Leslie Stephen, quoted in Horace Elisha Schudder, *James Russell Lowell* (Boston, 1901), vol. 1, p. 217.

36. 1961 Senate *Hearings*, p. 446 (in transcript of *CBS Reports* program).

37. Robert L. Tienken, *Proposals to Reform Our Electoral System*, Legislative Reference Service, Library of Congress (Washington, D.C., 1966), pp. 9–11 (hereafter cited as 1966 LRS *Report*).

38. Source for 1948 example: U.S. Congress, House Committee on the Judiciary Subcommittee No. 5, *Hearings, Amending the Constitution with Respect to Election of President and Vice President*, 81st Cong., 1st sess., 1949, p. 148 (hereafter cited as 1949 House *Hearings*). Source for 1972 example: presidential campaign involvement of one of this book's authors. Source for 1992 example: Timothy Noah, "Perot Could Face Hurdle of Reversals in Electoral College: Some Electors No Longer Back Texan, Threaten Attempt to Give His Race Meaning," *Wall Street Journal*, Oct. 28, 1992. Source for 1980 example: Anderson presidential campaign management role of one of this book's authors.

39. The fifteen states (and the District of Columbia) that as of 1966 required electors by law to vote for their party's presidential candidate: Alaska, California, Connecticut, Colorado, Florida, Hawaii, Idaho, Maryland, Nevada, New Mexico, New York, Oklahoma, Oregon, Tennessee, Virginia, and the District of Columbia. See 1966 LRS *Report*, pp. 13–17.

40. *Ray v. Blair* (1952); see also "Presidential Electors," *Columbia Law Review*, April 1965: 606.

41. Kirby, "Limitations on the Power of State Legislatures," p. 509.

42. Before the 1964 election, substantial efforts were made to open the way for unpledged-elector slates in Florida, South Carolina, Virginia, and Georgia, in addition to Alabama and Mississippi. In each case, an attempt was made to get the legislature, or party committees if they had sufficient authority under state law, to authorize unpledged states. Democrats loyal to the national party, however, were able to thwart most of these moves. In the case of Florida, President Kennedy reportedly made a personal telephone call to the Florida House Speaker to prevent passage of enabling legislation for independent electors. (See *Congressional Quarterly Weekly Report*, June 14, 1963: 969, and Sept. 13, 1963: 1572.) Alabama governor George C. Wallace announced on July 4, 1964, that he had "definite, concrete plans" to run for president in sixteen states: Alabama, Arkansas, Florida, Georgia, Illinois, Indiana, Kentucky, Louisiana, Mississippi, Missouri, New York, North Carolina, South Carolina, Tennessee, Virginia, and Wisconsin. But he withdrew on July 19, four days after Goldwater's nomination. (See *Congressional Quarterly Weekly Report*, July 17, 1964: 1499, and July 24, 1964: 1547.) For further background on the 1960 effort, see *Congressional Quarterly Weekly Report*, April 1, 1960: 569; and 1961 Senate *Hearings*, pp. 562 ff., especially pp. 622–25, describing plans to mobilize independent electors for subsequent elections.

43. Rufus King in 1824. See *Annals of Congress*, 18th Cong., 1st sess., I, p. 355.

44. Dougherty, *Electoral System of the United States*, p. 226.

45. See U.S. Code, Title 3, chap. 1, which establishes statutory provisions regarding the meeting of electors. This is reprinted in Appendix E at the back of this book.

46. Dixon, "Electoral College Procedure," pp. 218–19.

47. *Ann Arbor News*, Dec. 14, 1948, cited in *Congressional Record*, April 13, 1949: 4449.

48. Dixon, "Electoral College Procedure," p. 220.

49. Cited in ibid., p. 221. Using the 1948 Ohio electoral college as an example, Dixon listed the array of political processes and paraphernalia at times involved in electoral college proceedings: (1) opening of the session with the secretary of state presiding; (2) calling of the roll to ascertain if a quorum is present; (3) prayer; (4) election of a temporary chairman; (5) calling of the official roll and swearing in of members (the point at which vacancies are filled, if necessary); (6) oral statement by governor of electors' duties; (7) appointment of four committees—rules and order of business, permanent organization, mileage and per diem, and resolutions; (8) recess for lunch; (9) reconvening, report of committee on permanent organization, and election of permanent chairman and of the secretary of

state as the ex officio secretary of the college; (10) address by the permanent chairman; (11) reports of committees on rules and order of business, on mileage and per diem, and on resolutions; (12) casting and counting of ballots for president and vice president of the United States; (13) signing of the requisite certificates of votes and establishing provisions for their disposition; (14) authorizing printing the proceedings of the college; (15) reading a letter regarding a dinner planned in Washington for members of all the electoral colleges in the various states, to take place on the eve of the inauguration; and, finally, (16) adjournment (pp. 219–20).

50. See Lawrence D. Longley, "Why the Electoral College Should Be Abolished," speech to the 1976 electoral college, Madison, Wis., Dec. 13, 1976. In 1988 the Wisconsin electoral college voted overwhelmingly to adopt a similar resolution: "Resolved: That the 1988 Wisconsin Presidential Electoral College goes on record as calling upon Congress to act to abolish the Electoral College—including the office of Elector; The U.S. President instead should and must be elected directly and equitably by a vote of the American people."

51. Dixon, "Electoral College Procedure," pp. 220–21.

52. James Cheetham to Thomas Jefferson, Dec. 10, 1801, in *Proceedings of the Massachusetts Historical Society*, 3d ser., vol. 1, p. 47; cited by Wilmerding, *Electoral College*, p. 183.

53. William Purcell, cited by Dougherty, *Electoral System of the United States*, p. 253.

54. See U.S. Code, Title 3, chap. 1, repr. in Appendix E above; see also Dixon, "Electoral College Procedure," p. 222.

55. David A. McKnight, *The Electoral System of the United States* (Philadelphia, 1878), p. 15.

56. Dougherty, *Electoral System of the United States*, pp. 51–57 and 86–87; 1949 House *Hearings*, p. 15.

57. The congressional debates on the challenge to Dr. Bailey's electoral vote are summarized in *Congressional Quarterly Weekly Report*, Jan. 10, 1969: 54–55; the House and Senate roll call votes can be found on p. 49. A useful summary of these events can be found in Congressional Quarterly, *Guide to Congress*, 2d ed. (Washington, D.C., 1976), pp. 8–9. Congressional reform efforts of the 1960s and 1970s are analyzed in Neal R. Peirce and Lawrence D. Longley, *The People's President: The Electoral College in American History and the Direct Vote Alternative*, rev. ed. (New Haven, 1981), chap. 7.

58. Cited by John B. Andrews, "Should the President Be Elected by Direct Popular Vote? Yes!" *Forum*, October 1949: 231.

59. Cited by Dougherty, *Electoral System of the United States*, pp. 23–24.

60. Paul J. Piccard, "The Resolution of Electoral Deadlocks by the House of Representatives," in *Selecting the President: The Twenty-seventh Discussion and Debate*

Manual (1953–54), vol. 1, repr. in 1961 Senate *Hearings,* pp. 826–43. See also the excellent summary discussion of the power of Congress to elect the president in the Congressional Quarterly's *Guide to Congress,* pp. 5–7.

61. Sidney Hyman, *The American President* (New York, 1954), p. 145; Wilmerding, *Electoral College,* p. 209.

62. Edward Stanwood, *A History of the Presidency from 1788 to 1897* (Boston, 1898), pp. 187–88.

63. For a recent examination of issues arising in the case of the death of a presidential candidate or president-elect, see U.S. Congress, Senate Judiciary Committee, Subcommittee on the Constitution, *Hearings on Presidential Succession Between the Popular Election and the Inauguration,* 103d Cong., 2d sess., Feb. 2, 1994 (cited as the February 1994 Senate *Hearings*). Included in these *Hearings* (pp. 43–46) is an overview document, "Prepared Statement of Lawrence D. Longley on Presidential Candidate and President-Elect Death, Disability, or Resignation," from which this section is adapted.

64. John D. Feerick, *From Failing Hands: The Story of Presidential Succession* (New York, 1965), pp. 271–72 and 324–25.

65. Ibid., pp. 161 and 271.

66. Ibid., pp. 271–72.

67. Corwin, *President,* pp. 339–40; Stanwood, *History of the Presidency,* pp. 353–54.

68. Feerick, *From Failing Hands,* p. 274. The 1873 precedent, in which Congress refused to count the Greeley votes, would not be binding because Greeley was already dead when the electors cast their votes.

69. For further background, see *Congressional Quarterly Weekly Report,* Nov. 18, 1960: 1901.

70. 1961 Senate *Hearings,* pp. 1–2.

Chapter 5

1. In an attempt to show that voters in population-heavy states have inordinate power in presidential elections, the Committee on Electoral College Reform of the American Good Government Society and Sen. Karl Mundt (R., S.Dak.) some years ago advanced a curious method of computing "votes" as opposed to "voters." In the 1960 election, for instance, they claimed that the 7,290,823 voters in New York State actually cast an astronomical 328,000,000 "votes" for president, since each voter chose 45 presidential electors. The 60,762 voters of Alaska similarly were claimed to have cast "only" 182,286 votes, since each Alaskan voter chose only 3 presidential electors.

This remarkable way of counting may be an interesting mathematical game, but it is no substitute for serious analysis. The method overlooks the fundamental fact that the number of voters per electoral vote is actually much less in Alaska (where there were at the time 20,254 voters for each electoral vote) than in New York (where there were 162,018 voters per electoral vote). This is a situation that arises, of course, from the two "extra" votes corresponding to each state's two senators, which effectively gives individual voters in smaller states greater proportionate power per electoral vote than their counterparts in more populous states. Therefore, the fact that New Yorkers in 1960 voted for 45 electors, while Alaskans voted for only 3, is more than overbalanced by the electoral vote/population disparity between the two states—and this in turn (as we shall see) is itself far outweighed by the consequences of the general winner-take-all determination of each state's bloc of electoral votes.

2. In the nineteenth century a few states averaged the number of votes received by the various members of an electoral slate, rather than taking the highest electoral vote. This practice has been discontinued. The only difficulty in the prevailing method arises in rare instances, like that of Alabama in 1960, when the members of the same electoral slate in a particular state favor different candidates (see Chap. 3).

3. One calculation shows that in the eleven presidential elections from 1908 through 1948, a total of 372 million votes were cast for president, but 163 million (44 percent) of these votes were cast by supporters of losing candidates in various states who failed to see a single electoral vote cast representing their votes. Figures presented by former Rep. Clarence F. Lea of California in U.S. Congress, House, Committee on the Judiciary, Subcommittee No. 5, *Hearings on Amending the Constitution with Respect to Election of President and Vice President*, 81st Cong., 1st sess., 1949, p. 28 (hereafter cited as 1949 House *Hearings*).

4. Similarly, in the neighboring states of Illinois and Indiana in 1960, Nixon won a total of 3,554,108 votes to Kennedy's 3,330,204. But Kennedy narrowly won Illinois, thus receiving its 27 electoral votes, while Nixon won a strong victory in Indiana, bringing him 13 electoral votes. Thus the two-state electoral vote was 27 for Kennedy, 13 for Nixon—or 67.5 percent of the electors for Kennedy, based on only 48.4 percent of the two-state popular vote total. In the adjoining states of Maryland and Virginia in the same election, the discrimination worked the other way. Kennedy won 50.9 percent of the two-state popular vote but received only 43 percent of the two states' electoral votes because he won by a large majority in Maryland (with 9 electoral votes) but lost by a smaller margin in Virginia (with 12 electoral votes). See plaintiff's complaint in *Delaware v. New York*, a legal challenge to the general ticket system filed in the U.S. Supreme Court in 1966; quoted in *Congressional Quarterly Weekly Report*, Aug. 19, 1966: 1812.

5. J. Hampden Dougherty, *The Electoral System of the United States* (New York, 1906), p. 73.

6. U.S. Congress, Senate, Committee on the Judiciary, Subcommittee on Constitutional Amendments, *Hearings on Nomination and Election of President and Vice President and Qualifications for Voting,* 87th Cong., 1st sess., 1961, p. 670.

7. See "The Electoral College: Operation and Effect of Proposed Amendments," memorandum prepared by the staff of the Senate Judiciary Committee, Subcommittee on Constitutional Amendments, Oct. 10, 1961; see also fact sheet on voting participation, *Congressional Quarterly Weekly Report,* Sept. 18, 1964: 2181.

8. Adapted from material presented by C. S. Potts, Dean Emeritus, Southern Methodist University, 1949 House *Hearings,* p. 181.

9. For further discussions of partisan biases in the electoral college, see Michael C. Nelson, "Partisan Bias in the Electoral College, *Journal of Politics* 37 (November 1974): 1033–48; Carleton W. Sterling, "The Electoral College Biases Revealed, The Conventional Wisdom and Game Theory Models Notwithstanding," *Western Political Quarterly* 31 (June 1978): 159–77, also in July 1977 Senate *Hearings,* pp. 432–54; and other studies cited in the Select Bibliography.

10. The following discussion is based on Lawrence D. Longley and James D. Dana, Jr., "The Electoral College's Biases in the 1992 Election—and Beyond," paper delivered at the Annual Meeting of the American Political Science Association, Sept. 3–6, 1992; "The Biases of the Electoral College in the 1990s," *Polity* 25, no. 1 (Fall 1992): 123–45; and "The Electoral College's Biases in the 1992 Election— and Beyond," U.S. Congress, Senate, Committee on the Judiciary, Subcommittee on the Constitution, *Hearings on the Electoral College and Direct Election of the President,* 102d Cong., 2d sess., July 22, 1992, pp. 38–76. These 1992 studies also draw upon earlier research reported in Longley and Dana, "New Empirical Estimates of the Biases of the Electoral College for the 1980s," *Western Political Quarterly* 37 (March 1984): 157–75; Lawrence D. Longley, "Electoral College Reform: Problems, Politics, and Prospects," in *Paths to Political Reform,* ed. William J. Crotty (Lexington, Mass., 1980); John H. Yunker and Lawrence D. Longley, "The Biases of the Electoral College: Who Is Really Advantaged?" in *Perspectives on Presidential Selection,* ed. Donald R. Matthews (Washington, D.C., 1973); and John H. Yunker and Lawrence D. Longley, *The Electoral College: Its Biases Newly Measured for the 1960s and 1970s,* Sage Professional Papers in American Politics (Beverly Hills, Calif., 1976). This last work contains the most complete statement of the methodology followed.

11. See works cited in the Select Bibliography. See also Lawrence D. Longley and Alan G. Braun, *The Politics of Electoral College Reform,* 2d ed., (New Haven, 1975), pp. 121–28; Yunker and Longley, "Biases of the Electoral College," pp. 190–95; Lawrence D. Longley and John H. Yunker, "The Changing Biases of the Electoral

College," paper delivered at the Annual Meeting of the American Political Science Association, New Orleans, La., Sept. 4–8, 1973, also in U.S. Congress, Senate, Judiciary Committee, Subcommittee on Constitutional Amendments, *Hearings on Electoral College Reform*, 93d Cong., 1st sess., Sept. 26–27, 1973, pp. 187–212; and Yunker and Longley, *Electoral College*, pp. 31–44. This literature is subject to a very thoughtful and complete critique in William R. Keech, "Background Paper," in *Winner Take All: Report of the Twentieth Century Fund Task Force on Reform of the Presidential Election Process* (New York, 1978), chap. 2.

12. Longley and Dana, "Electoral College's Biases," "Biases of the Electoral College," and "New Empirical Estimates"; Longley and Braun, *Politics of Electoral College Reform*, p. 115; Yunker and Longley, "Biases of the Electoral College," p. 182; Longley and Yunker, "Changing Biases of the Electoral College," pp. 189–200; Yunker and Longley, *Electoral College*, pp. 9–21.

13. Longley and Dana, "Electoral College's Biases" and "New Empirical Estimates of the Biases of the Electoral College"; Longley and Yunker, "Changing Biases of the Electoral College," p. 193; Yunker and Longley, *Electoral College*, p. 13.

14. See discussions in Longley, "Electoral College Reform;" Peirce and Longley, *People's President*, esp. chaps. 5 and 8; and Longley, "Electoral College and Minorities."

15. For discussion and analysis of this hypothesis and the conventional wisdom surrounding it, see Longley and Yunker, "Who Is Really Advantaged by the Electoral College?" pp. 3–7; and Longley and Braun, *Politics of Electoral College Reform*, pp. 96–103.

16. Much of the following discussion was originally prepared by John H. Yunker of the University of Minnesota for the Senate Judiciary Committee, and can be found on pp. 498–500 of U.S. Congress, Senate, Judiciary Committee, Subcommittee on the Constitution, *Hearings on the Electoral College and Direct Election*, 95th Cong., 1st sess., Jan. 27, Feb. 1, 2, 7, and 10, 1977. Appreciation is expressed to John H. Yunker for permission to use this analysis here.

For further discussion of the controversy concerning the voting power of blacks under the electoral college and direct election system, see the December 1977 Senate *Report*, especially "Racial and Minority Group Voting Power Under the Electoral College and Direct Election Systems," pp. 20–23; Lawrence D. Longley, "Minorities and the 1980 Electoral College," paper delivered at the Annual Meeting of the American Political Science Association, Washington, D.C., Aug. 28–31, 1980; and Longley, "The Electoral College and the Representation of Minorities: Myths and Realities," in *The President and the Public*, ed. Doris A. Graber (Philadelphia, 1982).

select bibliography

Recent Major Senate Documents on the Electoral College

U.S. Congress, Senate, Judiciary Committee, *Hearings on the Electoral College and Direct Election,* 95th Cong., 1st sess., Jan. 27, Feb. 1, 2, 7, and 10, 1977 (cited as the February 1977 Senate *Hearings*).

U.S. Congress, Senate, Judiciary Committee, Subcommittee on the Constitution, *Hearings on the Electoral College and Direct Election,* 95th Cong., 1st sess., July 20, 22, and 28 and Aug. 2, 1977 (cited as the July 1977 Senate *Hearings*).

U.S. Congress, Senate, Judiciary Committee, *Direct Popular Election of the President and Vice President of the United States,* December 1977 (cited as the December 1977 Senate *Report*).

U.S. Congress, Senate, Judiciary Committee, Subcommittee on the Constitution, *Hearings on Direct Popular Election of the President and Vice President of the United States,* 96th Cong., 1st sess., March 27 and 30 and April 3 and 9, 1979 (cited as the 1979 Senate *Hearings*).

U.S. Congress, Senate, Judiciary Committee, *Direct Popular Election of the President and Vice President of the United States,* 1979 (cited as the 1979 Senate *Report*).

U.S. Congress, Senate, Judiciary Committee, Subcommittee on the Constitution, *Hearings on the Electoral College and Direct Election of the President,* 102d Cong., 2d sess., July 22, 1992 (cited as the July 1992 Senate *Hearings*).

U.S. Congress, Senate, Judiciary Committee, Subcommittee on the Constitution, *Hearings on Presidential Succession Between the Popular Election and the Inauguration,* 103d Cong., 2d sess., Feb. 2, 1994 (cited as the February 1994 Senate *Hearings*).

Recent Research and Articles on the Electoral College

Abbott, David W., and James P. Levine. *Wrong Winner: The Coming Debacle in the Electoral College.* New York: Praeger, 1991.

Amar, Akhil Reed, and Vik Amar. "Split Decision." *Washington Monthly* 24 (November 1992): 22–23.

———. "President Quayle." *Virginia Law Review* 78 (1992): 913ff.

Anglim, Christopher. "A Selective, Annotated Bibliography on the Electoral College: Its Creation, History, and Prospects for Reform." *Law Library Journal* 85, no. 2 (1993): 297–327.

Archer, J. Clark, Fred M. Shelly, Peter J. Taylor, and Ellen R. White. "The Geographic Cleavages Divide the Electorate: They Weigh Heavily in the Electoral College System and Demand That a Winning Candidate Build a Geographic Coalition." *Scientific American* 259 (July 1988): 44.

Arrington, Theodore S., and Saul Brenner. "The Advantages of a Plurality Election of the President." *Presidential Studies Quarterly* 10 (Summer 1980): 476–82.

———. "Electoral College Misrepresentation: A Geometric Analysis." *Polity* 13 (Spring 1981): 425–49.

Ball, William J., and David A. Leuthold. "Estimating the Likelihood of an Unpopular Verdict in the Electoral College." *Public Choice* 70 (1991): 215–24.

Barnes, Fred. "College Counseling." *New Republic,* July 18, 1988: 13.

Bartels, Larry M. "Resource Allocation in a Presidential Campaign." *Journal of Politics* 47 (August 1985): 928–36.

Bates, Stephen. "How Dukakis Can Still Be President, and You Thought Dan Quayle Was Next in Line." *Washington Monthly* 20 (December 1988): 34.

Berns, Walter, ed. *After the People Vote: A Guide to the Electoral College,* revised and enlarged edition. Washington, D.C.: American Enterprise Institute, 1992.

Best, Judith. *The Case Against Direct Election of the President.* Ithaca: Cornell University Press, 1975. Chaps. 1 and 7 can also be found in the July 1977 Senate *Hearings,* pp. 65–113. Chap. 3 can be found in the 1979 Senate *Hearings,* pp. 264–305.

———. "The Case For the Electoral College." Paper delivered at the Annual Meeting of the American Political Science Association, Sept. 1–4, 1977, Washington, D.C. Also in the July 1977 Senate *Hearings,* pp. 56–64.

———. *The Choice of the People? Debating the Electoral College.* Lanham, Md.: Rowman and Littlefield, 1996.

Blair, Douglas H. "Electoral College Reform and the Distribution of Voting Power." The Wharton School Department of Economics, Discussion Paper no. 362. Repr. in the February 1977 Senate *Hearings,* pp. 503–14.

Brams, Steven J. *Game Theory and Politics.* New York: Free Press, 1975, esp. pp. 191–92 and 243–78.

———. "How the Presidential Candidates Run the Final Stretch." In the February 1977 Senate *Hearings,* pp. 538–40.

———. "Bias in the Electoral College." In the February 1977 Senate *Hearings,* pp. 540–42.

———. *The Presidential Election Game.* New Haven: Yale University Press, 1978, esp. chap. 3, "The General Election: How to Run the Final Stretch." This section can also be found in the 1979 Senate *Hearings,* pp. 477–531.

———. "Resource Allocation in the 1976 Campaign." In the 1979 Senate *Hearings,* pp. 455–62.

Brams, Steven J., and Paul J. Affuso. "Power and Size: A New Paradox." *Theory and Decision* 7 (1976): 29–56.

Brams, Steven J., and Morton D. Davis. "Resource-allocation Models in Presidential Campaigning: Implications for Democratic Representation." *Annals of New York Academy of Sciences* 219 (1973): 105–23.

———. "The 3/2s Rule in Presidential Campaigning." *American Political Science Review* 68 (March 1974): 113–34. Repr. in the February 1977 Senate *Hearings*, pp. 515–37.

Brams, Steven J., and Peter C. Fishburn. "Approval Voting." Paper delivered at the Annual Meeting of the American Political Science Association, Sept. 1–4, 1977, Washington, D.C. Also in *American Political Science Review* 73 (September 1978): 831–47.

Brams, Steven J., and Mark Lake. "Power and Satisfaction in a Representative Democracy." Paper prepared for delivery at the Conference on Game Theory and Political Science, July 10–17, 1977, Hyannis, Mass. Also in *Game Theory and Political Science,* ed. Peter C. Ordeshook. New York: New York University Press, 1978.

Breckenridge, Adam C. *Electing the President.* Washington, D.C.: University Press of America, 1982.

Colantoni, Claude S., Terrence J. Levesque, and Peter C. Ordeshook. "Campaign Resource Allocations Under the Electoral College." *American Political Science Review* 69 (March 1975): 141–54. "Comment" by Brams and Davis, pp. 155–56. "Rejoinder" by Colantoni, Levesque and Ordeshook, pp. 157–61.

Congressional Research Service, American Law Division. "Majority or Plurality Vote Within State Delegations When House of Representatives Votes for the President." Washington, D.C.: Congressional Research Service, June 10, 1980.

Cook, Rhodes. "Assault on Two-Party System May Find Toehold in '96." *Congressional Quarterly Weekly Report,* Sept. 9, 1995: 2735–41.

———. "In Surprise Move, Perot to Launch Third Party." *Congressional Quarterly Weekly Report,* Sept. 30, 1995: 3022–24.

Cronin, Thomas. "Choosing a President." *Center Magazine,* September–October 1978: 5–15.

———. "The Direct Vote and the Electoral College: The Case for Messing Things Up!" Paper delivered at the Center for the Study of Democratic Institutions, June 26, 1978, Santa Barbara, Calif. Also in *Presidential Studies Quarterly* 9 (Spring 1979): 144–63.

———. "The Electoral College Controversy." In Judith A. Best. *The Choice of the People? Debating the Electoral College.* Lanham, Md.: Rowman and Littlefield, 1996.

Diamond, Martin. *The Electoral College and the American Idea of Democracy.* Washington, D.C.: American Enterprise Institute for Public Policy Research, 1977. Repr. in the July 1977 Senate *Hearings*, pp. 161–85.

————. "The Electoral College and the Idea of Federal Democracy." *Journal of Federalism* (Winter 1978): 63.

Dolan, Joseph, and Frank Chmelik. "Role of the Courts in Election '80: A 3-Ring Circus for a 3-Way Race." *National Law Journal,* Aug. 18, 1980: 24.

Duffy, Michael. "The 34% Solution." *Time,* June 1, 1992: 34.

Dunn, Katheryn A. "Time for Fairness in the Presidential Electoral Process: Major and Minor Candidates in Competition." *Journal of Law & Politics* 6 (Spring 1990): 625.

Durbin, Thomas M. "The Anachronistic Electoral College." *Federal Bar News & Journal* 39 (October 1992): 510.

————. "The Electoral College Method of Electing the President and Vice President and Proposals for Reform." Washington, D.C.: Congressional Research Service, Aug. 8, 1988.

————. "The 1992 Electoral College Dilemma: The H. Ross Perot Factor." Washington, D.C.: Congressional Research Service, American Law Division, n.d.

Durbin, Thomas M., and L. Paige Whitaker. "Nomination and Election of the President and Vice President of the United States, 1992." Washington, D.C.: Congressional Research Service, January 1992.

Final Report of the Commission on National Elections, Georgetown University. *Electing the President: A Program for Reform,* ed. Robert E. Hunter. Washington, D.C.: Center for Strategic and International Studies, 1986.

Flood, Emmett, and William G. Mayer. "Third-Party and Independent Candidates: How They Get on the Ballot, How They Get Nominated." In *In Pursuit of the White House: How We Choose Our Presidential Nominees,* ed. William G. Mayer. Chatham, N.J.: Chatham House, 1996.

Frost, Congressman Martin. "Election of the President in the House of Representatives." Unpublished memorandum to Richard Bolling, chairman, House Rules Committee, July 1, 1980.

Galvin, Thomas. "House Warily Dusts off Rules on Choosing a President." *Congressional Quarterly Weekly Report,* May 23, 1992: 1420.

Garand, James C., and T. Wayne Parent. "Representation, Swing, and Bias in U.S. Presidential Elections, 1872–1988." *American Journal of Political Science* 35 (November 1991): 1011–31.

Germond, Jack W., and Jules Witcover. "Another Electoral College Graduation." *National Journal,* Dec. 19, 1992: 2914.

Gewirtz, Paul. "House Party: How Not to Elect a President." *New Republic,* July 27, 1992: 38.

Glennon, Michael J. *When No Majority Rules: The Electoral College and Presidential Succession.* Washington, D.C.: Congressional Quarterly, 1993.

Goetz, Charles J. "Further Thoughts on the Measurement of Power in the Electoral College." Paper delivered at the Annual Meeting of the Public Choice Society, May 4, 1972.

———. "An Equilibrium-Displacement Measurement of Voting Power in the Electoral College." Paper delivered at the Annual Meeting of the American Political Science Association, Sept. 4–8, 1973, New Orleans.

Gorman, Joseph. "Election of the President by the House of Representatives and the Vice President by the Senate: Relationship of the Popular Vote for Electors to Subsequent Voting in the House of Representatives in 1801 and 1825 and in the Senate in 1837." Washington, D.C.: Congressional Research Service, Nov. 20, 1980.

Gossett, William T. "Electing the President." *Detroit College of Law Review* 4 (1983): 1283.

Hardaway, Robert M. *The Electoral College and the Constitution: The Case for Preserving Federalism.* Westport, Conn.: Praeger, 1994.

Hinich, Melvin J., and Peter C. Ordeshook. "The Electoral College: A Spatial Analysis." Paper delivered at the Annual Meeting of the Midwest Political Science Association, May 1973, Chicago. Also in *Political Methodology* 1 (Summer 1974): 1–29.

Hinich, Melvin J., Richard Michelsen, and Peter C. Ordeshook. "The Electoral College vs. a Direct Vote: Policy Bias, Indeterminate Outcomes and Reversals." *Journal on Mathematical Sociology* 4 (1975): 3–35.

Huckabee, David C. "Electoral Votes Based on the 1990 Census." Washington, D.C.: Congressional Research Service, Nov. 19, 1991.

Keech, William R. "Background Paper." In *Winner Take All: Report of the Twentieth Century Fund Task Force on Reform of the Presidential Election Process.* New York: Holmes and Meier, 1978.

Levesque, Terrence J. "Measuring State Power in Presidential Elections." *Public Choice* 42, no. 3 (1984): 295–310.

Longley, Lawrence D. "The Electoral College." *Current History* 67 (August 1974): 64–69 ff.

———. "Prepared Statement of Lawrence D. Longley," Feb. 1, 1977. In the February 1977 Senate *Hearings,* pp. 88–105.

———. "The Case Against the Electoral College." Paper delivered at the Annual Meeting of the American Political Science Association, Sept. 11, 1977, Washington, D.C.

———. "Electoral College Reform: Problems, Politics, and Prospects." In *Paths to Political Reform,* ed. William J. Crotty. Lexington, Mass.: D.C. Heath-Lexington for the Policy Studies Organization, 1980.

———. "Minorities and the 1980 Electoral College." Paper delivered at the Annual Meeting of the American Political Science Association, Aug. 28–31, 1980, Washington, D.C.

————. "The Electoral College and the Representation of Minorities: Myths and Realities." In *The President and the Public,* ed. Doris A. Graber. Philadelphia: Institute for the Study of Human Issues, 1982.

————. "Changing the System: Electoral Reform Politics in Great Britain and the United States." Paper delivered at the Thirteenth World Congress of the International Political Science Association, July 15–20, 1985, Paris.

————. "The Politics of Electoral Reform in Great Britain and the United States." *Parliamentary Affairs: A Journal of Comparative Politics* (U.K.) 41 (October 1988): 527–35.

————. "Changing the System: Anticipated Versus Actual Results in Electoral and Legislative Reform." Paper delivered at the Annual Meeting of the Midwest Political Science Association, April 13–15, 1989, Chicago.

————. "The American Electoral College." In *Political Parties and Elections in the United States: An Encyclopedia,* ed. L. Sandy Maisel. New York: Garland, 1991.

————. "The Electoral College: A Fatally Flawed Institution." In *Controversial Issues in Presidential Selection,* ed. Gary L. Rose. Albany: State University of New York Press, 1991.

————. "Prepared Statement of Lawrence D. Longley," U.S. Senate Judiciary Committee, Subcommittee on the Constitution, *Hearings on the Electoral College and Direct Election of the President,* 102d Congress, 2d session, July 22, 1992, pp. 29–76. Also in Judith A. Best, *The Choice of the People? Debating the Electoral College.* Lanham, Md.: Rowman and Littlefield, 1996, pp. 85–97.

————. "Prepared Statement of Lawrence D. Longley on Presidential Candidate and President-Elect Death, Disability, or Resignation." U.S. Senate Judiciary Committee, Subcommittee on the Constitution, *Hearings on Presidential Succession Between the Popular Election and the Inauguration,* 103d Congress, 2d sess., Feb. 2, 1994, pp. 43–46.

————. "The Electoral College Should Be Abolished." In *Controversial Issues in Presidential Selection,* ed. Gary L. Rose. 2d ed. Albany: State University of New York Press, 1994.

————. "The American Electoral College." *The Encyclopedia of Democracy,* ed. Seymour Martin Lipset. Washington, D.C.: Congressional Quarterly, 1996.

Longley, Lawrence D., and Alan G. Braun. *The Politics of Electoral College Reform.* New Haven: Yale University Press, 1972, 1975.

Longley, Lawrence D., and James D. Dana, Jr., "New Empirical Estimates of the Biases of the Electoral College for the 1980s." *Western Political Quarterly* 37 (March 1984): 157–75.

————. "The Electoral College's Biases in the 1992 Election—and Beyond." Research monograph published in U.S. Judiciary Committee, Subcommittee on the Constitution, *Hearings on the Electoral College and Direct Election of the President*, 102d Cong., 2d sess., July 22, 1992, pp. 38–76.

———. "The Electoral College's Biases in the 1992 Election—and Beyond." Paper delivered at the Annual Meeting of the American Political Science Association, Sept. 3–6, 1992, Chicago.

———. "The Biases of the Electoral College in the 1990s." *Polity* 25, no. 1 (Fall 1992): 123–45.

Longley, Lawrence D., and John H. Yunker. "Who Is Really Advantaged by the Electoral College—and Who Just Thinks He Is?" Paper delivered at the Annual Meeting of the American Political Science Association, Sept. 7–11, 1971, Chicago.

———. "The Changing Biases of the Electoral College." Paper delivered at the Annual Meeting of the American Political Science Association, Sept. 4–8, 1973, New Orleans. Also in U.S. Congress, Senate Judiciary Committee, Subcommittee on Constitutional Amendments, *Hearings on Electoral Reform*. 93d Cong., 1st sess., Sept. 26–27, 1973, pp. 187–212.

McCaughey, Elizabeth P. "Democracy at Risk: The Dangerous Flaws in the Electoral College." *Policy Review* 63 (1993): 79–81.

McLaughlin, John. "The Electoral-Vote Lock." *National Review*, Aug. 5, 1988: 26.

Margolis, Howard. "The Banzhaf Fallacy." *American Journal of Political Science* 27 (May 1983): 321–26.

Merrill, Samuel, III. "Citizen Voting Power Under the Electoral College: A Stochastic Model Based on State Voting Patterns." *SIAM Journal on Applied Mathematics* 34 (March 1978): 376–90.

———. "Empirical Estimates for the Likelihood of a Divided Verdict in a Presidential Election." *Public Choice* 33, no. 2 (1978): 127–33.

Michelsen, R., and P. C. Ordeshook. "The Electoral College and the Probability of Reversals." In *Modeling and Simulations*. Pittsburgh: University of Pittsburgh Press, forthcoming.

Mikva, Abner J. "The Electoral College: How Democratic Was—and Is—the Constitution?" *Prologue* 19 (Fall 1987): 177.

Millus, Albert J. "The Electoral College—Should Anything Be Done About It?" *New York State Bar Journal*, February 1982: 84.

Neale, Thomas H. "Contingent Election: Congress Elects the President and Vice President." Washington, D.C.: Congressional Research Service, May 20, 1992.

———. "Presidential Elections in the United States." Washington, D.C.: Congressional Research Service, June 6, 1991.

Nelson, Michael C. "Partisan Bias in the Electoral College." *Journal of Politics* 37 (November 1974): 1033–48.

Nicola, Thomas J. "Meaning and Implications of Twelfth Amendment Requirements that House Vote for President 'by Ballot.' " Washington, D.C.: Congressional Research Service, June 10, 1980.

Niemi, Richard, and William H. Riker. "The Choice of Voting Systems." *Scientific American* 234 (June 1976): 21–27.

Noah, Timothy. "Perot Could Face Hurdle of Reversals in Electoral College: Some Electors No Longer Back Texan, Threaten Attempt to Give His Race Meaning." *Wall Street Journal,* Oct. 28, 1992.

O'Sullivan, Michael J. "Artificial Unit Voting and the Electoral College." *Southern California Law Review* 65 (July 1992): 5.

Owen, Guillermo. "Evaluation of a Presidential Election Game." *American Political Science Review* 69 (September 1975): 947–53. Also, "Communication" by Chester Spatt, "Evaluation of a Presidential Election Game." *APSR* 70 (December 1976): 1221–23, and "Rejoinder" by Guillermo Owen, *APSR* 70 (December 1976): 1223–24. The Spatt and Owen exchange is reprinted in the February 1977 Senate *Hearings,* pp. 549–53.

———. "Multilinear Extensions and the Banzhaf Value." *Naval Research Logistics Quarterly* 22 (December 1975): 741–50.

Peirce, Neal R., and Lawrence D. Longley. *The People's President: The Electoral College in American History and the Direct Vote Alternative.* Rev. ed. New Haven: Yale University Press, 1981.

Power, Max S. "A Theoretical Analysis of the Electoral College and Proposed Reforms." Ph.D. diss., Yale University, 1971.

———. "The Logic and Illogic of the Case for Direct Popular Election of the President." Paper delivered at the Western Political Science Association Meeting, April 8–10, 1971, Albuquerque.

———. "Logic and Legitimacy: On Understanding the Electoral College Controversy." In *Perspectives on Presidential Selection,* ed. Donald R. Matthews. Washington, D.C.: Brookings Institution, 1973.

Rabinowitz, George, and Stuart Elaine MacDonald. "The Power of the States in U.S. Presidential Elections." *American Political Science Review* 80 (March 1986): 65–87.

Reidinger, Paul. "Still Ticking After All These Years." *Journal of the American Bar Association,* Sept. 1, 1987: 42.

Reuven, Frank. "Election Night." *New Leader,* Oct. 5, 1992: 20.

Sayre, Wallace S., and Judith H. Parris. *Voting for President: The Electoral College and the American Political System.* Washington, D.C.: Brookings Institution, 1970.

Schneider, William. "Electoral College's 'Archaic Ritual.' " *National Journal,* Dec. 10, 1988: 3164.

Sindler, Allan. "Basic Change Aborted: The Failure to Secure Direct Popular Election of the President, 1969–70." In *Policy and Politics in America,* ed. Allan Sindler. Boston: Little, Brown, 1973.

Slonim, Shloma. "Designing the Electoral College." In *Inventing the American Presidency,* ed. Thomas E. Cronin. Lawrence: University Press of Kansas, 1989.

———. "The Electoral College at Philadelphia: The Evolution of an Ad Hoc Congress for the Selection of a President." *Journal of American History* 73 (June 1986): 35–58.

Smith, R. A. N., and Peverill Squire. "Direct Election of the President and the Power of the States." *Western Political Quarterly* 40 (March 1987): 31–44.

Smolka, Richard G. "Possible Consequences of Direct Election of the President." *State Government* 50 (Summer 1977): 134–40. Repr. in the 1979 Senate *Hearings,* pp. 629–36.

Spilerman, Seymour, and David Dickens. "Who Will Gain and Who Will Lose Influence Under Different Electoral Rules." Discussion paper, Institute for Research on Poverty, University of Wisconsin, Madison, December 1972. Also in *American Journal of Sociology* 80 (September 1974): 443–77. Repr. in the February 1977 Senate *Hearings,* pp. 554–91.

Sterling, Carleton W. "The Political Implications of Alternative Systems of Electing the President of the United States." Ph.D. diss., University of Chicago, 1970.

———. "The Failure of Bloc Voting in the Electoral College to Benefit Urban Liberal and Ethnic Groups." Paper delivered at the Annual Meeting of the American Political Science Association, September 1970, Los Angeles.

———. "The Electoral College: The Representation of Non-Voters." Manuscript.

———. "The Electoral College and the Impact of Popular Vote Distribution." *American Politics Quarterly* 12 (April 1974): 179–204.

———. "Biases of the Electoral College Evaluated through Mathematical Models." Manuscript.

———. "Electoral College Misrepresentation: A Geometric Analysis." *Polity* 13 (1981): 425–49. Also in the July 1977 Senate *Hearings,* pp. 409–32.

———. "The Electoral College Biases Revealed, the Conventional Wisdom and Game Theory Models Notwithstanding." In the July 1977 Senate *Hearings,* pp. 432–54. Also in *Western Political Quarterly* 31 (June 1978): 159–77.

Straffin, Philip, Jr. "Homogeneity, Independence and Power Indices." *Public Choice* 30 (Summer 1977): 107–18.

Tipy, Thomas B. "Would the District of Columbia Be Allowed to Vote in the Selection of a President by the House of Representatives?" Washington, D.C.: Congressional Research Service, July 7, 1980.

Tribe, Laurence H., and Thomas M. Rollins. "Deadlock: What Happens If Nobody Wins." *Atlantic Monthly* (October 1980): 49.

Twentieth Century Fund. *Winner Take All: Report of the Twentieth Century Fund Task Force on Reform of the Presidential Election Process*. New York: Holmes and Meier, 1978.

Uslaner, Eric M. "Pivotal States in the Electoral College: An Empirical Investigation." *Annals of New York Academy of Science* 219 (1973): 61–76.

———. "Spatial Models of the Electoral College: Distribution Assumptions and Biases of the System." Paper delivered at the Annual Meeting of the American Political Science Association, Aug. 29–Sept. 2, 1974, Chicago. Also in *Political Methodology,* Summer 1976: 335–81.

Walser, George. "Electoral College: Bibliography-in-Brief, 1958–1988." Washington, D.C.: Congressional Research Service, October 1988.

Weinhagen, Robert F., Jr. "Should the Electoral College Be Abandoned?" *Journal of the American Bar Association* 67 (July 1981): 852–57.

Weisberger, Bernard A. "Electoral Headaches." *American Heritage* 43 (November 1992): 22.

Young, H. P. "The Allocation of Funds in Lobbying and Campaigning." *Behavioral Science*. Forthcoming.

Yunker, John H. "Prepared Statement of John Yunker." In the February 1977 Senate *Hearings,* pp. 498–500.

Yunker, John H., and Lawrence D. Longley. "The Biases of the Electoral College: Who Is Really Advantaged?" In *Perspectives on Presidential Selection,* ed. Donald R. Matthews. Washington, D.C.: Brookings Institution, 1973.

———. *The Electoral College: Its Biases Newly Measured for the 1960s and 1970s.* Sage Professional Papers in American Politics. Beverly Hills, Calif.: Sage, 1976.

Zeidenstein, Harvey. *Direct Election of the President.* Lexington, Mass.: Heath-Lexington Books, 1973.

Materials Criticizing and Defending the Electoral College
Works on the Electoral College Generally Supporting Its Abolition

Abbott, David W., and James P. Levine. *Wrong Winner: The Coming Debacle in the Electoral College.* New York: Praeger, 1991.

Arrington, Theodore S., and Saul Brenner. "Should the Electoral College Be Replaced by the Direct Election of the President?: A Debate." *P.S.* 17 (Spring 1984): 237–50 (esp. sections by Arrington supporting abolition of the electoral college).

Broder, David S. "Admirable Case, Wrong Defendant." *Washington Post,* March 21, 1979. Also in the 1979 Senate *Hearings,* pp. 57–58.

"Demolish the College." Editorial, *Washington Post,* Feb. 1, 1977. Also in the February 1977 Senate *Hearings,* p. 114, and the July 1977 Senate *Hearings,* pp. 493–94.

Feerick, John D. "The Electoral College and the Election of 1976." *Journal of the American Bar Association* 63 (June 1977): 757–75. Also in the July 1977 Senate *Hearings*, pp. 360–63.

———. "Electoral College Archaic, Dangerous: Democracy Demands Popular Vote." Syndicated column, Jan. 21, 1977. Also in the July 1977 Senate *Hearings*, pp. 490–92.

Lewis, Anthony. "Again: Why Keep the Electoral College?" *New York Times*, Nov. 7, 1976.

Longley, Lawrence D. "Abolish the Electoral College." In *The New Federalist Papers*, ed. J. Jackson Barlow, Dennis J. Mahoney, and John G. West. Washington, D.C.: University Press of America, 1988.

———. "The Electoral College: Archaic, Uncertain, Unfair." *This Constitution: A Bicentennial Chronicle* 12 (Fall 1986): 22–25.

———. "The Electoral College: A Fatally Flawed Institution." In *Controversial Issues in Presidential Selection*, ed. Gary L. Rose. Albany: State University of New York Press, 1991.

———. "The Case Against the Electoral College." In *Point-Counterpoint*, ed. Herbert M. Levine. 5th ed. New York: St. Martin's, 1994.

———. "The Electoral College Should Be Abolished." In *Controversial Issues in Presidential Selection*, ed. Gary L. Rose. 2d ed. Albany: State University of New York Press, 1994.

———. "The Case Against the Electoral College." In *Points of View*, ed. Robert DiClerico and Allan Harnmock. 6th ed. New York: McGraw-Hill, 1995.

———. "The American Electoral College." *The Encyclopedia of Democracy*, ed. Seymour Martin Lipset. Washington, D.C.: Congressional Quarterly, 1996.

Longley, Lawrence D., and Alan G. Braun. *The Politics of Electoral College Reform.* New Haven: Yale University Press, 1972, 1975.

Peirce, Neal R. "Electoral College: Its Time Has Run Out." *Washington Post*, Dec. 3, 1976. Also in the July 1977 Senate *Hearings*, pp. 485–86.

Peirce, Neal R. and Lawrence D. Longley. *The People's President: The Electoral College in American History and the Direct Vote Alternative.* Rev. ed. New Haven: Yale University Press, 1981.

Wayne, Stephen J. "Let the People Vote Directly for President." In *The Quest for National Office: Readings on Elections*, ed. Stephen J. Wayne and Clyde Wilcox. New York: St. Martin's, 1992.

Wicker, Tom. "An Old Idea Still Needed." *New York Times*, Nov. 16, 1976. Also in the July 1977 Senate *Hearings*, p. 480.

———. "One Person, One Vote." *New York Times*, March 27, 1977.

———. "Black Voting Power." *New York Times*, Sept. 16, 1977.

See also various statements contained in the February 1977 Senate *Hearings,* especially those by Senators Hubert Humphrey and Robert Dole; Lawrence D. Longley, John H. Yunker, and Alan G. Braun; Justin Stanley and John Feerick of the American Bar Association; Gus Tyler of the International Ladies' Garment Workers Union; and Clark MacGregor of the U.S. Chamber of Commerce. Additional statements supporting the abolition of the electoral college can be found in the reopened July 1977 *Hearings,* esp. those by Paul A. Freund, Richard M. Scammon, Lance Tarrance, Douglas L. Bailey, and Senator Dole. The July 1977 Senate *Hearings* contains an extensive selection of newspaper and magazine editorials and articles favoring electoral college reform, pp. 471–503.

Further testimony in favor of abolishing the electoral college can be found in the 1979 Senate *Hearings,* especially in statements by John D. Feerick, Doug Bailey, and James A. Michener; and in the July 1992 and February 1994 Senate *Hearings* in statements by Lawrence D. Longley.

An excellent summary of the case for the abolition of the electoral college will be found in the December 1977 Senate *Report,* pp. 1–23. This report includes discussions of the defects and deficiencies of the present electoral college system; the opponents' arguments and some counterpoints; the effects of direct election on the two-party system, federalism, and direct election; the impact of direct election on the smaller states; its consequences in terms of voter fraud, vote recounts, and possible run-offs; and social- and minority-group voting power under electoral college and direct electoral systems.

Works on the Electoral College Generally Supporting Its Retention

"A Bad Idea Whose Time Has Come." Editorial, *New Republic,* May 7, 1977. Also in the July 1977 Senate *Hearings,* pp. 525–28.

American Enterprise Institute. *Direct Election of the President.* Washington, D.C.: American Enterprise Institute for Public Policy Research, 1977. Repr. in the July 1977 Senate *Hearings,* pp. 384–97.

Arrington, Theodore S., and Saul Brenner. "Should the Electoral College be Replaced by the Direct Election of the President?: A Debate." *P.S.* 17 (Spring 1984): 237–50 (esp. sections by Brenner supporting the retention of the electoral college).

Berns, Walter, ed. *After the People Vote: A Guide to the Electoral College.* Revised and enlarged edition. Washington, D.C.: American Enterprise Institute, 1992.

Best, Judith A. *The Case Against Direct Election of the President.* Ithaca: Cornell University Press, 1975.

———. "Why the Electoral College Keeps Winning: The Federal Principle in Presidential Elections." In Judith A. Best. *The Choice of the People? Debating the Electoral College.* Lanham, Md.: Rowman and Littlefield, 1996.

———. "The Electoral College: A Paradigm of American Democracy." *This Constitution: A Bicentennial Chronicle* 12 (Fall 1986): 19–22.

Brown, Robert D. "The Electoral College Should Not Be Abolished." In *Controversial Issues in Presidential Selection*, ed. Gary L. Rose. 2d ed. Albany: State University of New York Press, 1994.

"Busybody 'Reform.' " Editorial, *Wall Street Journal*, March 28, 1977. Also in the July 1977 Senate *Hearings*, pp. 511–12.

Diamond, Martin. *The Electoral College and the American Idea of Democracy*. Washington, D.C.: American Enterprise Institute, 1977. Repr. in the July 1977 Senate *Hearings*, pp. 161-85.

———. "Testimony in Support of the Electoral College." Reprint no. 76. Washington, D.C.: American Enterprise Institute for Public Policy Research, 1977.

———. "The Electoral College and the Idea of Federal Democracy." *Journal of Federalism*, Winter 1978.

"Election Reform." Editorial. *New Republic*, June 25, 1977. Also in the July 1977 Senate *Hearings*, pp. 534–35.

"Electoral College Reform." Editorial. *New York Times*, Nov. 16, 1976.

Hardaway, Robert M. *The Electoral College and the Constitution: The Case for Preserving Federalism*. Westport, Conn.: Praeger, 1994.

Kilpatrick, James J. "Yes, an 18th-Century Idea." Syndicated column, *Washington Star*, Aug. 11, 1977. Also in the July 1977 Senate *Hearings*, pp. 536–37.

Hunt, Albert R. "Don't 'Fix' the Electoral College." *Wall Street Journal*, July 5, 1979.

"Making the Vote and Voting More Popular." Editorial. *New York Times*, March 23, 1977. Also in the July 1977 Senate *Hearings*, pp. 510–11.

"Old Reform, New Risks." Editorial. *New York Times*, Feb. 6, 1977. Also in the February 1977 Senate *Hearings*, p. 357, and the July 1977 Senate *Hearings*, pp. 506–7.

Perkins, Paul M. "What's Good About the Electoral College." *Washington Monthly*, April 1977: 40–41. Also in the 1979 Senate *Hearings*, pp. 658–59.

Piland, Denny. "The Electoral College Should Not Be Abolished." In *Controversial Issues in Presidential Selections*, ed. Gary L. Rose. Albany: State University of New York Press, 1991.

"The 'Plebiscitary Presidency.' " Editorial. *Washington Star*, April 6, 1979.

Ranney, Austin. "Keep the Electoral College." *Baltimore Sun*, April 28, 1977. Also in the 1979 Senate *Hearings*, pp. 655–56.

Rapoport, Ronald B. "The Electoral College: Still the Best Alternative." In *The Quest for National Office: Readings on Elections*, ed. Stephen J. Wayne and Clyde Wilcox. New York: St. Martin's, 1992.

" 'Reforming' the Electoral College." Editorial. *Wall Street Journal*, Jan. 6, 1977. Also in the July 1977 Senate *Hearings*, pp. 505–6.

Schlesinger, Arthur M. "The Electoral College Conundrum." *Wall Street Journal*, April 4, 1977. Also in the July 1977 Senate *Hearings*, pp. 514–16.

"Senator Bayh's Nightmare." Editorial. *Washington Star*, Nov. 18, 1976.

Weinhagen, Robert F., Jr. "Should the Electoral College Be Abandoned?" *Journal of the American Bar Association* 67 (July 1981): 852–57.

Weissberg, Robert. "In Defense of the Electoral College." In *Points of View*, ed. Robert DiClerico and Allan Hammock. 5th ed. New York: McGraw-Hill, 1992.

Wildavsky, Aaron. "The Plebiscitary Presidency: Direct Election as Class Legislation." *Commonsense* 2 (Winter 1979): 1–10. Also in the 1979 Senate *Hearings*, pp. 533–42.

Will, George F. "Don't Fool with the Electoral College." *Newsweek*, April 4, 1977: 96. Also in the July 1977 Senate *Hearings*, pp. 509–10, and the 1979 Senate *Hearings*, pp. 231–32.

———. "Constitutional Numbers Games." *Washington Post*, Aug. 18, 1975. Also in the July 1977 Senate *Hearings*, pp. 519–20.

———. "Why Electoral College Is Best." Syndicated column. *Post-Crescent* (Wisconsin), April 20, 1992.

———. "Don't Scrap the Winner-Take-All Electoral System." Syndicated column. *Post-Crescent* (Wisconsin), June 27, 1992.

Williams, Eddie N. "Would Popular Election Dilute the Black Vote?" *Washington Post*, April 14, 1977. Also in the July 1977 Senate *Hearings*, pp. 518–19, and the 1979 Senate *Hearings*, p. 628.

See also the various statements contained in the February 1977 Senate *Hearings* and in the reopened July 1977 Senate *Hearings*, esp. those by Austin Ranney, Aaron Wildavsky, Martin Diamond, Herbert Storing, Judith Best, and Eddie Williams. The July 1977 Senate *Hearings* contains an extensive selection of newspaper and magazine editorials opposing electoral college reform, pp. 505–37.

Further testimony in favor of retaining the electoral college can be found in the 1979 Senate *Hearings*, esp. by Harry Bailey, Walter Berns, Judith Best, Vernon Jordan, Jeane Kirkpatrick, Howard M. Squadron, Theodore White, and George Will; and in the July 1992 Senate *Hearings* in statements by Judith Best, Norman Ornstein, and Thomas Mann.

A comprehensive summary of the case against the abolishment of the electoral college will be found in the December 1977 Senate report "Minority Views of Messrs. Eastland, Allen, Thurmond, Scott, Laxalt, Hatch, and Wallop on S.J. Res. 1," pp. 24–32:

> In summary, we believe that the proposal should be rejected for the following reasons:
> It would cripple the party system and encourage splinter parties;
> It would undermine the federal system;

It would alter the delicate balance underlying separation of powers;

It would encourage electoral fraud;

It could lead to interminable recounts and challenges;

It would necessitate national control of every aspect of the electoral process;

It would give undue weight to numbers, thereby reducing the influence of small states;

It would encourage candidates for President to represent narrow geographical, ideological, and ethnic bases of support;

It would encourage simplistic media-oriented campaigns and bring about drastic changes in the strategy and tactics used in campaigns for the Presidency; and,

It would increase the power of big city political bosses.

index

Page numbers in italics represent
tables.

Act of *1792*, 98. *See also* Electors, presidential

Acting president, 14, 43, 165–66

Adams, John, 25

Adams, John Quincy, 30, 91

African Americans. *See* Black voters

Agnew, Spiro, 68

Alabama: in *1960* election, 29–30, 47–49; in *1964* election, 49–50, 128

Allen, James B., 118

Amendments, constitutional. *See* Constitutional amendments

American Independent party, 58

Anderson, John B., 78–80, 158

Anti-Mason party, 91

Apportionment, congressional: and population shifts, 94, 119; unfairness of, 21, 119, 153, 155; and voter turnout, 128

Article II (U.S. Constitution), 111; text of, 184–86

Automatic Succession Act of *1947*, 13, 124, 165. *See also* Presidential succession

Bailey, Lloyd W., 63, 105, 117

Baker, Howard H., 117

Ballot controversies, 100–101, 115–18

Ballot designation, official, 2–3, 83

Ballot, long, 100–101

Ballot, short, 98, 100–101, 102

Baring, Walter S., 66

Barkley, Alban W., 43

Barnett, Ross, 52

Bayh, Birch, 117

Becker, Carl, 89–90

Bell, John, 131

Benton, Thomas Hart, 102–4

Bischoff, Charles W., 136–38

Black voters, voting power of, 146–47, *148*, 149, *150–51*, 152–53

Bolton, Francis P., 56

Bradley, Joseph P., 28, 103

Breckinridge, John C., 56, 131

Brewster, Robert L., 76

Brown, Jerry (Edmund G.), 82

Buchanan, Patrick J., 82, 86

Burr, Aaron, 25, 114

Bush, George, 81, 82

Butler, Nicholas Murray, 122

Byrd, Harry Flood, 46, 52, 56

California: in *1912* election, 128; in *1992* election, 129; number of electors, 94; voting power of, 152

Campaign strategies: in *1960* election, 54–55n; in *1992* election, 84, 86; influenced by electoral college, 154, 156, 157; and large-state bias, 54–55, 68–69, 157–58

Candidates, independent. *See* Independent candidates

Candidates, third-party. *See* Independent candidates

Carter, Jimmy, 67, 72, 79

Central-city residents. *See* Inner-city residents
Clay, Henry, 30, 91
Cleveland, Grover, 29
Clinton, Bill, 82–83; in *1996* election fable, 1–2, 5, 6
Clinton, De Witt, 114
Cohen, Alfred M., 113
Committee of Eleven, 17–18. *See also* Constitutional Convention
Compromise of *1877*, costs of, 29, 61. *See also* South
Congressional caucus, 91
Congressional Quarterly, 82; and "First Method," 48, *49;* and "Second Method," 48, *49*
Connecticut Plan (Great Compromise), 17, 19. *See also* Constitutional Convention
"Constant two," 128, 130, 145, 153, 155, 156. *See also* Electoral vote
Constitutional amendments and articles: Article II, 111, 184–86; Fifteenth Amendment, 188; Fourteenth Amendment, 96, 187; Nineteenth Amendment, 188; Seventeenth Amendment, 188; Twelfth Amendment, 9, 12, 22, 26, 102, 110, 111, 114–15, 118, 123, 186–87; Twentieth Amendment, 13, 43, 112, 120, 121, 123, 165, 188; Twenty-fifth Amendment, 68, 123, 190; Twenty-fourth Amendment, 189; Twenty-second Amendment, 44, 189; Twenty- third Amendment, 94, 189
Constitutional Convention, 16–21, 91; adoption of intermediate election plan, 19; and Committee of Eleven, 17–18; representational conflicts, 17; support of electoral college system, 19–21

Contingent election. *See* House of Representatives contingent election procedure
Crawford, William H., 105
Curtis, Carl, 56

Daley, Richard, 157
Daniel, W. C., 66
Davis, David, 28
Death of presidential candidate. *See* Presidential succession
Delaware, and small-state bias, 157
Democratic Executive Committee (Alabama), 108
Democratic party, 28–29; and death of nominee, 121, 123; in *1948* election, 39–41, 128; in *1960* election, 44; in *1964* election, 128; in *1968* election, 65; in *1992* election, 86; in *1996* election fable, 10; and popular vote analysis, *139, 140*
Dewey, Thomas E., 40
Dickinson, John, 17
Direct election: analysis of, 136–38, 156–57; arguments for, 124–26; problems of, 6, 18. *See also* Popular vote
Direct popular vote. *See* Direct election; Popular vote
District of Columbia, 9, 22, 119, 142, 164; and number of electors, 94
District plan, 95, 99–100
Divided verdict, 5, 101–2, 161. *See also* District plan
Dixiecrat (States' Rights) party, 40, 41, 42, 110
Dixon, Robert G., 113
Dole, Bob: in *1996* election fable, 1, 5, 7; on electoral college, 76
Douglas, Stephen A., 131

Dual-count system. *See* Electoral college system

Dubinsky, David, 97–98

Eagleton, Thomas F., 122

Edgar, Jim, 157

Eisenhower, Dwight D., 44

Election fraud. *See* Fraud, election

Election of *1796*, 25, 104

Election of *1800:* and House contingent election procedure, 25–26, 30, 118

Election of *1820*, 104–5

Election of *1824:* and House contingent election procedure, 30, 31, 104, 118

Election of *1836:* and vice president, 120–21

Election of *1860, 131;* and electoral votes, 128; and voter turnout, 131

Election of *1876:* electors in, 107; and popular vote reversal, 27–29

Election of *1888:* and popular vote reversal, 29; winner-take-all feature, 29

Election of *1892*, 95, 99

Election of *1904:* voter confusion in, 101

Election of *1912:* results of, *132;* and unpledged electors, 109–10; and voter turnout, 131–32

Election of *1936, 132;* and voter turnout, 132, *132*

Election of *1948*, 38–43; crisis elements of, 41–43; and Dixiecrat party, 40, 41, 42, 110; faithless elector in, 105; results of, *42;* voter confusion in, 101

Election of *1960*, 44–57; counting of electoral votes, 55–57; counting of popular vote, 29–30, 47–49, 54; crisis elements in, 55; effects on *1964* election, 50; faithless elector in,

52–54, 105; popular vote, 46–49; results of, *49*, 57; similarities to *1948*, 45; and unpledged electors, 46–48, 51–52, 111

Election of *1968*, 57–67; analysis of, 64–67; crisis elements of, 62–67; faithless elector in, 63, 105, 117; results of, 62, *63;* winner-take-all feature, 61–62

Election of *1972, 133;* faithless elector in, 105; and voter turnout, 133

Election of *1976*, 67–78, 113; analysis of, 74–78; crisis elements in, 75–78; faithless elector in, 75, 106; popular vote, 77; results of, *75*

Election of *1980*, 37, 78–81; crisis elements in, 80–81; results of, *81, 134;* and voter turnout, 133

Election of *1988:* faithless elector in, 106

Election of *1992*, 81–88; analysis of, 87–88; crisis elements in, 88; and effects of winner-take-all feature, 129; popular vote, 87, 135–36; potential for House contingent election procedure, 84–85; results of, *87, 135*

Election of *1996:* fable of, 1–15; hypothetical results of, *5;* possible scenarios for, 154–66

Electoral college lock, 158

Electoral college system: abolishment of, 113, 118, 166 (*See also* Electoral reform); biases of, 141–53; changes in, 21–26; as counting device, 22, 50, 116, 155–56; creation of, 16–21; deadlock of (*See* House of Representatives contingent election procedure); membership summary, *177–81;* summary of problems of, 17–18, 38, 118–21, 125, 135–36,

Electoral college system (continued)
155–67. *See also* "Constant two";
Multiplier effect; Voting power;
Winner-take-all feature

Electoral Commission of *1877*, 103

Electoral reform, 21–26, 113, 117–18,
126, 166; and Twelfth Amendment,
26

Electoral vote: counting of, 55–57, 114–
21; disputed, 115, 116; and popular
vote summaries, *182–83*. *See also*
Apportionment, congressional;
"Constant two"; Electoral college
system; Winner-take all feature

Electors, faithless, 104–6, 117–18; in
1796 election, 23, 104; in *1820* election, 104; in *1824* election, 104–5;
in *1960* election, 52–54, 105; in
1968 election, 60, 63, 105, 117–18;
in *1972* election, 106; in *1976* election, 74–75, 105; in *1980* election,
80–81; influence on election results,
155, 159–60; lack of, in *1992* election, 88

Electors, free, 22, 23, 103–4, 108

Electors, presidential, 6, 63, 98–102;
creation of, by Constitutional Convention, 19; in early elections,
20–21; influence of, 160–61; legal
restrictions on, 23, 109; loyalty
pledges from, 107–9; numbers of,
93–94; qualifications of, 22, 84,
97; replacements for, 112; role of,
102–3, 107; selection of, 24, 47, 84,
95–96, 98–102; voting by, 111–14

Electors, unpledged: in *1912* election,
109–10; in *1948* election, 110–11;
in *1960* election, 46–48, 51–52,
111

Ervin, Sam J., 117

Faithless electors. *See* Electors, faithless

Far West. *See* West

Federalist, The, 19, 88

Feerick, John P., 22

Fifteenth Amendment, text of, 188

"First Method," 48. *See also* Election of
1960

Fitzpatrick, Benjamin, 122

Florida, in *1992* election, 129

Ford, Gerald R., Jr., 67–68

Foreign-born voters, voting power of,
147, *148,* 149

Founding fathers, 25, 26, 90, 97, 102,
111

Fourteenth Amendment, 96; text of,
187

Fraud, election: in *1960* election,
50–51; in *1976* election, 76; potential for, 69–70

Free electors. *See* Electors, free

Frémont, John C., 91

General ticket system. *See* Ballot, short;
Winner-take-all feature

Gingrich, Newt, in *1996* election fable,
14

Giuliani, Rudolph, 157

Goldwater, Barry, 111

Gore, Al, 12, 165

Granger, Francis, 121

Greeley, Horace, 123

Hairbreadth election, 35–36, 141; definition of, 34

Hamilton, Alexander, 19, 26, 88

Harkin, Tom, 82

Harris, R. Lea, 53

Harrison, Benjamin, 29, 104

Hayden, Carl, 56

Hayes, Rutherford B., 27, 29, 61

Hispanic voters, voting power of, 147, *148*, 149, 157

House Judiciary Committee, 84

House of Representatives: counting of electoral votes, 55–57, 114–21; partisan bias of, 164, 166; tellers, 56, 116

House of Representatives contingent election procedure, 9, *31;* description of, 118–21, 195–97; in election of *1800*, 25–26, 30, 118; in election of *1824*, 30, 31; as emergency step, 24; objections to, 119–20; potential in *1948* election, 42–43; potential in *1968* election, 64; potential in *1976* election, 74–75; potential in *1992* election, 84–85; potential in *1996* election, 161–62; questions about, 85; state delegations and, 65–66, 164–65

Humphrey, Hubert H., 40, 44, 58

Illinois, in *1960* election, 50–51

Illinois Democratic party, 28–29

Independence party. *See* Reform party

Independent candidates; in *1948* election, 40–42; in *1968* election, 58–62; in *1976* election, 70–71; in *1980* election, 78–80; in *1992* election, 83–86, 87, 88; in *1996* election fable, 2–15; and electoral college effect on, 154, 158; in future elections, 159. *See also* Splinter parties; Spoiler candidate

Indirect election. *See* Electoral college system

Ingalls, John J., 103

Inner-city residents, voting power of, 146, *148*

Intermediate election plan, 18. *See also* Constitutional Convention

Irwin, Henry D., 52–54, 105

Jackson, Andrew, 30, 91

Jackson, Robert H., 103

Jefferson, Thomas, 25; on contingent election, 30

Jewish voters, voting power of, 147, *148*, 149, 157

Johnson, Herschel V., 122

Johnson, Lyndon B., 44, 57

Johnson, Robert M., 120–21

Jones, Walter E., 105

Kefauver, Estes, 124

Kelly, Edna F., 56

Kennedy, Edward M., 79

Kennedy, John F., 44–46, 54

Kennedy, Robert F., 58

Kerrey, Robert, 82

King Caucus. *See* Congressional caucus

Kingmaker, concept of, 8, 61, 70

Kirby, James C., Jr., 109

Knight, Goodwin, 107

Landon, Alfred M., 132

Large-state bias, 17, 21, 43, 94; and campaign strategies, 54–55, 68–69, 156–58; and voting power, 142–47

Laws, summary of federal election, 191–94

Legislative choice of electors, 24, 95–96

Levy, J. J., 112

Lispenard, Anthony, 114

Lodge, Henry Cabot, 46, 103

Long ballot. *See* Ballot, long

Longley, Lawrence D., 72

Louisiana, and selection of presidential electors, 96

Lowell, James Russell, 107
Lucey, Patrick, 79, 113

MacBride, Roger, 105
Madison, James, 18, 21
Maine, in 1972 election, 99
Marsh, John O., Jr., 66
Mason, George, 20
Massachusetts, and selection of presidential electors, 24
McGovern, George S., 133
McMaster, J. B., 104
McPherson v. Blacker, 95, 96, 99. See also District plan; Divided verdict
Media, national: in 1960 election, 47; in 1976 election, 72–74; in 1980 election, 37; in 1992 election, 83; in 1996 election fable, 1–2; focus on state-by-state results, 4; in presidential campaigns, 92–93
Merrill, Samuel, III, 146n
Michener, James A., 64, 97
Michigan, in 1892 election, 95, 99
Midwest, voting power of, 147, 148, 149
Miles, Samuel, 23, 104
Minehart, Thomas, 64
Minority presidents, 30–31, 32–34, 77–78, 125, 135
Mississippi: in 1960 election, 52; in 1976 election, 73–74
Mitchell, Albert K., 53–54
Mondale, Walter F., 67
Morris, Gouverneur, 18
Morton, Oliver P., 119
Morton, Thurston B., 50, 54
Mountain states, voting power of, 147, 148, 149
Multiplier effect, and electoral college majority, 34, 132, 133, 134
Mundt, Karl E., 117
Muskie, Edmund, 117

National nominating conventions, 89–92; delegates to, 91–92
National Republican Convention, 91
National Republican party, 91
Nebraska, in 1992 election, 99–100
New Jersey Plan, 17. See also Constitutional Convention
News Election Service, 74, 93. See also Media, national
New York, number of electors, 94
Nineteenth Amendment, text of, 188
Nixon, Richard M.: in 1960 election, 44, 45, 46, 49, 54–55n; in 1968 election, 58; in 1972 election, 133
North Carolina, and faithless electors, 104

O'Connor, Thomas, 97
Official ballot designation. See Ballot designation, official
O'Hara, James G., 117

Padden, Mike, 75, 106
Parks, Preston, 105
Pataki, George, 157
Patman, Wright, 107–8
Peirce, Neal R., 59, 60; and "First Method," 48; on popular vote, 71–72
Pennsylvania, selection of electors, 98
People's President, The (Peirce and Longley), 136
Perot, Ross: in 1992 election, 83–86, 158; in 1996 election fable, 2–4, 7–11. See also Independent candidates
Plumer, William, 104
Plurality election. See Direct election
Political participation. See Voter turnout

Political parties, 91; effects of, 25, 91; rise of, 22, 90–91. *See also* Democratic party; Independent candidates; Republican party

Popular vote, 5, 7, 8; definition of, 127–28; effects of shifts in, 41, 62, 77, 141; and percentage of electoral votes, 128, 134–35, 136–41; reversal of, *27*, 27–29, 71–72; statistical analysis of, 136–38, *139, 140,* 142–53. *See also* Direct election; Election of [year]; Voter turnout

Population, principle of: as factor in elections, 21, 130, 142, *143–44,* 145–46, 149, 155. *See also* Apportionment, congressional

Presidential electors. *See* Electors, presidential

Presidential succession, 13, 121–24; to president-elect in case of death, 123. *See also* Automatic Succession Act of *1947*; Vice president

Progressive party, 40, 101

Rayburn, Sam, 56

Reagan, Ronald, 68, 78–79, 80–81

Reform of electoral college. *See* Electoral college system; Electoral reform

Reform party, 2–3

Republican party: and death of nominee, 121–22; in *1948* election, 39–41; in *1960* election, 44, 50–51, 54–55; in *1968* election, 64, 65; in *1996* election, 163; in *1996* election fable, 10; and popular vote analysis, *139, 140*

Riordan, Richard, 157

Robertson, Pat, 86

Roche, John, 20

Rockefeller, Nelson A., 44

Roosevelt, Franklin D., 38, 124, 132

Roosevelt, Theodore, 131

Rural voters, voting power of, 147, *148,* 149

Sanders, Bernard, 10, 163

Satterfield, David E., III, 66

"Second Method," 48. *See also* Election of *1960*

Senate contingent election of vice president. *See* Vice president

Senate Judiciary Committee, 76

Seventeenth Amendment, text of, 188

Sherman, James S., 122

Short ballot. *See* Ballot, short

Shriver, Sargent, 122

Small-state bias, 17, 142–46, 157–58

South: and Compromise of *1877,* 29, 61; in *1948* election, 40, 110–11; in *1960* election, 44–45, 111; in *1968* election, 58–62, 59; and unpledged electors, 46–48, 51–52, 110–11; voting power of, 147, *148,* 149, 152

South Carolina, and selection of electors, 24

South Dakota, and unpledged electors, 109–10

Speaker of the House, in presidential succession, 13–14, 165. *See also* Presidential succession

Splinter parties, effects of, 42, 43, 70. *See also* Independent candidates

Spoiler candidate, concept of, 3, 7–8. *See also* Independent candidates

Stassen, Harold E., 41

States' Rights (Dixiecrat) party, 40, 41, 42, 110

Stevenson, Adlai E., 44

Storms, Henry R., 95–96

Symington, Stuart, 44

Taft, Robert A., 41
Taft, William H., 131, 165
Tellers of House of Representatives, 56, 116. *See also* Electoral vote
Third-party candidates. *See* Independent candidates
Thurmond, Strom, 40, 110
Tilden, Samuel J., 27
Tombstone voting. *See* Fraud, election
Truman, Harry S, 38–41
Tsongas, Paul, 82
Turner, W. F., 105
Twelfth Amendment, 9, 12, 22, 26, 102, 111, 118, 123; and counting of electoral votes, 114–15; text of, 186
Twentieth Amendment, 13, 43, 112, 120, 121, 123, 165; text of, 188
Twenty-fifth Amendment, 68, 123; text of, 190
Twenty-fourth Amendment, text of, 189
Twenty-second Amendment, 44; text of, 189
Twenty-third Amendment, 94; text of, 189

U.S. Senate, president of, 114, 115, 116, 165
U.S. Supreme Court, 95, 96, 99, 108–9
Unit-vote system. *See* Winner-take-all feature
Unpledged electors. *See* Electors, unpledged
Urban voters, voting power of, 147, 148, *148*

Van Buren, Martin, 118–19, 120–21
Vice president: replacement of, in case of death, 123; Senate contingent election of, 9, 12, 43, 120–21, 165. *See also* Presidential succession
Virginia, number of electors, 94
Virginia Plan, 17. *See also* Constitutional Convention
Vote, disputed. *See* Electoral vote
Vote, electoral. *See* Electoral vote
Vote, national, historical summary of, *167–76*
Vote, popular. *See* Popular vote
Vote, shifts in, effects of, 41, 62, 77, 141. *See also* Hairbreadth election
Vote, wasted, 4, 5, 79–80, 86, 159
Voter apathy, 2
Voter confusion, effects of, 100–101
Voter turnout, 130–35, 153, 155. *See also* Popular vote
Voting power: of population groups, 146–53, *148, 150–51;* relative, 142; and state of residence, 142–47, *143–44*

Wallace, George C., 58–61, 80
Wallace, Henry A., 40, 43, 101
Warren, Earl, 41, 43
Washington, George, 20
West, voting power of, 147, *148,* 149
Whig Convention, 91
White Citizens Council, 52
Wilder, L. Douglas, 82
Wilson, James, 18
Wilson, Pete, 157
Wilson, Woodrow, 131
Winner-take-all feature, 24–25, 145, 153, 155, 156; in choosing electors, 99–102; definition of, 4; and effects on popular vote, 128, 129–30; support for, 24–25, 61–62. *See also* Electoral college system; Electoral vote
Wisconsin, 113, 115–16
Wright, Fielding, 110

The Electoral College Primer
Lawrence D. Longley and Neal R. Peirce

What is the electoral college? Why do we have it? How does it work? What is its impact on presidential elections? Most Americans remain only dimly aware of the operations of the electoral college and feel little concern about a system that seems to be working. Yet our archaic electoral college has the potential to thwart popular will, warn Lawrence Longley and Neal Peirce, two leading national authorities on the subject. In this complete guide to the electoral college, Longley and Peirce explain how the U.S. electoral college was created, how it has evolved, how it has influenced various "crisis" elections (including that of 1992), how it works today, and how it might affect future elections.

The electoral college is a "system of disastrous failings," the authors say, and it could lead to a political and constitutional crisis. To highlight the shortcomings of the system, they create a fictitious, but not impossible, 1996 election scenario in which neither Sen. Robert Dole nor President Bill Clinton can claim a victory in the electoral college. A surprising chain of events set off by a strong third party eventually confers the presidency on the Speaker of the House—a man who received not a single vote in the popular election. Whatever the outcome of the real election, this useful handbook will provide all the information a citizen needs to understand our baffling electoral college.

Lawrence D. Longley is professor of government at Lawrence University and coauthor of *Bicameral Politics: Conference Committees in Congress,* published by Yale University Press. He was a presidential elector in the 1988 and 1992 presidential elections. Neal R. Peirce, a prominent Washington journalist, writes a national column on state and local government themes syndicated by the Washington Post Writers Group.

A Yale Fastback